GW00585316

QUOTES FROM REVIEWS ON
LANDSCAPES UNDER THE LUGGAGE RACK...

"The next best thing to a journey in the carriages themselves!" *Railway Magazine*

"A delightfully nostalgic book... it should enthral almost anyone with an eye for a gift that is rather different and rather special" *Scotsman*

"This delightful and beautifully produced book is a poignant memoir of the steam age" *Heritage Today (English Heritage) Magazine*

"One of the great railway books of all time... it is unquestionably the most attractive book produced so far on any aspect of railwayana" *Railway Collectors Journal*

"An ideal Christmas gift... his book is one of the best of its kind I have ever seen" *Runcorn Weekly News*

"Numerous superb colour illustrations" *The Scots Magazine*

"Thorough and painstaking research, not only into the life and work of the artists but also into the scenes they depicted, is evident in this beautifully produced book" Roly Smith - *Countryman Magazine*

"A superb compilation" *Lincolnshire Life Magazine*

"A Who's who of prominent watercolour artists for the period" *Antiques Bulletin Magazine*

"Undoubtedly the definitive work on the subject" *Steam World Magazine*

"Well-captioned pictures are complemented by a very readable and often humorous text" *Rail News*

"Represents extraordinary good value for money" *Great Eastern News*

"Every now and again, the publishing world is blessed by the arrival of a book providing a refreshing change - this is such a publication and will delight all." Nick Pigott - *Railway Magazine*

"A sumptuous full-colour volume" Cathy Brown - *East Anglian Daily Times*

"The book provides useful information on the artists and prints" *The Artist Magazine*

"Beautiful pictures... thoroughly researched" *Hertfordshire Countryside Magazine*

"A delightful book... highly recommended" *Friends of the National Railway Museum*

"There can be no finer present... a treasured book that will remind you of a lost Britain" *Best of British Magazine*

LANDSCAPES under the luggage rack

Greg Norden

Greg Norden *October 2002*

LANDSCAPES
under the luggage rack

Great paintings of Britain

Published by GNRP 2001

www.carriageprints.com

Acknowledgements

Great Norden Railway Publications
PO Box 485
Bugbrooke,
Northampton NN7 3ZY

Tel: +44 (0)1604 830031
E-mail: greg@carriageprints.com
Web site: www.carriageprints.com

Copyright © Greg Norden 2001
All rights reserved. This book is protected by copyright.
No part of this publication may be reproduced, stored in a
retrieval system, or transmitted in any form or by any means,
electronic, mechanical, photocopying or otherwise, without
written permission from the publisher.

The moral right of the author has been asserted.

British Library Cataloguing in publication data.
A catalogue record for this book is available from the
British Library.

ISBN 0 9529602 1 4 popular edition 2001

All illustrations are from the author's collection unless stated.

Conceived and produced by Greg Norden.
Designed by Dr. Roger Denning & Associates.
Typeset in Rockwell and Gill Sans by Caroline Archer.
Photography by Nick Hughes, Northampton.
Maps drawn by the author.
Origination, printing and binding in Singapore, under the
supervision of MRM Graphics Ltd., Winslow, Bucks.

Original (collectors) edition 1997 [ISBN 0 9529602 0 6]

Front cover illustration: A view of Leonard Squirrell's *Bible
Hedingham, Essex,* displayed in the beautifully preserved,
Southern Railway Maunsell coach No. 6575 on the Bluebell
Railway, Sussex.
The author acknowledges the kind help received from the
Railway in producing the photograph.

Many thanks to those who have freely given their assis-
tance in the task of producing this book. In particular to
Matthew White, a generous Scotsman, who gave me
practical encouragement when my writing pistons began
to run out of steam in the early stages, and for his commitment to the project and help with certain captions.
Alan Bowman assisted by acquiring materials and
dashed madly around the north east with his camera,
photographing and researching some of the print locations. To Beverley Cole, pictorial curator at the National
Railway Museum, York, for suggesting I write the book in
the first place and for remaining calm enough not to
throttle me whenever I tried to use a pen instead of a
pencil in the archive store.

Artists were more than helpful, too. To Ronald Maddox,
not only for his artistic expertise, but particularly for the
great enthusiasm he has shown for the book since its
inception and for his personal encouragement. James
Fletcher-Watson, Frederick Donald Blake and James
Mcintosh Patrick were also more than willing to wind
back the clock and remember their days of artwork for
the railways. Barbara Buckle, the late Grace Steel and
Hilda Merriott, wives of artists Claude, Kenneth and Jack,
were also very helpful and assisted with information on
their late husbands' work. Jim, another member of the
artistic Merriott family, has been most enthusiastic in the
project too, and is pretty good with a paintbrush himself.

Thanks also to a very helpful Andrew Dow, former Head
of the National Railway Museum at York, for information
on his father, George Dow, and for casting his learned
eyes over the draft text. To Malcolm Guest, who, without
knowing it, was an answer to prayer when he filled in a
missing gap in my knowledge of the Western Region
prints and to Martin Marix Evans, whose experience in
book production proved invaluable.

To Selina Charlton, for her comments on the draft and
her herculean efforts to teach me Queen's English, like
the stuff what I now write. Bill Hamilton, too, gave me his
time to read the original text and gave constructive sug-
gestions. Sir William McAlpine and his curator Fred Gray
provided material on the GWR royal train panels and
gave a pleasant tour around the Fawley museum in the
process. To Glenn Foxley from the Keighley & Worth
Valley Railway, David Jones, the late Stan Burn, Allan
Middleton and Michael Max for providing material for
illustrations.

At this point, most authors normally acknowledge their
long-suffering families who had coped with the author's
madness during the production of the book. I was fortunate, however; my own loyal and supportive crew had all
doubted my sanity long before the project anyway.

The surprise success of the first edition, which brought
a nomination for the McColvin Medal as the Librarian's
Association 'best reference book of the year', was
helped by many supporters, including John Yellowlees
of Scotrail, Margaret White, Percy Norden, Roger
Osbaldeston, Helen Norden, Fred Bliss (one of the last
of the great British goons), and many other helpful folks
in the book trade and elsewhere. Your encouragement
was greatly appreciated.

A final thanks to those big-hearted people in the Jesus
Fellowship who kept faith in me throughout my very long
period of illness and, last but not least, to the British
Railways Board for their kind permission to use many of
the print illustrations in these pages.

Greg Norden May 2001

Dedication

Dedicated to Jesus Christ, who has radically changed
my life, and made the present and the future even
more attractive and exciting than the past.

Contents

Abbreviations

Names of railway companies are abbreviated as follows:

BR	British Railways
CLC	Cheshire Lines Commitee (GCR/GNR/MR)
CR	Caledonian Railway
ER	Eastern Region (BR)
FR	Furness Railway
GCR	Great Central Railway
GER	Great Eastern Railway
GNR	Great Northern Railway
GNSR	Great North of Scotland Railway
GSWR	Glasgow & South Western Railway
GWR	Great Western Railway
HR	Highland Railway
LBSCR	London Brighton & South Coast Railway
LMR	London Midland Region (BR)
LMS	London Midland & Scottish Railway
LNWR	London & North Western Railway
LNER	London & North Eastern Railway
LSWR	London & South Western Railway
LT	London Transport
LT&S	London Tilbury & Southend Railway
L&Y	Lancashire & Yorkshire Railway
M&GN	Midland & Great Northern Joint Railway
MR	Midland Railway
M&SWJ	Midland & South Western Junction Railway
NBR	North British Railway
NER	North Eastern Railway
NLR	North London Railway
NSR	North Staffordshire Railway
SECR	South Eastern & Chatham Railway
S&MJ	Stratford on Avon & Midland Junction Railway
SR	Southern Railway
S.Region	Southern Region (BR)
ScR	Scottish Region (BR)
WR	Western Region (BR)

Information

Would you like more information on.....

Collecting, selling or exchanging carriage prints?

The railway collector's market?

The *Rarity & Price Guide to Carriage Prints* ?

Carriage print greetings cards?

Then either.....

Visit website: www.carriageprints.com

Or write (with sae) to   Landscapes
                             c/o PO Box 485
                             Bugbrooke
                             Northampton NN7 3ZY

Or Telephone/fax: +44 (0)1604 830031

Or E- mail: greg@carriageprints.com

Foreword

Ronald Maddox PRI Hon RWS

When I was first approached by Greg several years ago about the possibility of a book featuring railway carriage pictures I was immediately excited about the idea. As he later visited and we went through his enormous collection of prints in the studio here, I was able to view again the commissioned artwork from many artists, some of whom I have known over many years and whose work is reproduced in this book and whose names became familiar to those travelling by train on the different regions. My enthusiasm for the project grew and memories of my own involvement with artwork for the railways began to flood back.

My interest in the compartment paintings began when travelling to and from school on the Eastern Region of British Railways, and seeing the many lovely views of Britain featured in these pictures. Later my rail journeys became part of my route to Art School in St Albans and, as a result of my course and being encouraged to draw and paint at locations around the city, I took an even greater interest in the carriage panels and railway posters. I studied the styles and techniques used by these selected artists, who mainly worked in watercolour, my own favourite medium.

The contrasting places of beauty depicted were intended to entice the travelling public to possible holiday locations, most of which could at that time be reached by train. The war years with petrol rationing, and the smaller number of people owning cars, meant that a great many families still travelled by railway to reach their holiday destinations.

My research into the artists made me aware that many had the affixes RI, RWS or RSW after their names, which I discovered meant Royal Institute of Painters in Watercolours, Royal Watercolour Society and Royal Scottish Watercolour Society, and I started sending paintings to the exhibitions of the RI, which was the only one that would show work of non-members at that time.

This was at the start of my career as an artist and designer and I was already producing drawings and paintings featuring many aspects of Britain, building up a library of sketchbooks. As a result, my paintings came to the attention of British Railways London Midland Region at Euston and a Mr Savage commissioned me to design and illustrate leaflets and posters, and a set of compartment paintings of the Lake District, featuring National Trust properties.

It was an interesting experience travelling north by train in 1956 on an Artist's Pass from Euston to Kendal so that I could work on the first drawings and colour sketches of Sizergh Castle, and on to Ambleside to paint the Bridge House. Townend House at Troutbeck was the next subject, although this involved a bus trip and walk! Finally, I travelled on a small diesel train on the single track railway from Penrith, to paint Wordsworth's birthplace at Cockermouth. The town was still relatively industrialised then and, during my hotel stay here, I remember being awakened by the sound of clogs in the street below!

The watercolour roughs had to be approved by the London Midland Region Publicity Board before I went ahead at home with the final paintings for reproduction and, incidentally, these were almost the last set of compartment illustrations ever commissioned.

The number of noted artists working on the series of paintings for all the Regions showed that British Rail played a major part in the commissioning of works of art, along with companies such as Shell, BP and London Transport, carrying on a tradition established by the original railway companies.

Now we can look again at some of these paintings of landscape and architecture which once appeared above our carriage seats and I am pleased to recommend this beautiful and thoroughly-researched book to all those who love Britain, its railways and the art of watercolour painting.

Ronald Maddox

Preface

Was it once possible to travel on a Waterloo to Exeter train and see Brighton Pier en route? – or travel on *The Flying Scotsman* and gain a view of Durham, ten minutes out of Kings Cross? Or could you once catch a suburban train from Euston and see a boat on Lake Windermere before you reached Watford? The answer to each question was **yes** – if you had a carriage panel to gaze at on your journey!

Carriage panels were the frames or recesses above the seats inside railway carriages, which allowed the insertion of photographs, prints, maps or advertisements, where they could be viewed by the passengers. Many people can remember the days when framed pictures kept them company in their compartments on journeys in the days of steam. Like the pictorial posters on railway stations, and often by the same artists, these landscapes brought a splash of colour to a dreary or routine journey and would reveal much about the railway company's image and objectives.

It is a fact of life that common, everyday objects become most interesting and collectable when they are disappearing or obsolete. Consequently, vast numbers of books on railway locomotives have appeared since steam's decline. In addition to books on railway companies and their services, there have been books on rolling stock and their decor, books on civil engineering works and architecture and books on posters and printed ephemera. Curiously, scarcely anything has been written on the railway carriage print.

Views from a railway carriage

Although the historians have ignored the subject, the passengers certainly appreciated the colourful pictures – the world of fine art had, at last, become accessible to the general public. Even *The Times* newspaper got excited about the panels when it carried a lengthy, semi–humorous editorial on the subject just after the war, entitled *A Picasso under the Parcels?* This extolled the work of watercolour artists . . . 'Rowland Hilder, Frank Sherwin and Claude Buckle, who for years have kept the flag of art flying even in the darkest of third class smokers.'

The article was rather uncomplimentary, however, about the carriage panel photographs . . . 'they were not always compositions of the highest standard. By a stroke of bad luck the photographer doing his best for the Grand [Hotel] at Midlandville failed to notice that a chambermaid was grinning from an upstairs window. On the day he went to Beachleigh quite a number of the holiday makers on the Grand Parade were wearing overcoats.'

Enlightened management's over the years have changed all that. Art conquered the compartments as it had conquered the hoardings and the ticket hall . . . The bulkhead beneath the parcel rack is, on the evidence of the railway authorities themselves, of great commercial value for it is seen by millions of travellers each week. Who knows what changes in public taste might not be wrought if from time to time a few Old Master prints were to be displayed . . .' A rather interesting suggestion – at least passengers would have been getting value for their Monet.

There is much truth in John Ruskin's theory that . . . 'all travelling becomes dull in the exact proportion to its rapidity' – and so it is difficult to reminisce over air travel, where you see less and less of more and more, or road journeys, where you are often a human sandwich with assorted traffic jams spread before you. Rail travel, though, with its roots in the 19th century, has created its own nostalgia. Winston Churchill even likened the past itself to rail travel when he wrote that . . . 'History with its flickering lamp stumbles along the train of the past, trying to reconstruct its scenes, to revive its echoes, and kindle with pale gleams the passion of former days.'

A century ago, the railways, with all their separate companies, certainly had enormous *character*, even if their services were often slow and erratic. With the advent of privatisation and the introduction of today's independent train operating companies with their own logos and liveries, plus a growing public opinion against the high level of road vehicle traffic, a golden opportunity exists for a new flair, verve and initiative in today's marketing of rail travel and the promotion of individual lines. The days of families enjoying a day trip to towns, cities, seaside resorts and historical sites are hopefully returning!

Recollections of journeys in the days of steam have bred a nostalgia unmatched by any other form of transport. The memories of childhood train journeys with the family remain firmly in the minds of many people – the excitement of waiting on station platforms with their enamel signs and colour posters; the sensations – at once velvety and prickly, of sitting in carriage compartments surrounded by antique hardwood panelling; views of the countryside and the telegraph poles flashing past; glimpses of stations and steam locomotives simmering in yards and sidings and the excitement of a holiday to come. Such vivid impressions are easily remembered. To the young at heart they were not just journeys but real adventures to far–away places. And the carriage pictures of seaside resorts, beauty spots and townscapes which accompanied the travellers were a small but unique characteristic part of those early pilgrimages.

The serious–looking fellow in the corner must have forgotten to shave that morning if the advertising panel above him carried any truth at all. Briefcase on luggage rack, newspaper in hand, carriage panel to gaze at and another long, hard day in the city to tackle in this typical, period snapshot of the immediate post–war era. This was an official photo of a Metropolitan Railway compartment and was used to draw attention to commercial advertising spaces in London Transport stock. [LT]

A travelling picture show

Between the late 1930s and the mid–1960s, when the railway publicity departments moved into colour reproduction and commissioned some of the leading watercolour artists of the day to paint scenes from all around Britain, the trains became travelling art galleries.

Considering its size, Britain is blessed with a gloriously varied landscape and, within a relatively short distance, the scenery (and, it must be said, the weather!) can change dramatically. This is a facet of our island which most inhabitants take for granted. But an artist, with his reliance on careful observation and sensitivity to his surroundings, is better disposed to appreciate Britain's landscape than most. If the paintings illustrated in this book convey something of this wide variety of rich scenery then it will largely have achieved its purpose.

The landscapes revealed in the carriage panel pictures of this period portray a very different country from that of today. Roads were then largely empty except for horses and carts; fashions were different and any vehicles included in the pictures looked positively prehistoric. Many towns and villages were unspoilt by major building developments; the steam locomotive was still king and – of course – most people still travelled by train! The railways of that era were different, too: the widespread closure of a large proportion of the rail network in the early 1960s had not yet taken place and most of the country could still be reached by train – often on pleasant but, sadly, little used, rural and branch lines. The four large companies controlling the railway system were in the process of being nationalised and the early years of British Rail and its dieselisation and electrification programmes were only just beginning.

A large proportion of this book is therefore devoted to a tour around England, Scotland and Wales between the years of 1937 and 1960, using many of the standard sized, beautiful fine art prints from my own collection which were issued in this period – a pictorial tribute to an era regarded by many as the heyday of advertising graphic art.

The pictures may bring back to you old memories of past visits. And you may find that looking again at the pictures – perhaps for the first time for 20, 40 or even 60 years – confirms that perceptive old saying about nostalgia . . . 'When you return to your boyhood town, you find that it wasn't the town you longed for – it was your boyhood'.

Starting in the sunshine of the Southern we shall work our way, breezily, through the east of England and up and across the Highlands of Scotland. After traversing southwards via some of the old railways in London Midland territory, we will then 'Go Great Western' for a while – all without the need to leave our seats. As the final stop on the itinerary we shall visit London – a capital end to a tour of Britain.

Choosing the illustrations for this travelling picture show has been no easy task, particularly in the Eastern and London Midland areas where the huge choice of views has necessitated a rather merciless approach to editing. This is in complete contrast to the Southern and Western regions, where very few prints were produced. The following criteria were therefore necessary for the selection of illustrations:

a) An attempt has been made to show, with relatively few exceptions, at least one example of each artist's work.
b) Some priority has been given to those prints containing railway interest such as architecture and trains.
c) An effort to provide a good geographical spread of locations was important. This has largely been achieved with the exception of the print-less South Wales area.
d) The selection has been made with a bias towards human, rather than natural, interest in order that city, town and village scapes predominate. The fact that these views are likely to have changed over the years, gives added interest to the subject. Quaint pictures of old stone bridges over streams and castle ruins have been allocated a low profile as they will probably remain the same for years to come and, besides, travel guides are full of these vistas. However, a sprinkling of this type of picture has been included in order to balance the overall effect – they did, after all, make up a fair percentage of the prints.
e) Some prints were simply chosen on their artistic merit alone. Deeping St James by Freda Marston is a good example of this.

A narrow perspective

If the choice of print illustrations was a difficult one, then the possible final size and format of the book proved an even more perplexing problem to solve. Just as the long lengths of the carriage pictures gave the artists a compositional headache, the same dimensions have not been easy to adapt to the printed page without ending up with an enormous book! In the end, the format used here was considered to be the most satisfactory compromise.

The purpose of the book can be summarised as fourfold: to resurrect a largely–forgotten or even unknown aspect of railway history; to tour nostalgically around the Britain of yesteryear in print form, as seen through the eyes of the gifted artists who painted them; to appreciate and study the different artistic styles of these painters and, finally, to help the many collectors, or would-be collectors and antique lovers, with information including print listings, and sources for the original pictures.

It is, of course, the illustrations which make this subject attractive to the non–railway enthusiasts amongst us. Without the evocative views by these top artists the purpose of the book appears rather esoteric. Some friends of mine who hadn't seen the landscape views even suggested a book on something less specialised - such as an architect's guide to window design for yak-herder's huts in central Tibet . . . As it transpired, the success of the first edition was largely due to the huge interest shown in the subject by the nostalgic, general public.

The large degree of interest in the first edition wasn't entirely unexpected, apart from the nomination for the 'best reference book of the year' award which, both took me by surprise, and resulted in some helpful TV news coverage! I was, however, taken back by the number of enthusiastic responses from many people who told me how much they appreciated the rekindling of happy memories of times spent admiring art during their train journeys. Indeed, many (including some well-known artists today) were influenced by the pictures they saw.

Since the first edition other helpful people have furnished me with extra information on the artists and the listing of prints and these revisions are all included in this edition. One correspondent also gave me an interesting account of London humour which is worth relating here. Whilst travelling on the Underground he saw a carriage advertisment showing Henry VIII with a tube ticket, with the caption "A return to Tower station please". Beneath it someone had scrawled in pen "....and a single for the missus!"

More interest in the carriage prints has been generated by the recent cinema film Enigma, starring Kate Winslet and set in Britain during the Second World War. This features some of my prints in a couple of railway carriage scenes, including one (commisioned for the occasion!) which directly involves a turning point in the plot to break the Nazi code. So, even according to the film industry, the outcome of the war turned on a humble carriage print!

Let us start, then, by having a look at the evolution of railway art and, particularly, the use of carriage panels for communicating the railway's services to its passengers.

Chapter 1
Scene in a railway coach— a century of carriage art & advertising

Early days of railway art (1830–1883)

The first carriage panels in 1884 sprang, no doubt, more from aesthetic considerations than purely commercial reasons. Just as new house owners sitting in their bare–walled lounges think it essential to have a few framed pictures around the room to brighten the surroundings and provide focal points for the household, so the compartments of the early railway carriages must have appeared rather naked without some form of adornment above the seats.

The thesis that the panels were first produced in order to attract passengers onto the railways is easily refuted by the fact that people viewing them had to be already travelling by train to do so! The most valid claim you could make for the importance of the early panels was that, apart from decorating the carriages, they broadened the public's travel horizons and encouraged more of the use of the company's network and subsidiary services. It was not until the advent of mass–produced photographs that the railways had suitable material to display in their rolling stock, and carriages began to exude this more homely atmosphere.

Ever since J. M. W. Turner's atmospheric image in 1844 of a Great Western train in his painting *Rain, Steam and Speed,* art and the railways seem to have developed a warm affinity for one another. Prints of railway subjects became fashionable in extolling the virtues of rail travel when the earliest railways were being built but they were not suitable for use in carriage rolling stock. This was hardly surprising, really, since many passenger coaches of the period had no roof! Two thousand of these prints alone were produced between 1830 and 1850; the works of John Cooke Bourne and Thomas Talbot Bury probably being the best known, especially for their drawings of the engineering feats undertaken in building these early lines. Shaw's hand-coloured 'long prints', published by Rudolph Ackerman in 1831, entitled *Travelling on the Liverpool and Manchester Railway* became the most famous of these and, with their generous length and narrow wooden frames, looked remarkably like early versions of the carriage panels of the mid 1900s. In fact, because of their popularity, they were re-published by Raphael Tuck in 1894 and were used in carriage panels in LMS days.

After 1860 few prints were being produced – the need had disappeared now that the railways had established

themselves. Indeed, any idea of decorating the railways with posters and prints was ridiculed at first, as can be deduced by the following quote from the *Railway Chronicle* . . . 'The suggestion that railway stations can be enlivened with pictures is as ridiculous as painting a madonna on a butcher's tray! How could jostling, panting crowds spare the time to look at art?' – hardly prophetic!

Carriage panels of the pre–grouping period (1884–1922)

Early photograph panels

The earliest known official photograph of railways, taken in 1851, was of a South Eastern Railway, Crampton locomotive *Folkstone* at the Great Exhibition, but the mass production of photographs did not really begin until just before the turn of the century.

The first company to enhance the interiors of their rolling stock with scenic photographic panels was the Great Eastern Railway, under Thomas William Worsdell, who began displaying them in their carriages in 1884. These were produced by Payne Jennings Ltd, and often consisted of seven small, black and white, mounted photographs. The locations were hand–written in ink on the mount under each view – unattractive in their own right, perhaps, but they certainly added to the carriage decor and set the trend for British coaching stock for the next hundred years.

In 1895 the Great Western Railway also began to include photographic panels in their clerestory coaches and, surprisingly enough, these were not black and white, but beautiful colour–tinted photographs. Landscape features were given highlights of colour over the top of black and white photographs and these views were attractively mounted. Every effort was made to create a stylish finish and, in view of the numbers produced, must have been very expensive. The company responsible for all of the artificially-coloured photographic work for the railways in those days (and the manufacture of the carriage panel frames themselves) was the Photocrom Company of Cheapside, London – a pioneering world–wide business with their works at Tunbridge Wells in Kent. Some of their statistics make interesting reading: eight men were employed by the company solely in the taking of railway company photographs for use in carriages and railway stations and 12,000 different subjects were photographed for this purpose, involving 250,000 prints in stock! The works despatched an average of 10-12 tons of finished photos daily and cut up 24 miles of moulding

1

every year for the frames! Most of the major railway companies later followed the example of the GWR who were still Photocrom's largest customer in 1000 and had views in most of their coaches. The LSWR and SECR (1898), MR, GCR and GNR (1899) also began to place orders for their carriage stock.

Photocrom also supplied the colour-tinted photographs which graced the panels in Queen Victoria's *Diamond Jubilee* Royal Train. Built in 1897 by the GWR at Swindon, this was, possibly, the only royal train to include carriage panels and they were superb and unique examples. The frames were constructed in sycamore and walnut hard-woods, with hand carved corner flutings and gilded surrounds. They contained photographs of locations around the GWR territory (including Windsor Castle!) and each hand–painted title was recessed into the frame. After all this work, Queen Victoria should have been suitably 'amused'.

Even though many smaller companies had been taken over by larger concerns before the turn of the century, the railway network still consisted of a sizeable number of independent companies who had grown out of the railway mania years of the 1840's. Passenger comfort in carriage rolling stock saw a vast improvement by the late

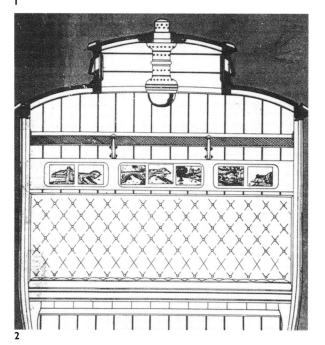

2

3

1 **The Great Eastern Railway was the first railway company to display photograph views inside their carriages. They commissioned Payne Jennings to produce these panels consisting of small, mounted photographs of locations within their area and these first appeared in 1884. The titles were hand-written in ink on the mounts. This particular example is dated 1889 and contains views of Hertfordshire and Suffolk. [NRM]**

2 **A cross-section of a GWR clerestory coach in 1895, showing the layout of panels.**

3 **The *Royal* approach. The superb interior of Saloon 283, one of the coaches in the Diamond Jubilee Royal Train built for Queen Victoria by the GWR at Swindon in 1897. The gilded and hand carved, hardwood panels with their colour–tinted photographs, complete a magnificent decor and were possibly the only panels to have been produced for royal trains.**

4 **The *giant* approach. Possibly the largest carriage panel ever! A huge framed picture adorns Director's Saloon No.1, belonging to the Lancashire & Yorkshire Railway. [NRM]**

5 **The *art gallery* approach. Very large photographic panels and adverts in a North Eastern Railway open coach enhance the surroundings and provide attractive focal points for the passengers. [NRM]**

4

5

The *sumptuous* approach. The magnificent interior of a North Eastern Railway, first class open coach, showing how the different–sized carriage pictures blended in with the beautiful hardwood panelling. Craftmanship of a bygone age. [NRM]

The *front room lounge* approach. These mounted photograph panels provide a homely and finishing touch to the decor of this Midland Railway, Bradford–Morecambe club saloon in 1921. [NRM]

19th century with the Midland Railway pioneering the way. In this period it was often only these larger main line companies who displayed panels in their coaches.

By the early 1900s the carriages of most major companies were enlivened by photographs in colour, black and white, and sepia. These came framed in all varieties of shapes and sizes, some of them huge, and largely depended on the space available or the contour of the carriage walls and partitions. Frames were sometimes hexagonal, octagonal and even oval; often being a part of the carriage interior itself and sometimes a separate addition. In many companies' coaches, scenic photos were also located between the windows along the length of the carriage – no doubt their rivals were quick to point out that this was due to the scenery outside being too depressing to view by the passengers.

Similar notices appeared in the coaching stock of some companies – particularly those of the London, Brighton & South Coast Railway and another unusual but attractive way of producing panels, which was certainly adopted in North Eastern Railway carriages, was to print photographic images straight onto a rectangular piece of wood. This was then varnished and slotted into the carriage panel itself. Similarly, this company, along with the Great Northern and the North British, also used panels

The *elegant* approach. Beautiful 'swept head', framed photographs bring a touch of style to this Lancashire & Yorkshire Railway, first class open saloon No.109, in 1911. [NRM]

The *basic* approach. Carriage pictures were not only provided for the benefit of the wealthy, first class clientele in pre-grouping days. Mounted photographs are here displayed in an open, third class carriage, owned by the London & South Western Railway, although it appears that passengers needed to be giraffes in order to view them! [NRM]

made up of transfers mounted on boards. These transfers chiefly advertised their railway hotels and, in the case of York, bore at the base the legend . . . 'Dinner is ready at York on arrival of the Scottish expresses which are allowed not less than 20 minutes in the station' – an interesting reminder of the railways before buffet and restaurant cars came into being and a probable cause of an increase in the cases of indigestion around station platforms in those days.

The interior decor of railway carriages in this era was relatively luxurious. Even third class stock gave off an aura of craftsmanship with their wooden bodies, detailed hardwood panelling and sweeping curves. They were also superbly painted and protected by abundant layers of varnish. The carriage photograph panels blended in well with this decor and enhanced the elegance, too.

Some companies' carriages, such as the Lancashire & Yorkshire's Southport coaches, even managed to contain framed and glazed posters in them. These posters advertised the large hotels and other locations and resorts in their domain and the slogans on them seemed to be tongue–in–cheek, such as . . . *'Come to Southport for mild winters!'* Visitors to this amazing resort were also assured by the Cheshire Lines Committee brochures, that if . . .' a shower should happen to fall, the porous nature of the soil ensures that it should not have a permanent effect upon the health and spirits . . .' After reading this soothing and imaginative nonsense, readers must have wondered if the only real shower they were likely to be affected by in Lancashire, were those responsible for the company publicity.

Oh I do like to be beside the seaside
At the turn of the century, companies saw the need actively to promote their local resorts. These were often compared to those on the continent, particularly on the Mediterranean coast. The object of this was to encourage the public to see Britain first before travelling overseas, or, as Charles Kingsley put it . . .

While we find God's signet
Fresh on English ground,
Why go gallivanting
With the nations round?

This approach produced some rather outrageous comparisons. The Great North of Scotland Railway, for example, saw the Moray Firth coast as 'The Scottish Riviera'; the Great Northern Railway likened Ullswater to 'The English Lucerne' and – wait for it – the Furness Railway

portrayed Grange over Sands as 'The Naples of the North'! It would not have surprised too many people if the Metropolitan Railway had attempted to advertise Neasden as 'The Nice of the North Circular'.

Since the day in 1841 when Thomas Cook had become inspired by the idea of temperance excursions and had begun organising them on a commercial basis, the railways had run special trains which, in the early days, reached enormous lengths and were drawn by a string of locomotives. With their cheap fares and potential to cover long distances, the railways brought a new host of opportunities for leisure travel to the common man. *The Railway News* remarked on this in 1889 when it stated that . . . 'Hundreds of thousands of dwellers in "populous cities pent" would, but for the railways, have been compelled to pass their holidays amid the familiar squalor of their everyday life . . . Our great manufacturing cities pour forth their tide of human life into the neighbouring hills and moorlands and seaside places of resort.' It was thus the railways themselves who, indirectly, created large holiday resorts. This was especially the case in the mid–1800s just after the railways had been built. When the railway reached Brighton in 1841, the population increased by 20,000 in ten years – an enormous metamorphosis for those days.

Companies like Bass, the brewers, began to charter fleets of special trains on a yearly basis to these popular seaside destinations, albeit not to publicise temperance! One day in 1893, for example, they hired 15 trains for their *10,000 workforce* which left Burton for a day out in Great Yarmouth, at ten minute intervals – a works outing on a huge scale! It was around this time that a mass holiday–making industry began to appear. By 1937, it was estimated that the number of people taking holidays away from home had risen to 15 million – a vast (potential) source of revenue for the railways and the prime advertising target for the carriage panels and the posters.

Early advertisements & maps
At the same time that photographs were being employed to enhance the carriage interiors, companies also realised the commercial potential offered by the captive audience sitting in the railway carriages. Advertisement panels began to appear in coaches. These often promoted the hotel, shipping and associated facilities of the operating company or its subsidiaries. One colourful panel, advertising the South Eastern & Chatham Railway's refreshment rooms, also reminded passengers: '. . . In the interests of cleanliness and public health, passengers are earnestly requested to refrain from spitting in the

carriages or on the station platforms'. It seems strange now, but the habit presented a major health problem in those days when many died from the spread of tuberculosis.

Most pre-grouping companies managed to maintain the stylish look of their carriage interiors, even when filling them with advertisements. A close study of the compartment wall in a London, Brighton & South Coast Railway, second class carriage, shows how adverts were adapted to fit the contours of the stock. The unusual handle in the centre of the mirror is a heat regulator. [NRM]

Attractive advertisements in a Lancashire & Yorkshire Railway, Liverpool to Southport coach in 1920. Adverts had become a familiar sight in carriages by this time and were often administered by W H Smith and Sons Ltd. Note the large system map above the doorway. [NRM]

1

2

1 **Chee Tor & Ashwood Dale (MR)**
The Midland Railway used Photocrom's colour–tinted photographs in their panels, which also displayed the Company's 'Wyvern' crest on the mount and a title, including the nearest station. Scenes of the Peak District were very popular in carriages. Here we see a typical MR panel with views of the limestone scenery of Chee Tor and a Midland express with its red coaches steaming through Ashwood Dale, between Millers Dale and Buxton.

2 **Shoreham Harbour, Sussex & Bourne Bridge, Guildford, Surrey(LB&SCR)**
An attractive Edwardian panel for the LB&SCR, with its elegant lettering, featuring views of Shoreham Harbour and Bourne Bridge at Guildford.

3 **Pannal Links, Yorkshire (NER)**
'I said aim for the middle arch of the viaduct – not the train on top!' Golf courses were common subjects for posters and panels. Here we see a lovely period snapshot of golfers on the course at Pannal, near Harrogate – a popular area for visitors to the north east. The impressive structure in the background is the 31-arch, 1,873 foot long, railway viaduct at Crimple. [NRM]

4 **The Sands, Bridlington, Yorkshire (NER)**
This NER panel has a marvellous, spontaneous feel about it – children seem to be enjoying themselves in the sand at Bridlington, although the girl in the moat *(centre right)* appears to have wet herself! The lad in the centre seems content to fling sand at the boy with the spade, too – all good, dirty fun in this sepia photograph panel from the early 1900s. The photographs were taken by Thomas Illingworth & Co. and were produced by Payne Jennings Ltd. [NRM]

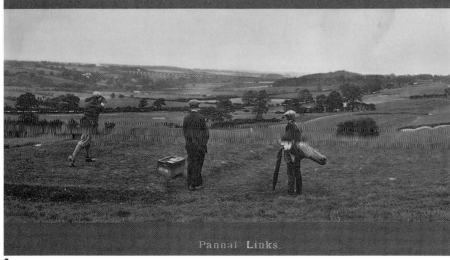

3

4

Pre-grouping panel illustrations

One of the panels from coach 233 of Queen Victoria's *Diamond Jubilee* royal train of 1897. Only hand–carved, gilded hardwoods, with colour–tinted photographs and hand–written, recessed titles were thought fit enough for royalty. The GWR photographs show *(from left to right)* the Water Tower at Chester; Eccleston Ferry, Chester; and Magdalen Tower in Oxford.

Clifton Suspension Bridge, Bristol (GWR)
Designed by Isambard Kingdom Brunel and built between 1836 and 1864, this elegant structure stands 245 ft above the river and crosses the Avon Gorge just to the west of Bristol. In this photograph of around 1895, the Bristol to Portishead branch line can be seen running along the river on the right. A fine bridge from a fine engineer. *(Bottom right)*

The Coracle men, Carmarthen (GWR)
A charming period view of fishermen with their coracle boats by the Afon Tywi, Carmarthen. Their faces give the impression that they'd caught nothing that day, or perhaps the photographer had captured them fishing on the Sabbath! *(Bottom left)*

Barmouth Bridge & Cader Idris (GWR)
A marvellous 19th century view across the Mawddach estuary as a Cambrian Railways train traverses the bridge, with Cader Idris in the background. *(Top left)*

Shrewsbury, The Square (GWR)
An interesting choice of transport exists in the Square at Shrewsbury in the days before motor cars or pedestrian precincts had appeared. *(Top right)*

Pre-grouping panel illustrations

Whitley Bay

Whitley Bay, Northumberland (NER)
The great British husband in his suit, tie and rolled up trousers, paddles in the water keeping a watchful, fatherly eye on his family down at the 'shallow end'. The poor lad in the centre looks rather frozen in this very natural photo of Whitley Bay beach, just north of Tynemouth on the NER coast line to Blyth. [NRM]

Gloucester Town Centre (GWR)
The photographer captures a nostalgic scene here, as a tram to Kingsholm trundles along busy Northgate Street in the centre of Gloucester. At this time, the town was an important railway centre, with the Midland and the Great Western Railways both having main stations here. How times have changed . . . and fashions too.

The Pier, Plymouth, Devon (GWR)
The Edwardians loved their seaside piers, including this short one at Plymouth. Whilst promoting the delights of 'Walter George's Komedy Koncert Kompany' (groan) it was also operating paddle steamer trips around the Plymouth Sound.

Jersey, St Aubins, Channel Islands (GWR)
One of the lesser known narrow gauge railways in Britain was the Jersey Railways and Tramways Line in the Channel Islands, which ran from St. Helier to Corbiere, via St Aubin station, shown here. The 3'6" gauge, 8½ mile long line was completed in 1899. It ran quite an intensive service, but struggled financially, and after a disastrous fire in 1936 which destroyed the coaching stock, the line was closed.

Pre-grouping panel illustrations

ROTHESAY TOWN & PIER, LOOKING EAST.

Rothesay, Isle of Bute (CR)
One of the very attractive Caledonian Railway panels,
showing Rothesay, the chief resort on the island, with its
ferry boat service to Wemyss Bay across the Firth of Clyde.
It seems amazing that this was produced nearly 100 years ago.

Pre-grouping panel illustrations

Maps of the companies' systems also became a common companion on travellers' journeys for there was little point in encouraging travel in the future to the scenic views displayed if the passengers weren't even sure where they were at the time. It seems that the pioneering Great Eastern were the first company to display maps inside their trains. These were issued just after 1900, were very colourful (see p.19), and appeared in all their main line compartment stock. Other companies began to produce maps which, more often than not, resembled a network of rather illegible spidery lines. They tended more towards decoration than information. Mirrors located above the seats also became a common feature and added a final touch of sophistication to the carriage decor.

Due to the limited scope of printing techniques in those pre–grouping days, most panels contained photographs instead of prints, but companies like the Metropolitan Railway did occasionally reproduce some very simple sketches in pencil and charcoal. The Great Western Railway, too, had introduced some 'fine art engravings' in 1907 and an advertisement appeared in their *Holiday Haunts* book during that year . . . 'Arrangements have been made for fine art engravings to be exhibited in the Great Western Railway carriages. These engravings are printed on India paper, mounted on plate paper and consist of the beautiful scenery at places served by the GWR lines and, for the guidance of travellers, views of the principal hotels . . . .An illustrated catalogue of the views is now available'. Copies were sold, ready for framing, at the nominal charge of one shilling (5p) each. The engraved surface was 8 inches by 6 inches and the full size of the copies on sale, including the mount, was 16 inches by 12 inches. The advert omitted to say, however, that the pictures were, in fact, gravure prints over photographs. Advertising techniques were ever devious!

Panels abound – Underground

The first tube lines in London were opened by the Underground in the early 1900s. The panels in these early trains invariably carried commercial advertisements because of the number of passengers and the nature of their journeys. These revenue-earning panels have been the staple viewing diet of most commuter journeys for many years. Indeed, the layout of the panels inside London Transport stock has changed little since these early days, and the advertisements are still as prolific as ever. LT have tried a few experiments to relieve passenger boredom amongst their more intellectual clientele, such as the use of poetry in their panels (what I term the 'tube of smarties' approach), but at least these

make a pleasant change from the usual adverts for 'temps and typists' and cheap holiday flights.

By 1911 the *Railway Gazette* was asking the question . . . 'Is the railway advertising manager properly recognised as a force in modern railway work?', and most correspondents were of the opinion that they were not. Much of the advertising was channelled through the press in these days and the railway companies didn't compete with the roads but with each other, which was often unhelpful. In this era the choice of panel photograph views were proposed by the photograph companies and not the railways, in much the same way that the views for posters were submitted by the printers concerned. However, from this time on the railway advertising manager began to carry more initiative, influence and imagination as to how the railway was to promote itself.

The railways were undoubtedly at their zenith during the reign of Edward VII. The only real competition they faced at this time was with the trams in urban areas (in 1907 more people travelled in Greater London by tram than by train). Between 1870 and 1912 passenger carryings had quadrupled to 266.9 million train miles and 95 per cent of these passengers travelled in third class carriages, where panels were often scarcer than those in first class rolling stock.

GWR First World War carriage notice

By 1914 the total number of independent companies had condensed to 100, of which 15 controlled 84 per cent of the total mileage of the country. The First World War effort, however, had burdened the railways considerably and, by 1920, the system was in a poor physical condition and in a far weaker financial state at a time when new and difficult challenges were appearing on the horizon.

A typical interior view of London Transport pre–war tube stock, showing the panel adverts above the windows and at the coach ends and, also, the standard linear route map near the ceiling. Advertisements include parcels and house clearance operations by the LMS. The coach is No. 2212 from the Bakerloo Line and the photograph was taken in 1936. [LT]

A reproduction of a GER colour map, which dates from the early 1900s, and a Caledonian Railway map issued a little later. The former was probably the first map to be displayed in railway carriages, and featured in all GER main line compartment stock. The GER London suburban network was then the most intensive suburban steam service in the world, and the locomotive and the bus depicted were both built at Stratford, the famous GER London works.

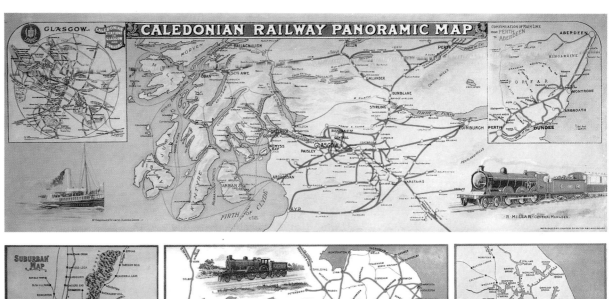

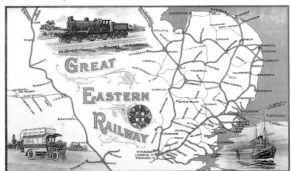

Older maps were often more attractive than modern versions, yet were very difficult to read! This is a Manchester, Sheffield & Lincolnshire Railway example, with its spidery web of lines.

Passengers looking at this attractive LB&SCR map and advert panel were tempted to take a journey to the continent or to move to the . . . 'Healthy country residential resorts of Croydon and Sutton'!

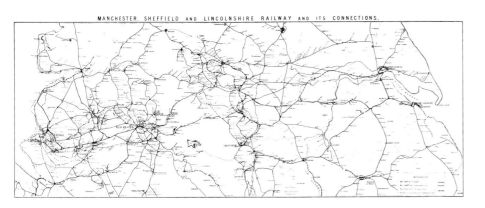

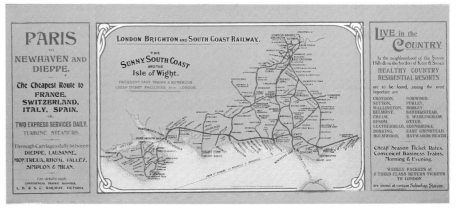

Pre-grouping advertisements and map panels

An intriguing comparison in detail between the carriage maps of rivals **GWR** *(top)* and **LSWR** *(bottom)*. Although both companies operated lines into the west country, you would never have thought so looking at these maps! The **GWR** map shows only one **LSWR** line in the area (from Barnstaple to Ilfracombe), whilst the **LSWR** are far more gracious, particularly in the Cornwall area. Main lines are drawn remarkably straight in diagrammatic fashion, with each company's route appearing to be the most direct. Note how the long length of the **GWR** map has necessitated a rather narrow Wales and Somerset!

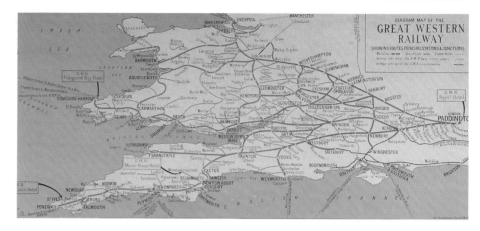

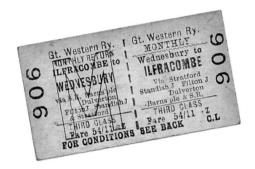

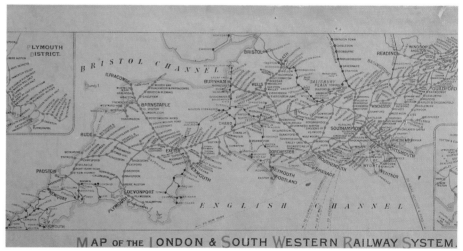

MAP OF THE LONDON & SOUTH WESTERN RAILWAY SYSTEM.

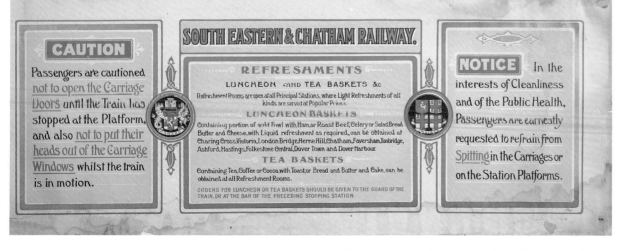

These notices were displayed in many **SECR & GWR** carriages. Whilst warning passengers not to mutilate the public by opening the doors of moving trains, and cautioning people against spitting all over the place, the **SECR** panel *(bottom)* also listed all the stations where luncheon and tea baskets were available – just in case travellers still had an appetite after reading the notice. It was the **LNWR**, in fact, who first advertised food baskets from their Chester station in 1876, in the days before dining cars came into use. The **GWR** advert *(top)* was issued in 1920 and included the standard instruction about pulling the communication chain. It was often situated below the carriage ventilator handles.

Pre-grouping advertisements and map panels

Carriage panels of the Big Four (1923–1938)

In 1923 the many existing railway companies were amalgamated into the 'Big Four' which consisted of the London & North Eastern (LNER), London Midland & Scottish (LMS), Great Western (GWR), and Southern (SR) Railways. As a result of this grouping, these companies acquired a large fleet of carriages – 20,000; 27,000; 10,100; and 10,800 respectively.

A call to competitiveness
Following the grouping, carriage panels started to assume a more standard (rectangular) pattern than they had previously. These new companies, too, began to realise the potential in creative commercial advertising. What is generally termed the 'golden era of posters' began and continued until the Second World War, with various competitions being run by the companies for the best designs and, in the case of the LMS, the use of top artists from the Royal Academy such as Augustus John and William Orpen to illustrate them. The output from these companies was prolific – the LNER advertising department, alone, employed 180 staff to handle the business.

Prior to 1923, most companies had given little thought to persuasive marketing. Companies generally concentrated on giving information on their services, rather than trying to persuade passengers to use them. For example, they crammed as much information into their posters as they could and Norman Wilkinson, one of the new breed of poster artists at the time, described them as being . . . 'An uninspired jumble of small views of resorts, frequently arranged in little circular frames, with a good deal of meaningless decoration interwoven between each picture. The effect was a hotchpotch which was quite unintelligible at a distance' (from his book *A Brush with Life*).

The size of the carriage panels, however, made it difficult to give scope to the same scale of imagination as the posters had, with all their extra space. Possible poster–like views of the solid dependable British husband, smoking a pipe on a perfect summer's day, accompanied by his perfectly–formed, and slightly top heavy, wife and their two happy children; one boy, one girl, playing in litter–less sand, which never seemed to stick to their tanned bodies, could never appear in the scenic panel views because of the picture size. However, commercial advertising in coaching stock certainly began to flourish as the railways realised that the travelling public were

Although the Metropolitan Railway was incorporated into the Underground system, its coaches (being surface stock), were similar to normal local carriage stock as can be seen from this interior view of a coach in 1934. Adverts abound, including one for *Wrigley's Chewing Gum* which claims to 'aid indigestion' – Hmmm? Note the Metropolitan carriages outside the window. [LT]

also interested in spending money on other items as well as railway tickets - at long last they started to see the passenger as one who has what it takes. A popular panel on the Southern and probably the longest running one, too, was the well known *Hovis* advert which appeared in 1926 and was still earning its bread at the beginning of the Second World War. It showed the word *Hovis* appearing on the headcodes of five Southern electric units with a caption : 'The route to health has *Hovis* at the end'.

As well as advertising brand names such as '*Jeyes fluid disinfectant*' and other well remembered commodities, railway companies also continued to make use of carriage panels to advertise their own services such as hotels, refreshment rooms, docks and cartage, for by this time, of course, wider roads and more widespread car ownership had made road travel a viable alternative. Motor vehicles were fast becoming a threat in the transport market of the future.

The railways were quite slow, in fact, to wake up from the sleep–induced years of competition–less complacency, and the need to sell themselves became more urgent. In September, 1931 the *Railway Service Journal* reported that the LMS passenger manager was telling his staff to . . . 'get in contact with as many members of the public as you can, and sell them rail travel. Give each one you

meet a strong selling talk on what we are doing for them this year'. By March, 1933 it carried a more positive note . . . 'Instead of letting the public come to the railway only when compelled to use the train service, railway companies now urge it by every possible means to use their services, creating reasons for people to travel by train and offering every kind of inducement to do so'.

However, road traffic continued to grow between the war years and the railways' attempts to salvage their position by initiating their own road transport services only met with limited success.

In 1926 the more commercially aggressive LNER had published a small booklet exalting the virtues of their carriage advertisements. This showed examples of their artistic, pencil drawn sketches, with a caption below each example: 'Say it in pencil to the buyer side of Britain' – a

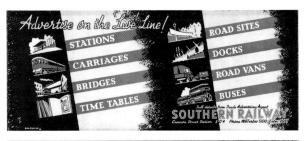

The railway companies operated a wide spectrum of services. Here we see a selection of SR panels. *The Advertise on the Live Line* panel lists the Southern's wide–ranging publicity facilities; the *Move your Furniture* advert shows the diversity of the railway's services; whilst the third example publicises one of the Company's hotels at Deal in Kent.

One of the LNER's pencil sketch panels issued in the mid–1920s. J W King drew these simple sketches of Scarborough, the 'Queen of Watering Places'. These panels, which involved the work of various artists, also advertised routes to the continent via the company's ports and shipping services.

pun on the LNER slogan 'Come to the drier side of Britain'. Perhaps it succeeded because, in 1932, the manufacturers of Shredded Wheat took 20,000 panels to advertise their product. These LNER sketches were produced in 1924 and extolled locations in their area such as Scarborough, Bridlington and cities in Northern Europe via their North Sea ferries. They actually evolved from earlier North Eastern Railway panel adverts and were produced in much the same format. The drawings were by well-known artists such as Fred Taylor, H.G.Gawthorn, Adrian Hill and J.W.King and listed the usual virtues of each resort : 'Bracing air'(roughly translated as arctic gale force winds), 'Good sands' (half an hour's walk to reach the sea), and a few facilities of each location. It all tended to make passengers think of the east coast in biblical terms – a place where 'many are cold but few are frozen'.

No comprehensive records appear to have survived of the photos and prints which went into railway carriage panels, even during British Rail days, so pre–war information is scarce. To give an example, a book of 55 miniature paintings, all approx. 4 inches by 2 inches, of scenes on the River Thames from source to sea by an unknown artist was sold by Phillips auctioneers in 1990 for £10,000. These were thought to have been painted for use as masters for carriage prints by the GWR but, as far as is known, no evidence, as yet, has appeared to substantiate it. It is more likely that these were produced for their travel publications and that the GWR were happy to remain loyal to their many photographic panels as far as their coaching stock was concerned.

Big Four photograph panels

The four companies were producing mainly black and white or sepia photographs of scenic views by the mid–1930s. Most local and express train carriages at this period carried these photographic panels and thousands were produced depicting scenic views in their own territories. Most of these featured beauty spots such as the Peak District, views of bays and beaches and mountain valleys. Some were of more man–made subjects such as cathedrals and seaside resort promenades. Rather than use outside suppliers, as in pre-grouping days, the railway companies now had the facilities to produce their own photographs. The GWR pictures, for instance, were taken by the staff of the photographic sections of their engineering departments and were sometimes used as illustrations for their company publications.

The difficulty with photographs as a long–term advertising medium is that they bring the dimension of real life with them, especially when it comes to people: the girl in the swimsuit on the beach near the Edwards arcade, for example, is middle–aged now with a few children, or perhaps she was killed in the blitz . . . Paintings are, generally speaking, far less realistic – their main job, in this case, is to project an image. After a while, most of the four companies' photos tended to appear rather outdated because of new developments, and had a sombre feel about them. They were also becoming very expensive to replace.

Photographs in a railway compartment
James Kirkup

In their oval frames, we contemplate
These old-fashioned landscapes, that do not,
Obscured by steam or nightfall, or merely
Distance, easily pass by. Occasionally
Sepulchred in tunnels, but always
Illuminated by the sun of holidays,
They travel changelessly behind
The mirror–glass that is another kind
Of window, and remain with us
All through our journey to the terminus.

In sepia tones we view the popular resorts,
Llandudno, Filey, Poole; the ports
Of Harwich, Dover; the fan–vault cloister
And the cathedral streets of Gloucester.
At Torquay, Frinton, Morecambe, we regard
White sails, tents, bathers, rose–beds on the promenade.
At Scarborough, the visitors recline upon the sands
Below the Grand Hotel, or listen to marine bands.
At Criccieth, Brighton, Buxton and Penzance
The couples loiter, waiting for the flannel dance.

A sympathetic cameraman recorded places
To which we never seemed to be going, faces
We never saw, now hardly distinguish
Under the deck-chair awnings; the anguish
Of time and place existing as if they
Were all time and everywhere. A sunny day
Flashed on the burn that clattered through a glen;
A wind blew spray upon a rock, then
As it appears to now, as if it would never
Happen here again: the pathetic moment, fixed for ever.

© James Kirkup. From *The Poetry of Railways* an anthology by Kenneth Hopkins, published by Leslie Frewin Ltd 1966.

Ilfracombe, Devon (SR)
An interesting view of the harbour from the hills above. The inset (from an earlier SR panel) shows the paddle steamer to Lundy Island and South Wales at the jetty. Ilfracombe was the destination for many holidaymakers to the lovely North Devon coast and the resort's ex LSWR station (now closed) was the terminating point for the *Atlantic Coast Express* and many other long express runs from Waterloo.

Westgate, Kent (SR)
People liked to be seen in their hats in this crowded seafront view of Westgate on Sea in Kent in the late 1920s. Perhaps this is why few people appear to be braving the sea.

Eastbourne, Sussex (SR)
Eastbourne looks very similar to Brighton here, with its pier, hotels and esplanade. The photograph was probably taken in the late 1920s as the row of cars in the left foreground indicates.

Big Four photograph panels

DEAL.

A LANE, KNUTSFORD   KNUTSFORD STATION

CHESHIRE LINES RAILWAY

A Lane, Knutsford, Cheshire (CLC)
The railways sometimes chose some strange views to portray in their carriages. Here, the Cheshire Lines Railway (using the standard **LMS** panel format) comes up with a, staggeringly breathtaking, panorama of a country road in Knutsford, Cheshire (and not too sharp a photo at that!).

Deal, Kent (SR)
A few children play amongst the boats and deckchairs on the pebble beach, whilst an East Kent bus approaches, centre right, in this interesting view of the Deal seafront in Kent. It was once a channel port, yet declined and later developed into a small resort. The town is located on the ex **SECR** line between Ramsgate and Dover, on a stretch of coast with few resorts. It even had its own pier, re-built in 1957 after this photo was taken.

Port Erin, Isle of Man(LMS)
A fine photograph of the beach and bay at this seaside town situated at the southern end of the island. Although there are many people on the beach, few seem to be braving the sea. Port Erin is the terminus station at the end of the Isle of Man Railway. The line was originally opened in 1873, as a 15$\frac{1}{2}$ mile, 3 ft gauge, single track line from Douglas. The Isle of Man Railway network finally spread to cover 46 route miles. The island was served by ferries from Liverpool and Heysham on the mainland.

PORT ERIN.   ISLE OF MAN.

Big Four photograph panels

Lime Street, Liverpool (LMS) *(top)*
A No. 24 tram to Seaforth approaches the photographer close to Lime Street station and hotel in this fascinating study of Liverpool city centre in the 1930s, before war time bombing destroyed many buildings.

The Promenade, Llandudno. (LMS) *(bottom)*
Llandudno has always been the most popular of the North Wales seaside resorts. Its station, which lies at the end of the ex **LNWR** branch from Llandudno Junction has seen countless holidaymakers and excursionists during the summer months over the last 100 years or more. The scene here has changed relatively little since this photo was taken before the war. The Grand Hotel, close to the pier, still appears impressive today and the large solid dwellings still cluster beneath Great Orme Head on the left. Crowds still like to stroll upon the prom, but at the Pavilion the brass band no longer plays tiddley om pom pom.

Big Four photograph panels

Blackpool, Lancashire (LMS)
It would be strange in a book containing pictures of seaside towns not to look at the most famous one of all. Blackpool certainly epitomises the British holiday resort in everything that is good, bad and, sometimes, downright ugly! The town saw its first railway excursion on the 3 July 1842. By 1880 it was attracting one million visitors a year and by 1903, there were a colossal *three million passengers* pouring into the town's two stations, jointly owned by the L&Y, and the LNWR. This influx sometimes necessitated an incredible *80 excursion trains* a day from locations all over the country and the town's 29 platforms could scarcely cope. In this classic view of the seafront, the 518 ft tall tower looks down on the masses below as they spend their money in vanity fair. Note the tram just visible on the promenade *(lower right)*.

Buxton, (Derbyshire) (LMS)
Numerous photographs of Derbyshire appeared in railway carriages in the early years of the century. This one shows an impressive view of the spa town of Buxton – the Peak District's 'Bath'. Here we look down upon the Crescent in the foreground, built by the 5th Duke of Devonshire at the end of the 18th century. The Devonshire Royal Hospital is situated behind it with its huge 156 ft dome and, for railway lovers, the station can clearly be seen on the right of the picture.

Morecambe, Lancashire (LMS)
'At Torquay, Frinton, Morecambe, we regard, white sails, tents, bathers, rose beds on the promenade'. Also note the *Winter Gardens* theatre *(centre)* and the **LMS** *art deco* style hotel *(right)*.

Big Four photograph panels

The River Looe, Cornwall (GWR)
The town and resort of Looe is located at the end of the pleasant branch line from Liskeard and was originally split into two distinct halves (East and West), situated on each side of the river. The bridge shown here was built in 1883 and connected the two. The location is now an attraction for sea anglers and also has some fine sandy beaches. The vehicles on the roads have also altered somewhat since then.

THE RIVER, LOOE.

THE BOATING LAKE, GOODRINGTON.

Boating Lake, Goodrington, Devon (GWR)
It often appears that the railways weren't too concerned if the public in their panel views didn't seem to be enjoying themselves! It is also interesting how often water, in one form or another, seemed to be a big attraction in the panels too – this time in a boating lake at Goodrington, near Paignton, one of the premier excursion centres on the GWR network.

The Beach, Borth, Cardiganshire (GWR)
The photographer seems to have chosen a bright day when taking this lovely sharp photo of the long Borth beach on the Cardiganshire coast. There is certainly room for a few more holidaymakers yet. The town lies in mid–Wales between Aberystwyth and Machynlleth on the ex Cambrian Railways main line from Shrewsbury.

THE BEACH, BORTH.

Big Four photograph panels

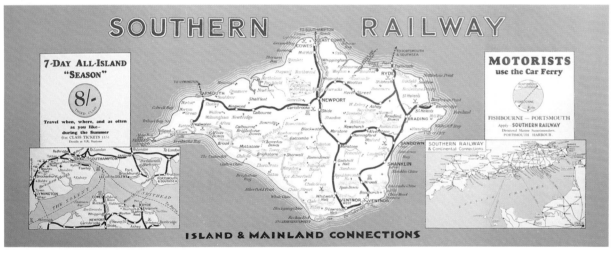

Hovis adverts *(top)* showing small bakeries in rural areas were both popular and prolific in Southern Railway carriages. Westerham station (now closed) lay at the end of the branch line from Dunton Green, 55 minutes from London, as the advert shows. David Burley was responsible for much of the Southern's advertisement artwork at this time, and this particular example was issued in 1947, just before nationalisation.

An attractive map of the Isle of Wight railways *(bottom)*, showing island and mainline connections, issued by the Southern Railway – the title appearing in their distinctive 'sunshine' lettering. A seven day 'rover' season ticket cost a mere eight shillings (40p) third class, and gave the owner the freedom to travel these quaint lines using any train.

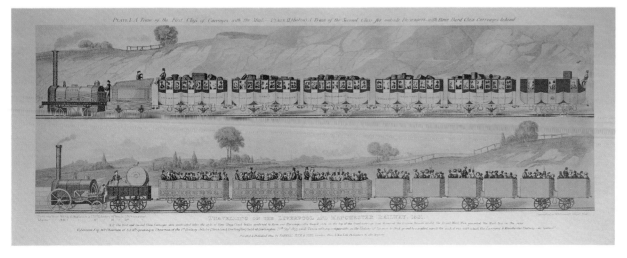

Travelling on the Liverpool and Manchester Railway 1831. (LMS Panel)

These quaint, hand coloured, 'long print' pictures by Shaw were originally printed in 1831, just after the opening of the world's first passenger railway on the 15 September 1830 – a landmark in the economic and social development of the world. They were reproduced by Raphael Tuck in 1894. The first class (covered) coaches, hauled by locomotive *Jupiter*, are shown above, and the second and third class coaches (open to the elements), hauled by *North Star*, are below. Plates 1 & 2 (passenger) and 3 & 4 (goods) were used as carriage panels in some LMS carriages, including their *American Set*. It would be interesting to know what the Department of Health & Safety would say about this mode of travel today.

Big Four advertisement and map panels

Early pioneering prints

In 1935, with the problem of ageing photographs and a reduced budget before them, both Cecil Dandridge, the LNER advertising manager and Cuthbert Grasemann, the Southern's public relations and advertising officer, looked at the possibility of replacing photographs with prints as new colour lithographic printing processes were now making this option feasible. Both managers were pioneering personalities and didn't always agree with each other at committee meetings of the 'Railway Clearing House', so it was nice to see them following the same path for once. It was the Southern who first launched their prints at the beginning of 1936 at a time when, under general manager Herbert Walker, they were pioneering electrification programmes and had the biggest electrified suburban system in the world. The former Artist to the Admiralty, Donald Maxwell, had been commissioned by them to produce some sketches of locations in their region and this was one of his last commissions in fact, as he died shortly afterwards. The sketches were fairly basic with a few added colours and were mounted in pairs, side by side in the carriage panels; simple but quite effective.

The LNER, however, had gone a little more 'upmarket' and commissioned artists Cyril Barraud and Frank Mason to produce 16 coloured etchings of scenic views around the region and even into Europe. These were used to produce mounted prints for displaying in the company's new express trains such as *The Silver Jubilee* and started to appear in the middle of 1936 at a time when many new innovations were being taken in the fierce inter-company battle between the LNER and the LMS. The LNER had commissioned well known poster artists such as Tom Purvis, Fred Taylor, Austin Cooper, Frank Newbould (and Frank Mason himself) under the previous advertising manager, Teasdale to paint creative railway poster designs – why not commission similar artists for carriage panel artwork, too? These artists were often proven in that field and were normally members of nationally recognised bodies of painters, such as the Royal Institute of Painters in Watercolours (RI) or the Royal Watercolour Society (RWS). In fact this move laid the foundation, in terms of style and size, and was therefore the forerunner of, the numerous standard scenic prints issued by the railways after the Second World War, which travellers can remember so well.

In a review of the SR and LNER panels in February 1937 the *Railway Gazette* noted . . . 'We have already emphasised . . . the growing importance (and publicity value) of railway carriage views in these days of increased

The forerunner of all the standard format carriage prints issued after the Second World War: Two of the new **LNER** Mason/Barraud, mounted, colour etching series in bakelite frames in an **LNER** first class compartment in 1936. The picture on the left is *The Night Parade, Harwich* and that on the right is *Western Highlands*.

opportunities for cheap long distance travel. Many in the Southern Railway series reflect most successfully in their colouring and execution that charm peculiar to the English scene which often eludes the camera, and the whole series is a valuable contribution to the incidental pleasures of travelling by train.'

Prints v photographs

The experience of the LNER was, undoubtedly, that paintings were more acceptable than photographs in view of the sanitised treatment that the artists could apply, the timeless appearance of the views and also the added attraction of colour. The artists could also be outrageously selective in the features they chose to include or omit in the paintings! In fact, the introduction of these colour pictures came at a time when the whole controversy of photographs versus prints was raging. The Advertising Convention Cruise aboard the *SS Voltaire* in 1936 had discussed the issue of 'Lens versus Brush' and, like so many other political debates – had concluded nothing. An F. Lambert of the Photocrom Co. wrote to the *Railway Gazette* in February 1937 putting forward the case for photograph panels. He mentioned that they allowed a larger variety of views and alleged that they were preferred by the public, but, in view of Mr Lambert's future livelihood, you might conclude that he was, just possibly, a little biased.

Because of the success of this project and the savings involved, the LNER commissioned Barraud, Henry Rushbury and W. Lee–Hankey to produce more etchings and paintings. These were given a second airing as

prints with titled mounts. All of these mounted prints are scarce now; no doubt most were removed from the carriages as the war started to disrupt the country. Just before the outbreak of hostilities, further well-known and proven artists, including Rowland Hilder, Ernest Haslehust and Fred Taylor were commissioned to produce watercolours of specified locations for which they were paid in the region of ten guineas each. The prints taken from these paintings were un-mounted, and were simply framed and glazed in the same 'Crommoid' (bakelite), 20 inch x 10 inch, ivory-effect, frames that were used for the earlier Barraud/Mason prints.

Maps become 'user friendly'

Carriage maps, too, were undergoing an evolutionary change in design at this point in railway history. Originally they were 'geographic' in design, but because the shape of the railway system was often incompatible with the landscape treatment the panels afforded, they often appeared severely distorted (see GWR map p.20). Companies also tended to exaggerate their maps to make them look as if they owned far more lines than was actually the case, by including those lines over which they ran 'through services'!

The pioneering of modern 'diagrammatic' maps has often, wrongly, been solely attributed to the draughtsman Harry Beck, who worked for London Transport during the immensely creative and successful reign of Frank Pick at 55 Broadway. He designed the diagrammatic maps of the London Transport system which were issued in 1933 and these were certainly models of clarity. These were not the first, however. George Dow, whilst working for the LNER, had already designed diagrammatic maps for the steam trains operating on the ex GNR and ex GER London suburban services from as early as 1928 – the first modern network diagrams to be issued. He later produced further examples for the Tyneside, Manchester–Altrincham and ex GCR suburban routes and also for the LMS Tilbury and Southend lines. This successful concept continued into British Rail days. Most trains which were confined to set LMR services carried these diagrams which were of a standardised style, commissioned by Dow, and designed by draughtsman Victor Welch. They were printed in maroon and black on white paper or card and embellished with the BR lozenge shaped totem (see p. 36). Nowadays, plastic diagrams with adhesive backings are simply stuck to the carriage walls.

Durham, from a colour etching by Frank H Mason RI (1936).
It has been commented that to look at Durham, sloping
away from the railway viaduct, on a misty day with the
smoke haze rising from the chimney pots below, is to look
back a century. Mason is situated in the park above the
south end of Durham station 'down' platform and he portrays this atmospheric panorama of castle and cathedral,
marvellously silhouetted against the skyline. Many passengers will recall this outline on their journeys between
Newcastle and York.

MAIDSTONE, KENT - MODERN.

Maidstone (Modern), from a sketch by Donald Maxwell (1936).
The picture shows the Medway as it passes through Maidstone
with its warehouses and tugs and barges. A few pencil lines
in grey and brown give a very adequate impression of
water. These sketches were issued by the SR in 1936 when
new lithographic processes had been developed. [NRM]

Early pioneering pre-war mounted prints

Peterborough Cathedral, Northamptonshire, from a water-colour by Henry Rushbury RA (1937).
Cathedrals were a very strong selling attraction for the LNER and they were privileged to have many notable examples in their area. Henry Rushbury is positioned just south of the River Nene, and is looking northwards towards the city. The cathedral was built in the 12th and early 13th centuries on the site of an old monastery. It is composed of local Barnack stone and two queens were buried here; Mary Queen of Scots and Catherine of Aragon. The town, which has recently seen much expansion, lies on the east coast main line, and the station was once an important junction.

York, from a colour etching by Cyril H Barraud (1936).
A classic railway lover's view of York from Barraud. It shows a class D49 locomotive with a Scarborough-bound train, traversing the Scarborough railway bridge over the River Ouse near to the old York steam shed. The site now houses the National Railway Museum collection and draws many tourists and enthusiasts each year. York Minster, the great cathedral built between 1220 and 1470, and containing half of England's surviving medieval stained glass windows, rises majestically above its surroundings in the centre.

Cambridge, from a colour etching by Cyril H Barraud. (1936).
Barraud, in one of the LNER original etching series, has chosen a classic vantage point for his painting of the university town of Cambridge. He is looking across the River Cam from 'The Backs' (the gardens and meadows running down to the water's edge), at the magnificent King's College Chapel in the centre. This building was begun in the mid 15th century by Henry VI, but was not completed for 100 years due to a lack of funds and, no doubt, a lottery grant. Clare College and Trinity Hall stand on the left and King's College is over to the right . The sights of ecclesiastical buildings were a common advertising feature for the railways, and Cambridge, a junction station with eight converging lines, profited from the many sightseers.

Early pioneering pre-war mounted prints

Wartime influence (1939–1947)

Unnecessary travel was discouraged when war broke out in 1939. After all their hard work in getting passengers on to their trains, the companies now had to concentrate on getting them off – thus most of the scenic pictures were temporarily abandoned during the years of hostilities. Carriage panel adverts and photographs were largely replaced by subtle hints such as 'Is your journey really necessary' or by passenger instructions in the event of air attacks. A chief concern was the drawing of carriage blinds, ensuring darkness during the 'black–out' conditions. Instructions to keep windows and ventilators closed in the event of air raids and the usual 'Careless talk costs lives' panels proliferated. 'Ensure that the train is at the platform before alighting' was another important one – especially during the 'blackout' when it was difficult to see just where the train had stopped.

These panels replaced many scenic views during the Second World War. Air raid and 'blackout' instructions, and 'careless talk' warnings became commonplace in carriage compartments between 1939 and 1945.

I remember hearing about the man who, on the false assumption that the train had stopped at his station, went to alight on one side of the compartment and was promptly restrained by a passenger next to the door who told him 'You can't get out here mate!'. He apologised, saying 'I'm sorry – you must think I'm very stupid', whereupon, thinking he'd attempted to get out on the wrong side, promptly rushed to the opposite door and plummeted feet–first into the darkness!

At the end of the Second World War many locations had changed dramatically from the photographs that had been displayed in carriages; enemy action had removed many signs and buildings; the iron railings had been donated for making weapons; the fashions and vehicles had altered and the roads were no longer so empty. It is a well–known saying that a photograph never lies, so a certain amount of 're–touching' to photographs went on at this period, removing such eyesores as overhead power

After the war the LNER continued to issue many mount–less, standard format, colour prints and these were housed in new, 20 inch x 10 inch, hardwood frames which became the standard issue in British Rail days. Alongside the classic oval mirror in this first class LNER corridor of 1947, are Fred Taylor's *Fountains Abbey* on the right and Henry Rushbury's *Rievaulx Abbey* on the left.

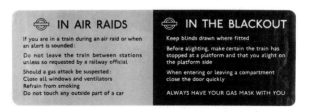

and telephone lines. No doubt in earlier days, piles of horse droppings were expertly touched out! It was impossible, in most cases, to disguise the effect that post–war development was having on the country and the process was a developing one so that one year's photo could be out of date the next. The days of the photographic panels were therefore numbered.

When the hostilities had ended, the LNER continued their pre–war colour print policy with prolific output. They often commissioned further paintings of subjects already covered before the war, because their pre–war stocks

had either been utilised or dispensed with between 1939 and 1945.

The Southern, however, in seeking to make use of their 16 inch x 10 inch panels, tried another style of format and produced some borderless prints of paintings by the well–respected artists Hesketh Hubbard and Adrian Allinson of locations in the south and south west. In fact these ended up having a fairly short life span and were mostly replaced when the BR standard series were issued in the early 1950s.

The GWR and LMS chose to remain loyal to their many, well-produced, black and white and sepia photographic panels right up to nationalisation, mainly because their large fleets still had some years of useful life ahead of them. Some black and white prints by the poster artist Norman Wilkinson had appeared in LMS stock during this period but it seems that very few were produced.

The railways had played a major part in the fight against Germany between 1939 and 1945, and had run a staggering 538,559 special trains for the Government. The end of the war saw the system in a very run down state with a large proportion of antiquated rolling stock. A colossal 14,000 passenger vehicles, alone, had been damaged or destroyed during the hostilities. In 1947 the management of the railways passed to the Railway Executive, but it was often well into the British Railways regime before improvements could be made or corporate designs instituted.

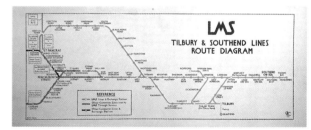

This was one of George Dow's designs for the LMS, and followed on from his pioneering diagrammatic maps produced for the LNER in 1928. It shows the ex London, Tilbury & Southend suburban lines from Fenchurch Street and bears Dow's signature at the bottom, dated 1935. Historically, the acquisition of the LTS by the Midland Rly in 1912, represented a significant coup over the GER. The line subsequently came under the jurisdiction of the LMS in 1923.

Hockworthy Bridge, Dartmoor, Devon, from a gouache painting by Hesketh Hubbard (1945–48).
After the Second World War the SR issued a series of prints by Hubbard and Allinson to use in their 16 inch x 10 inch frames. This is a pleasant painting by Hubbard of the stream running under Hockworthy Bridge. The title is misleading as Hockworthy lies between Tiverton and Taunton – hardly Dartmoor.

Hampshire Coast, from a gouache painting by Langhammer (1965).
This is one of three prints in the last series to be issued by BR in 1965. Langhammer gives this landscape the real Mediterranean treatment, using his vivid poster technique. Aiming at effect rather than detail – it looks as though the turquoise sea has been borrowed from Corfu, the trees from Majorca and the painting outfit from Mothercare. I believe this is a view of the entrance to Christchurch Harbour (now in Dorset).

Cornish Vale, from a pastel by Allinson (1945-48).
A simple, but effective, use of pastels by Adrian Allinson gives a peaceful feel to this composition, yet it still remains full of colour in order to brighten the carriage interior. These SR prints only covered locations in the ex LSWR area.

Post-war non-standard prints

The British Railways era (1948–1970)

In 1948, under a Labour Government, the railway companies were nationalised and amalgamated to become simply 'British Railways' (BR) and the British mainland was divided into six separate regions.

A general co-ordinated move was encouraged at this time to convert the sombre photographic panels to the coloured print variety. This sometimes proved a slow process. A standardisation of frame sizes was obviously necessary, too, for the sake of convenience and BR adopted the 1936 LNER bakelite panel size (itself a copy of the NER wooden frame) as the 'standard'. Its 20 inch by 10 inch measurement, after allowing a couple of inches for a small white margin, left space for a 16 inch by 6 inch picture. The panels were made of hardwood with brass fittings and were screwed into the compartment walls with chrome plated screws. One of the reasons for a standardised size was to make it possible for the different regional prints to be displayed in carriages belonging to the other regions as well, and a quantity of each print was often sent to other headquarters for this purpose – scenes of Scottish lochs appearing in Southern compartments etc. Unfortunately, many of the surviving Southern frames were 25½ inch by 10 inch and the ex LMS ones were 25 inch by 10 inch so a second 'picture' size of 23 inch by 7½ inch became necessary in order to use these panels, too.

British Rail print series

In early 1949 George Dow became the public relations and publicity officer for the new London Midland Region (LMR). He set out to make use of these larger frames in a more up to date, creative and economical way than the LMS had, especially when he was somewhat shocked to find, sepia photographs of Liverpool horse-drawn trams still in situ in ex LMS carriages! He therefore evolved four series of prints, three of which were for use in the stock just mentioned, and the fourth to be displayed in BR standard stock. Poster artists were commissioned to paint scenic views of interest and beauty for the first set of 16 pictures which were issued in 1950 and also a further set of 14 with their distinctive large titles in *Gill Sans* typeface.

Cuthbert Hamilton Ellis, the railway historian, was then commissioned by Dow to paint 24 views of the transport associated with some of the pre-grouping companies which formed the LMS. Known as the *Travel–In* series, these quaint and colourful pictures of railway history have

An external view of a new, Eastern Region suburban coach, E53171 in 1954. It is filled with panels containing the standard colour prints – but how many of them have survived? [NRM]

probably become the best known of all the carriage prints. They definitely have the ability to draw strong responses from their viewers – people either love them or find them rather overpowering! Just after this Dow, who was a railway historian himself, commissioned two eminent artists, Claude Buckle and Kenneth Steel, both of whom had already produced fine poster work for the railways, to paint eight views each of locations on the London Midland of architectural interest, known as the *Railway Architecture* series. Issued in 1952, the subjects selected gave a deliberate emphasis to certain features not wholly visible from the train such as tunnel entrances, bridges and viaducts.

It is interesting to note that Dow calculated the cost of using prints as being a quarter of that using the photographs. The prints were generally printed two at a time, side by side, on 30 inch x 20 inch (double crown) paper and then were split into two – this being the reason that some unused ones often have a wide margin on the left and right hand sides. The printers were normally the same firms that produced posters for the railways, such as Waterlow & Sons, Baynard Press, and Thos. Forman & Sons etc.

In 1952 the Southern Region publicity officer at Waterloo also produced a set, again in the larger size, of the five 'cinque ports' by poster artist Jack Merriott and four prints of cathedrals in the Southern's territory by Buckle.

A steady stream of standard sized pictures continued to be commissioned by the Eastern Region (ER) from many locally and nationally known artists during the late 1940s and early 1950s and these were issued in the same style as the previous LNER ones. By the mid 1950s there were over 200 views alone in this vast and varied series which, without doubt, contained some of the finest paintings produced for carriage prints.

When the LNER had produced their earlier prints, some Scottish locations were included (being part of their territory). But in 1956, the Scottish Region itself also issued its own series of 42 landscape views and these were produced in both standard and larger sizes to overcome the problem of the different frame dimensions on their own, and other, regions.

The Western Region appeared hesitant to conform with the overall policy of the other regions. After commissioning its paintings in 1949, they finally produced their standard sized series of 20 (18 views and two commercials) in 1954, only to withdraw most of them just six years later when the new diesel multiple units came on the scene! The few locations chosen on the Western (none were

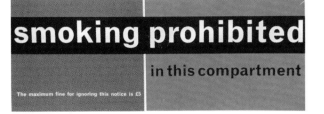

A selection of some of the notices displayed in coaching stock during the last years of the panels. *Smoking Prohibited* warnings were officially withdrawn in 1977, but probably survived for longer. *This is a Train Spot* advertised the services of British Transport Advertising Ltd., who managed the panel adverts during this period. The *It's not nice for you . . .* litter notice was a very common one in Southern Region, suburban electric units, as was the safety warning *Don't open the door*, showing the gallant, bowler–hatted, city gent coming to the aid of a damsel in distress. It was issued by **BR(S)** in 1962.

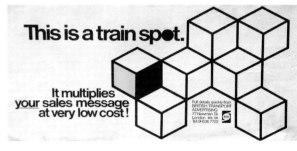

BR advertisements and notices

issued of views of South Wales), was largely due, in fact, to a commissioning error. Artists were sent to paint many scenic panoramas but, unfortunately, in the wrong sizes! Hence many of the paintings were unusable for the production of standard sized prints. This saga is dealt with in more detail on page 152.

By the middle years of the 1950s, it was obvious that the railways were in decline. The improving economy after the austerity years had created more road traffic than rail and it was apparent that initiatives would have to be taken to halt the slide. A modernisation plan was launched in 1955 by the British Transport Commission to re–equip the network and a £1,660 million programme for dieselisation, electrification and other projects began. However, Messrs. Ford and Morris were rapidly helping to ensure that private car production would almost treble in the ten years between 1953 and 1963 and it was becoming ominously certain that the railway network would not survive in its present form.

This situation didn't seem to affect the production of carriage prints and many more appeared during this period. The Southern issued its own small series of standard prints in 1956, mainly of coastal locations, and included a fine, imaginative set of four, of well known trains in its area by Richard Ward.

During 1955, J W Tonge who took over from George Dow at Euston, introduced a set of 48 prints showing historical events in the LMR area. These were commissioned from an artist's agency in London and, though differing completely from the style of previous series, did include some fine paintings by Edward Mortelmans of characters such as Florence Nightingale, Henry VIII & Ann Boleyn in their different surroundings. Whatever one's view of the *Historical* series, with their medieval battles and knights in shining armour – they were certainly a far cry from watercolour landscapes!

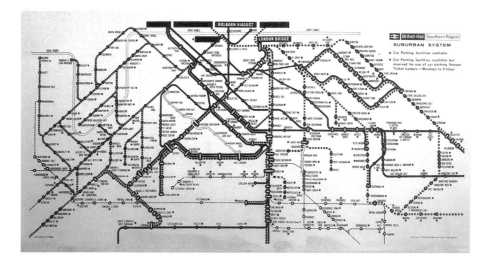

Originally designed by D A Lawrence, this diagrammatic map, issued by BR (Southern Region) in 1966, shows the complex network of lines south of the Thames, and was displayed in most of the Southern electric, suburban stock. By this time, many of the rural line closures envisaged by Beeching in Sussex and Kent had already taken place.

The LMR's sixth series of ten prints, which depicted certain historical buildings in the north west, appeared in 1957 in the larger size by courtesy of artists Ronald Maddox and Ronald Lampitt. This is known, affectionately, by me, as the *Two Ronnies* series.

Towards the end of the 1950s, the Region brought out its final offering of seven pictures to the public and issued the prints in both sizes. These included some fine paintings of boat services from the evergreen Buckle and were some of the last to be taken out of rolling stock when BR discontinued panels in the late 1970s.

The last prints remaining in carriage panels, however, and certainly the last to be produced, were the Southern's simple and margin–less *Coast* series by

Langhammer, issued in 1965. They were of the larger format, but were often folded to fit the standard 20 inches by 10 inches frames. These very basic prints will, no doubt, be remembered by those who travelled in Southern suburban stock in the latter years of BR.

Most compartments continued to display mirrors in British Railways days and the LMR used a large number of mirror–maps, showing their routes. These were held in place by four art deco corners and, contrary to expectations, they were easy to use. To look at the map you focused your eyes on the glass, but to look at yourself you focused on twice the distance, on the image reflected so the lines of the map didn't get in the way. It was an interesting way of combining the map and the mirror, so giving more space for panels. The idea came from George Dow's wife and he seized on it.

By the start of the 1960s, Britain's railway situation had become desperate. Passenger journeys had decreased from 1,579 million in 1920 to just over 800 million in 1960. As well as the upsurge in road traffic, increased domestic air flights were starting to eat into the long–distance travel market too. When it was revealed that

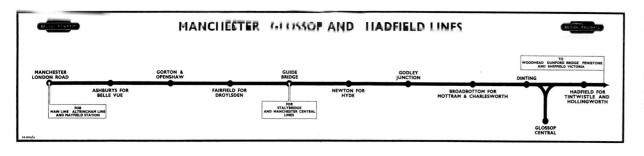

A typical example of a BR diagrammatic, route map, designed by Victor Welch for carriage stock confined to set services – in this case, the Manchester–Glossop–Hadfield line. The maps were printed in maroon and black, on white paper. The ex Great Central main line between Hadfield and Penistone via the Woodhead tunnel is now, sadly, closed.

50 per cent of all British Rail stations only produced two per cent of its passenger receipts then a radical remedy (and a ruthless doctor) were called for. The sad end to a once great system was close at hand.

In his infamous *Reshaping of British Railways* proposal document, Dr Richard Beeching advocated the closing of a vast 5,000 route miles and over 2,000 passenger stations. Carriage rolling stock was to be reduced by 45 per cent and locomotives by nearly two thirds. This devastation began to take effect at rapid speed. On Britain's main lines, hundreds of small stations which were, at one time, vital focal points of village life disappeared and many old branch lines – those endearing institutions of British rural life with their quaint, peaceful and slightly eccentric character – were abandoned. By 1970, the railway network map looked remarkably similar to that of 1850.

The surviving carriage rolling stock struggled on over the remaining network, and commercial adverts, maps, 'no smoking' panels and mirrors as well as the scenic prints, still continued to decorate them until the late 1970s. By this time many of the branch lines taking passengers to the picturesque locations displayed in the panels had closed, and the majority of these locations were now far easier to reach by car than by train. Advertisers, too, lost enthusiasm for advertising in 'closed sites' which could only be seen by a relatively small number of people each day. Poster hoardings and television, of course, offered better prospects. Carriage vandalism was also progressively rearing its ugly head and a decision was taken to discontinue and remove the panels from BR rolling stock.

A closure panel for the Mumbles Railway in 1960. Doctor Beeching's railway amputations were being experienced all over Britain during this period. No anaesthetic appeared to be given during the operation.

Postscript (1971–80)

In the late 1970s a friend and I went to Selhurst Depot on the Southern Region, armed with an authorisation to purchase any remaining glazed carriage frames as scrap. After going through a stack of soaking and damaged ones just outside the sheds, we were allowed to clamber inside the 4–SUB units lying condemned in the sidings of Norwood Yard. It was a strange feeling as we stood silently in the trains as the wind whistled through the open doors of this railway cemetery. We clambered through each compartment in the hope of finding a few panels that had been sheltered from the elements outside.

Originally, with two or three frames above each row of seats in every compartment, there must have been, on the Southern alone, a vast number of panels in suburban stock during the 50s and 60s. But how many of them had survived? When I worked for British Rail, I heard of thousands of these fine prints being destroyed for want of storage space at the distribution and 'bill' offices in much the same way that a friend of mine saw hundreds of Terence Cuneo posters cut up and used for wrapping paper at Liverpool Street station. They sell for hundreds of pounds each now – another case of 'if only . . .'

A gentle rain had started to blow into the compartments as we unscrewed what remaining panels we could find. Adverts declaring the wonders of 'Eucryl toothpowder', or 'This is a train spot' fell out and blew around in the wind. Appropriately enough, most of the surviving panels carried the reminder about not leaving litter : 'It's not nice for us, it's not nice for you' The majority had been stained by becoming damp over the years,.but, as usual, the railway works-made, hardwood frames were still solidly intact with their heavy, toughened glass and brass fittings. They had clearly been designed to withstand the rigours of climate and the human punishment inflicted on them over the years.

As we clambered down from the old coaches and walked back in the rain to the depot, laden with panels, I gazed back at the empty condemned carriages and realised that, like the end of steam . . . it was the close of another era of railway history.

Abandonment of the Mumbles Railway—Tuesday, 5th January, 1960

Normal train service will operate up to and including the following journeys :—
Rutland Street to Southend ———— 9.55 a.m.   Southend to Rutland Street ———— 10.20 a.m.
The first journeys on the substituted omnibus services will be :—
SERVICE No. 77 : PONTLASSE CROSS—MUMBLES PIER.
Pontlasse Cross to Mumbles Pier ———— dep. 10.5 a.m.   Mumbles Pier to Cwmrhydyceirw Cross dep. 10.26 a.m.
Cwmrhydyceirw Cross to Mumbles Pier ,, 9.31 a.m.   Mumbles Pier to Pontlasse Cross ———— ,, 10.38 a.m.
Guildhall to Mumbles Pier ———— ,, 10.0 a.m.
SERVICE No. 94 : RUTLAND STREET—OYSTERMOUTH SQUARE.
Rutland Street ———— dep. 1.0 p.m.   Oystermouth Square ———— dep. 1.25 p.m.
FULL DETAILS OF THE TIMETABLES OF THE SUBSTITUTED SERVICES ARE AVAILABLE FROM ANY OF THE COMPANY'S OFFICES OR DIRECT FROM THE HEAD OFFICE.
THE SOUTH WALES TRANSPORT CO., LTD.,
31, RUSSELL STREET, SWANSEA.
MERCURY, LLANELLY

Chapter 2
The Artists and the artwork

The London Midland & Scottish Railway caused quite a stir when they began to commission Royal Academicians to produce artwork for their railway posters. It quickly became clear from the early days of the 'Big Four' companies, that the railways were going to aim high in terms of the quality of artwork in their advertising departments. They were, therefore, careful in choosing their artists. Charles Knight, for example, who was commissioned by the London Midland Region, and who later became the vice-president of the Royal Watercolour Society, was asked by the Queen Mother in 1944 to give Princess Margaret painting lessons – whoever was good enough for royalty was good enough for the railways.

Britain has been pre–eminent in her contribution of watercolour to the world's art and the list of the artists employed by the railways for carriage prints appears a little like a *Who's Who* of prominent watercolour artists for the period. A sprinkling of artwork in oils appeared, too. Many of the painters were well known nationally for their works and the commissioning by the railways of advertising artwork was sometimes just a very small part of their working careers. As someone has drily commented . . . 'the most important thing an artist must draw is his wages'. There were some, however, who were embarrassed at having to produce commercial artwork to make a living. It is only in recent years that this form of artwork has gained the respectability it deserves. Painters such as Jack Merriott, Claude Buckle, Kenneth Steel, Fred Taylor and Frank Mason had no such qualms in this respect, and achieved a prolific output of artwork for the railways, especially in the realm of poster production. It is also clear from several interviews that they thoroughly enjoyed their work in the process.

Over 60 artists produced work for carriage prints and many were members of institutes and societies such as the Royal Institute of Painters in Watercolours (RI), the Royal Watercolour Society (RWS), the Royal Academy (RA) and so forth. The RWS was founded in 1804 as the 'Old Watercolour Society', with 10 members and the word Royal was added in 1881. Carriage panel artists William Lee–Hankey and Charles Knight both became vice-presidents. The RI was established in 1831 as a breakaway group called the 'New Watercolour Society' which became the 'Institute of Painters in Watercolours' in 1863, achieving Royal status in 1883. Rowland Hilder was a past president of the RI and has since achieved a world–wide reputation for his superb paintings. Ronald Maddox holds this position in the mid 1990s and Jack Merriott was a former RI vice–president. This helps to underline the quality of the painters commissioned by the railways. It is possible to see paintings by many of the artists connected with the production of railway commissioned artwork in art galleries and museums around the country.

Not all the artists were nationally recognised, however. Others were only known in their own localities and seldom painted further afield. F. W. Baldwin, for example, was self-taught and worked as a draughtsman but still accomplished some fine paintings for the railways of his own East Anglian territory and has since gained a solid reputation in his locality.

Top watercolour artists such as Rowland Hilder were commissioned by the railways for carriage panel artwork and railway posters. Whilst commercial artists were often disregarded by much of the art world of their day, their skill often brought colour and flair into the journeys of a large proportion of the travelling public. They thoroughly enjoyed their work for the railways too.

Norton, near Billingham, Co. Durham, from a watercolour by Kenneth Steel RBA/SGA (1948–55). It is an interesting exercise to compare the carriage print paintings with current photographs. Here we have the original painting by Kenneth Steel of Norton. The title should strictly read

Norton, near Stockton on Tees, as Norton is now incorporated into this town. This was the end of the tram line from Middlesbrough and has changed relatively little since it was painted. The duckpond area was tidied up in 1968 and the cottages on the left no longer house an old forge. The

butcher's shop on the right, with the green windows, is unchanged and the white building on the corner is now a newsagent. Set amidst an industrial area with its famous railway history, it is an unusual location to choose for a carriage print, but very pleasant, nevertheless. [A. Bowman]

After much research, a comprehensive listing of all the artists appears in Appendix A at the end of the book, with a little background information on them which may be of interest and help the reader to appreciate the person behind the painting.

Most watercolours tend to be representational rather than abstract and, unlike much of the artwork produced for railway posters, those for the carriage panels were very traditional in their realistic treatment of landscape styles and in their composition. Large areas of flat, bright colours were far better suited to the larger poster designs where visual impact was a key consideration, although Reginald Lander and Fred Taylor did try this approach with their panel work too (see Taylor's *Lincoln* on p.103). Not all the travelling public appreciated the modern use of flat, gaudy colour in railway art, as can be easily deduced from a poem by M.E.Durham, published in the *Manchester Guardian* in the 1920s which humorously tells a lament in cockney rhyme entitled *A Plaint to the Poster Artist:*

Oh I want to see the country
Like when I was a boy –
When the sky was blue and the clouds was white
And the green fields was a joy.

I want to see the country
But the posters seem to show
The country ain't no more the place,
Like what I used to know.

For the sky is pink and the fields are mauve
And the cottages all turned yellow
And the sheep all green or tangerine
Enough to stun a fellow.

Oh, I want to see the country
And I wouldn't mind where I went 'ter
So long as I knoo the trees weren't blue
And the cows all turned magenter!

This comical viewpoint regarding style was, like many other subjects of course, purely one of personal taste. But I suspect that most of the commissioned artists would have agreed with the need for the public to, at least, be able to recognise the subject depicted. The classic quote of Count Leo Tolstoy sums this up rather admirably . . . 'To say that a work of art is good but incomprehensible to the majority of men is the same as saying of some kind of food that it is very good, but most people can't eat it'. Whatever anyone's opinion of styles was during this time, there was certainly no room for the current abstract forms of art where the 'modern' artist throws paint onto a canvas, wipes it off with a cloth, and then sells the cloth.

Although there was little scope for alternative styles, there was certainly plenty of scope for the painters' use of artistic licence! Trees were often left out or painted in to help the composition, and unsightly objects were omitted. These types of careful alterations seemed to be acceptable to the famous artist Pablo Picasso, who once succinctly stated that . . . 'An artist must convince others of the truth of his lies'.

In the early days of railway posters and prints, the artists themselves were encouraged to submit speculative designs or landscapes in the hope that these would be found suitable. This situation largely changed in later years and artists were then specifically commissioned to paint certain subjects. The former approach tended to be

Two of the 'roughs' painted by F. Donald Blake for the Scottish series in 1956. His view of Ben Nevis *(top)* was accepted although, in the final painting, the vantage point had been changed to Corpach and the town of Fort William had been largely omitted (see p.110 for the final version). The 'rough' of Urquhart Castle, Loch Ness *(bottom)* was rejected by the commissioning department.

pretty flexible and unpredictable – fees were even decided on the spot and it is worth recounting here one of the more humorous outcomes of this hit and miss approach to commissioning . . .

Norman Wilkinson, one of the early poster artists, had approached the advertising manager of the Midland Railway with a poster design of the Heysham to Belfast steamship. The manager wasn't too impressed with it and offered only seven guineas for the artwork. Wilkinson, quite rightly, turned him down. He then noticed that if he changed the funnel markings and made a few simple alterations to the superstructure it looked like a Great Eastern vessel, so he approached that company instead. The Great Eastern Railway were very impressed and published it as a poster. When the directors of the Midland saw it they were keen on it too and

A selection of original artwork produced for various standard format print series. These paintings were normally executed on quality art paper or board and were sometimes mounted. The artwork was either the same size as the prints or was double the area and then reduced accordingly. Featured here clockwise from top left, are . . . *Welbeck Abbey, Notts* (Fairclough); *Langdale Valley, Lake District* (Greene); *Fountains Abbey, Yorks* (Taylor); *Anne Boleyn and Henry VIII* (Mortelmans); *Wolverton Viaduct, Bucks* (Steel).

asked their poor advertising manager to write to Wilkinson asking him why the Midland couldn't have such high standard poster work. How he extricated himself from that predicament is not certain!

There are, sadly, only a handful of the carriage panel artists alive at the time of going to print, but those surviving all proved most willing and helpful in assisting my research into the artist's involvement with the railways. Ronald Maddox has already given an account of his own commissioning in the foreword of this book and can add that the fee paid for these later panels was in the region of 18 guineas each. Working for the railways meant the obtaining of an Artist's Pass for free rail travel, so there was little need to 'take up thy "palette" and walk'!

The final artwork for carriage pictures was either produced to the same size as the intended prints or was double the area and then reduced accordingly at the printing stage. It was also possible for artwork to be rejected if the commissioners didn't appreciate it. In some cases the 'roughs', which were normally shown to the commissioners before getting the go ahead for the real thing, were preferred to the final painting. James Fletcher Watson, now a highly regarded artist and author, told me how he tried conscientiously to achieve the best possible painting of one of his Norfolk scenes only for the man in the London & North Eastern Railway offices at Liverpool Street to choose his 'rough' instead of his 'master' painting!

The railways retained the original paintings but the rough sketches and drawings remained in the artist's possession (if, indeed, they chose to keep them – see Claude Buckle's approach on p. 43).

The late James Mcintosh Patrick, a celebrated Scottish artist, mentioned that one of the difficulties with the carriage print paintings was the problem of composition because of the limitations imposed by the long length and narrow height of the artwork – 'the long perspective'. Posters obviously offered more scope, in terms of suitable subjects and composition.

It is an education to view the prints and see all the different watercolour styles used by the artists. From Leonard Squirrell's orderly and confident approach and Jack Merriott's enthusiastic, yet superbly controlled washes of colour, to Stanley Badmin's highly detailed paintings of bridges and viaducts in which almost every branch in the trees appeared to be drawn!

Michael Spender wrote in *Glory of Watercolour* . . . 'There is no successful painting if no sure drawing' and most of the carriage panel artists excelled in their draughtsmanship – the key foundation to good painting on paper. Like all human beings though, artists will have their good days and their bad and it's sometimes possible to tell the difference as you view the prints. However, an overall high standard of work was achieved for the railways and the artists were pleased to see their work appearing in these numerous mobile art galleries, which contained a constant flow of public viewers. It was a pity, though, that the prints were not displayed in something better than the un-mounted and cramped carriage panels, which never really brought out the best in the artwork and often failed to give the artists the recognition for their work that they deserved.

Portraits of the three most prolific artists

Having taken a broad–brush look at the world of carriage panel artwork it is helpful to focus on the lives of the three most prolific artists, Claude Buckle, Jack Merriott and Kenneth Steel. Considering the number of prints and posters they produced for the railways, it is surprising just how little is known about them. Havelock Ellis obviously thought that all painters described their own personalities as they wielded their brushes when he said that . . . 'every artist writes his own autobiography'. If this is the case, then most commercial artists lacked a reliable publisher! They were often overlooked or even scorned by much of the art world of their day, yet their skill and flair brought colour and the world of art to a far greater proportion of the public than most painters ever achieve.

As I visited the family and friends of the three artists it became noticeable just how much Claude, Jack and Ken enjoyed their work for the railway companies, so before we take a tour around Britain in the middle years of the century, I'll let these brief biographies paint their own background to a few of the artists behind the artwork . . .

Portrait of an artist
Claude Buckle RI RSMA

In his appreciation of the artist during the *Commemorative Exhibition of Claude Buckle,* held in London in 1974, Terence Cuneo, the late railway artist of international repute, wrote of his close friend . . . 'Claude was a gentle soul with a sympathetic understanding of the problems of others and this, together with a lively sense of humour, a steadfast determination and an unassuming humility, was, in part the secret of his success in achieving a position in the forefront of contemporary British watercolour painting.'

Claude had spent his early life in Wolverhampton, where his father was the agent for the Michelin Tyre Co. The young lad had an early desire to express himself with a pencil and brush and whilst at school, used to earn pocket money by painting 6ft. strips of sunsets. A shopkeeper would then cut them up, frame and sell them as originals. Upon moving to Bristol, Claude wanted to study at art school, but his father would have none of it . . . 'artists starve to death in attics' was his response! So when he left school at 15 he was articled to an architect and his father died a year later, leaving him penniless.

Claude Buckle – produced 25 illustrations for carriage prints

He was accepted at Frys, the chocolate firm, as assistant architect, despite forgetting to put his address on the application letter. His obvious ability convinced the chief architect to trace him and later send him to Bristol University to study architecture, specialising in architectural steel. Whilst in Bristol he submitted four paintings to the Savage Art Club, who invited him to become a member, more on the basis of his keenness than his ability, he learned later!

In 1926, Claude moved to London aged 21, and joined Wallis Gilbert & Partners, the large industrial architects responsible for building factories such as Fords at Dagenham. Whilst exceptionally capable in the architectural field, Claude's passion for painting was still bubbling below the surface, and he began a portfolio of his own sketches and paintings whilst making rough journeys as a galley boy on tramp steamers to Spain, North Africa and around the English coast.

In 1931 he decided to swap his secure career with its good financial prospects, for a much more unpredictable and precarious life as a freelance artist. The desire to paint purely for himself (albeit for his clients in the process) was starting to take shape. In those early days he would take any work he could get, including hotel brochures (these were the days before photos became popular), which he undertook largely for the fun of it. Much of his work also came from his past training – commissions for artistic impressions of building designs and engineering drawings and artwork at which he excelled.

Shortly after going freelance, Claude plucked up courage, took his portfolio and went, without appointment, to try his luck at the advertising manager's office at the GWR HQ at Paddington. After getting lost in the corridors he finally arrived at the office of the art commissioner. Sneaking past the receptionist and barging into the office, he showed Mr Beaumont his work and was taken on for poster work on the spot!

He was 34 when war broke out in 1939 and he tried to join the RAF but was considered too old. Rather than join the army, he was chosen (as an architect) as a leader of the 'Heavy Rescue Squad', based at a depot near the Old Kent Road in London where he trained a team of men to repair buildings and rescue trapped people. The locals he trained were an interesting bunch – largely from the South London criminal element – jailbirds, army deserters and racecourse gangs. As the bombs fell, they were, without doubt, excellent and courageous workers but had a slight tendency to return to the scene of the action several hours later and remove some of the contents. An interesting example of 'don't muzzle the ox whilst it's treading out the grain'!

This dirty, brutal and often humorous era was a real eye-opener for Claude – a time which he grew in maturity and confidence. Later war years were spent in Northern Ireland, building aerodromes for American bombers.

In 1946 he married Barbara, his supportive and appreciative wife, and, two years later, moved to a beautiful thatched cottage at Vernham Dene, a small hamlet in North Hampshire, where his twin children, Terence and

Barbara, were born. A large, old converted cow–byre at the back of the house became Claude's studio and Barbara would summon him by a bell whenever he was required for phone calls etc – not always a popular sound when in the middle of one of his watercolour washes! After the war years there was no hotel trade to find work from and it was a question of starting from scratch once more. He decided to try the railways again as they paid well. Claude renewed his friendship with Terence Cuneo and under the watchful eye of BR's Don Faulkner, the public relations officer at Waterloo (who Cuneo described as 'one of the most understanding men I have ever worked for and a fine friend and 'mother hen' to us both'), achieved a prolific output of posters and compartment illustrations for its Regions.

For these commissionings Claude would get a free rail ticket and hotel booking for the night and would inform the local council representatives who would meet him on the spot and suggest possible viewpoints. He would spend two days drawing the subject from various angles, including numerous pencil sketches of detail, such as arches, doors, horizon lines and eddies and swirls in rivers. One 'master drawing' was also made on the spot and served as a complete colour guide to the studio work which followed. When returning home, Claude, using the drawings (and his own excellent retentive memory), would prepare a rough sketch of the poster or panel. When this had been accepted by the railway authorities, most of the creative work was finished and it then became, using Buckle's own words . . . 'merely a matter of drawing and painting'.

To the layman it did not seem as simple as it sounded for, although as many as 30 or 40 colours may have been used in the 'master drawing', the rough and, more particularly, the finished drawing was worked in a much smaller selection of colours usually comparable to the number of 'runs' or coloured inks used in the printing process. This economy of colour helped to make the reproduction a more faithful copy of the original.. Once he was confident of the finished outcome, three to four hours of concentrated work was all it would take him to accomplish it and if he wasn't happy with the outcome he would tear it up! All his roughs would join the bin, too, when the work was complete.

Claude's sense of humour often found inspiration when Terence Cuneo was around and the two of them would get up to various pranks together . . . One day Claude found an old napoleonic cannon in a barn and with the help of his friend decided to test it out! After breaking open a lot of old gun cartridges to provide the gunpowder, they lit a (long) fuse which was connected to some touch paper and retreated to a safe distance. After some tense moments of waiting, the thing just fizzled out and the cannon remained silent – and probably just as well!

The late 1950s brought two great turning points in Buckle's life. Firstly, in 1958, he received a six month commission to depict in oils the first atomic power stations under construction for the British Engineering stand at the Brussels Fair. He found the rigid time schedule involved and the necessary tightness of the paintings hopelessly pressurising and, therefore, gave up commercial work completely and devoted himself to painting his own scenes for galleries.

When he first showed his work at the Royal Institute of Painters in Watercolour (RI) he was asked to become a member and exhibited at these and other galleries every year.

The second turning point came when Cuneo visited Buckle's studio as Claude was painting in oils and finding the waiting period for the oils to dry quite intolerable. Cuneo gave him some blunt advice . . . 'Chuck it' he said. 'Why labour away with a medium that obviously worries you when you have such a natural mastery for watercolour'. This finally clinched the decision Claude had already wanted to make, and his fluid skill in watercolour treatment never looked back. Because of his temperament, he even found the time it took for watercolour washes to dry almost as infuriating, and he once wrote for *The Artist* . . . 'so I used to find myself stamping up

and down, seething with impatience, cursing the moving shadows and the sky, which form a greater part of the composition'. He therefore adopted a technique of progressing from darker tones (which dried more quickly) to light, instead of the more, customary, reverse procedure. He disliked the idea of painting complete pictures outside and the additional complications it involved. As he once told Cuneo . . . 'I only use nature to build the picture I want; I never allow it to dictate to me'.

Claude had dropped the middle 'H' in his signature in 1960 and was regularly turning away all requests for him to lecture and teach by various societies and private individuals. He felt that time was not on his side and he wanted to be free to learn and experience more of the art of watercolour himself. He did contribute articles to *The Artist,* however.

Through a holiday to the Ile de Re in the Bay of Biscay in 1969, Claude found the marvellous combinations of light, sea and boats the inspiration and subject matter of his beautiful later works, and he visited France regularly for three months of every year, carrying on painting until his death in 1973.

It would be fitting to let the tribute of Claude's old friend, Terence Cuneo, finish this short biography . . .

'He was essentially a traditionalist and believed, as I do, that there are so many wonderful things in the world to paint, that there is little inducement to depart from representation and search for a fresh expression in more abstract spheres. If such conservatism puts Claude, in the eyes of some, beyond the pale of progressive art thinking and if he is to be branded as a traditionalist "square", there will always be countless others who will thank God for people who feel as he did. In any event, I have no doubt that such controversy in no way disturbs the peace of this fine artist who has contributed so much and whose work has brought pleasure to so many. '

Portrait of an artist
Jack Merriott

RI RSMA RSMA ROI

Jack Merriott – produced 38 illustrations for carriage prints

In the midst of a conversation with Jim Merriott, a relative of the great artist (and a devotee of watercolour himself), he suddenly remarked . . . 'If enthusiasm is an ingredient of success, then Jack had it by the wagon-load!' and this comment seemed to sum up Jack's character perfectly. Frank Sherwin, too, in his foreword to Jack's book *Discovering Watercolour,* echoed this when he said that . . . 'Anyone who met Jack Merriott could not fail to notice his enormous enthusiasm'. Jack's paintings certainly conveyed the excitement and warmth he felt for art and nature, especially in the medium of watercolour. Yet this

freedom of expression was built upon a solid foundation of draughtsmanship which hints at the more methodical side to Jack's character.

This balance of temperament and his love for the British landscape ensured a prolific output of paintings during his career. As Ernest Savage, the artist, once wrote about his friend . . . 'Jack Merriott was a traditional painter of long standing and much experience. His free impressionist style in oil, pastel, and particularly watercolour, is widely known. His pictures convey to the beholder, by subtle effects of light and atmosphere, a fine sense of tone, of delicate harmonious colouring and of sound draughtsmanship'.

Savage used to find the 'organised' side to Jack's nature amusing and the two of them would go through a humorous routine of dividing the furniture of their sleeping accommodation into two exact halves using ties etc, when staying at hotels on their teaching courses! Jack's brother, Albert, was also a painter but had a rather contrasting, 'laid back', personality to his brother's. On their painting outings when they were younger, Jack could be seen leaving the house with all his equipment neatly organised and ready long beforehand, whilst Albert would still be stuffing paintbrushes in his pockets and invariably clutching the remains of the breakfast toast in his hand!

Jack Merriott was born in London on the 15th November 1901 and was educated at Greenwich Central School. His artistic abilities were obvious from an early age and he naturally gravitated to the Croydon School of Art and on to St Martin's School of Art for his final training. He began to earn a living as a shipping clerk in an office near London Bridge and during this period spent most of his leisure time painting. He would often be seen sketching the shipping on the Thames on the backs of old invoices, during office hours! Even at this early age several of his pictures were appearing at the Royal Academy.

By the age of 28 he had decided to finish with routine work and trust his skills as a freelance artist – a decision which Claude Buckle later made at the same age. Important commissions were not long in coming and Jack rarely found himself idle. In 1930 he married Hilda, a choral soloist, in Croydon and they later had their only child, a daughter, Wenonah.

After the outbreak of war he applied to go into the Navy but failed his medical due to a colic condition. He tried again with the Army and was enrolled as a private. The war years seemed to produce some turning points in all of the lives of the three artists I have researched and Jack

Merriott was no exception. On the day before the 'D Day' landings in France he managed to break a knee during a practice exercise and had to remain in England. Most of his colleagues were killed the following day and Jack would almost certainly have been one of them. He recovered from his injury at an Army nursing home, where he helped with the funds of the British Red Cross by painting portraits of the staff and patients.

During the war he was elected a member of the Royal Institute of Painters in Watercolours in 1944 and later lectured in the Royal Army Education Corps between 1945–46, finding great enjoyment in the art of communicating his skill to others – an experience he would repeat in the years to come. Other activities followed the war years and he became a founder member and president of the Wapping Group of Artists between 1947 and 1960. He became a frequent contributor of illustrations to *Sphere* magazine and was commissioned by them to sketch the Queen's Coronation at Westminster Abbey – one of only two artists invited out of the many applicants. The weather was determined to do its worst on the day and Jack, dressed in his smart evening suit and carrying his materials, was confronted by a real downpour. Not to

be discouraged, he started to tie newspapers all around his suit until he emerged from the taxi, looking like a scarecrow, to be greeted by great cheers from the public! When asked whether he was nervous on the day, he said . . . 'not in the least – I loved every minute of it and I even think I felt more important than the Queen!'

He also produced some lovely watercolour landscapes for a second series of books called *Beautiful Britain*, published by Blackie. He found this commission a real challenge . . . 'How on earth do I follow in the footsteps of Ernest Haslehust?' (the gifted illustrator of the first edition), he remarked at the time. These paintings, however, and the posters he was producing for the General Post Office, were proving that he was equal to the task and his name was becoming increasingly prominent as a landscape painter. It was though, his posters and carriage panel landscapes for British Railways that, in the end, made Jack Merriott a household name.

He produced numerous naturalistic posters for the railways and a total of 38 landscapes for their carriage panels – a work he thoroughly enjoyed. There couldn't have been many stations or carriages in the 1950s or 60s which didn't have his name appearing somewhere. He travelled extensively by train and car around Britain in the process. As part of his lecturing and painting itinerary, Jack and Hilda would invariably be in Scotland in May and again in September (the former, in order to enjoy two springs in the U.K. in one year!) He found great beauty north of the border, but Yorkshire was, without doubt his favourite area . . . 'The best painting county in the country' he used to say.

Although he appreciated the work for the railways he would sometimes get annoyed at the railway department's insistence that railway subjects be included in certain paintings – something he could get quite stubborn over if he didn't think it helped the compositions!

Whilst he excelled in watercolour, he was no mean artist in other media too. He was elected to the Pastel Society in 1951, the Royal Society of Marine Artists in 1955 and the Royal Institute of Painters in Oils in 1959, which speaks of his all–round ability.

Although he enjoyed his commissioned work, Jack also found great fulfilment and recognition in passing on his knowledge and experience by teaching and lecturing. This formed a large part of his later career. Frank Sherwin once wrote . . . 'Jack was never happier than when out in the open with one of his many sketching parties'. He had produced an art course for *Leisure Painter* and travelled around the Art Societies of Britain giving demonstrations. He was also one of the first in the field conducting private painting courses for progressive amateurs and professional painters and was recognised as one of the best teachers of watercolour of his time – 'The Wizard of Watercolour' as he was known to many.

In 1953 he met Ernest Savage and persuaded him to help organise an expanding programme of painting courses around Britain and Western Europe, which continued over the next 15 years until Jack's death. As the Merriotts had moved from Storrington, Sussex, the engagements meant long hours and tiring journeys for Jack from his new home in Polperro, Cornwall to all parts of the U.K. and back – so much so that they moved back to Sussex again.

Pitman, the correspondence course company, commissioned Jack to produce a pioneering course for ardent amateurs at home which achieved immediate success. The volume of tutorial work that issued from this entailed the recruitment of other teacher artists to assist. Frank Sherwin RI and Oliver Bedford were brought in to cope with assessments. The course later became the foundation for the book *Discovering Watercolour* by Jack, published after his death in 1973.

He was absolutely devoted to the 'pure watercolour' tradition and hated the idea of using any innovations in technique such as masking fluid, wax resists etc. Of Merriott's own paintings, Savage wrote ' .   his own watercolours will be remembered for their purity of colour, the apparent

simplicity of their design and execution and the evidence of sound draughtsmanship despite the impressionistic quality of light and atmosphere he contrived always to portray'. He was a great believer in the need for constant observation of landscape detail and the prolific sketchings he produced proved his hard work in this department.

During his hectic career he made many friends around the country and in Europe. Edward Wesson, a great admirer of Jack's work, was one even though Jack used to tell him off for allowing too much unpainted paper in his watercolours – one of the few things Jack was probably wrong about! He knew William Russell Flint, Claude Buckle and Frank Sherwin well and was vice-president of the RI when Rowland Hilder was president. Jack's enthusiasm and energetic temperament sometimes used to clash with Hilder's quieter and more reserved character.

His closest friend was probably William Watkins, a co–member of the Langham Group of artists to which Jack also belonged. They would spend many happy hours together, constructively pulling each other's work to pieces. In 1964, whilst teaching at Rapallo in Italy, Jack was given the freedom of the town by the mayor (a great admirer of Merriott) and a medal in recognition of his work and the friendships he had made there. Jack's many painting courses meant that he was admired by so many of the people he taught, including the well–known artist and author John Blockley – arguably Jack's most successful student.

In 1968, Jack Merriott was driving back to his house at Storrington in Sussex from an art demonstration at the National Trust property, Killerton House. The car skidded on black ice and went over a wall into a field. Jack's injuries were very serious and he never recovered, dying later that year, aged 66 – a rather sudden end to one of art's great characters.

His memorial service was held at 'the artist's church', St James in Piccadilly, London in 1969.

Portrait of an artist
Kenneth Steel

RBA SGA

Kenneth Steel – produced 35 illustrations for carriage prints

It seems that the slogan 'Sheffield – Home of British Steel', can have more than just one application in this interesting English language of ours, for Kenneth Steel was associated with the great industrial city for most of his life. He was born here on the 9 July, 1906, the son of G. T. Steel, an artist and silver engraver – and with his brother, George Hammond Steel, they learned the skills of their dad's work as young men. George also became a

fine artist and lived in Eyam, Derbyshire. Ken's skills benefited from the time he spent at the Sheffield College of Art, where he studied under Anthony Betts.

The war years and, in particular, the Sheffield blitz, left its cruel mark on Ken's life. By this time he was married and lived at Eccleshall, a suburb of the city. He was on A.R.P. duty one night, leaving his family at home. His invalid mother was in the ground floor lounge and in the cellar below were his father and his wife. A bomb blew the building apart and his mother came through the floor into the cellar and was killed. His wife suffered serious injuries and was taken away by ambulance to hospital. En–route (and unbeknown to his family) the ambulance plunged into a bomb crater. Ken spent two whole days searching for her in various hospitals in the area only to find her dead in a mortuary. Another terrible example of the idiocy of war. His ability to bounce back after the family tragedy gives some indication of the zeal for life he carried and the lively character of the man. After the war, he and his father found temporary accommodation in a cottage at Fullwood and he worked at Sheffield Town Hall using his obvious skills as an architectural artist to produce drawings for the publication *After the Bombing – Sheffield Re–Planned.* This was a job he was well qualified for after his ordeal.

During the following years Ken began to take commissionings and produce artwork for the London & North Eastern Railway and the reputation as a painter grew. By this time he had become the youngest member of the Royal Society of British Artists and also a member of the Society of Graphic Artists and he would often combine his visits to Jack Souter, the commissioning manager for the railway at Marylebone, with his visits to these art societies. He was certainly a believer in the work ethic . . . 'you don't wait for work to come to you – you go out and get it!', hence he would often be contacting the railways and other organisations for work. He called them his 'little forages' and, if his prolific output for the railways is anything to go by, the principle certainly worked!

Ken re-married, and would sometimes drive to the subject locations for the posters and compartment illustrations with his second wife, Grace, in their car and caravan. He would spontaneously make up poems en–route and talk of many subjects on the way – he had an excellent general knowledge. Like most artists he would do 'on the spot' sketches and watercolour roughs at the location. He was particularly good with a pencil – no doubt a by–product of his etching skills. Sometimes they would travel to these

working assignments by train and would make the most of the trip, enjoying 'jugged hare' at a Newcastle Hotel whilst sketching the *King Edward Bridge* one day, or staying at a local hotel whilst painting the *Forth Bridge* on another. Painting the Forth Bridge in two days must have been a record – it normally takes years!

The final artwork was accomplished in his studio at the Steel's bungalow at Lodgemoor in Sheffield and there is little doubt that Ken was a perfectionist when it came to architectural detail as can be deduced from the following story . . .

Shortly after the print of his painting of *Lambeth Bridge* appeared in railway carriages, he was forwarded a letter via the LNER from a gentleman passenger who pointed out an error on the London skyline. Because of the confidence of Ken's own eye for detail (and, no doubt, a bit of the old Yorkshire pride!), he immediately replied, inviting the man to meet him on the spot in London to compare the print with the landscape. Needless to say that on the day Ken was proved right and the men departed as good friends.

Not surprisingly, given his father's occupation, Ken was a fine etcher and engraver and wrote the book *On Engraving,* published by Pitman. The numerous poster and carriage panel designs for the LNER and British Rail kept him busy and his reputation for watercolours meant that private tuition and week-long teaching courses became a part of his life. Peter Coulthard, the

well–known Sheffield artist was one of his best students and readily acknowledges that much of his skill was inspired by 'Uncle Ken'.

Unlike Claude Buckle, Ken was happy working with other mediums such as oils, charcoal and pen and ink, but it is fair to say that he excelled in watercolour. He contributed articles for *The Artist,* exhibited in larger shows and held one-man exhibitions in Dublin. He got to know some of the artists involved in railway commissionings, especially Jack Merriott, but was particularly close to William Russell Flint, one of the great British artists of the 20th century.

As you view Ken's paintings, you can't help feeling that behind them all was a man with a real jovial personality who enjoyed his work and was determined to get the best out of life whilst the days remained – a lesson learnt, perhaps, from his own experiences of the war years. He certainly loved and lived for his art too much to have time for any other hobbies, although he often found the time for dancing functions at the Cutler's Hall at Sheffield, where he was the life and soul of the party. It was certain, Grace recalls, that it took a lot to get Ken down. The only clue he gave that things weren't going too well was when he could be heard whistling *Tea for Two!* On the odd occasion when things were really grim, he would go off for a drive in the car to wind down a little . . .

One day Grace and Ken had their three year old granddaughter staying with them while Ken was just finishing a beautiful oil painting of a Scottish landscape in his studio. As he went indoors, little Susan crept in and began prodding the wet paint and found that, by sliding her hands backwards and forwards over the canvas, it produced some interesting patterns. On returning, Ken saw the rather altered 'finished' product. Seconds later, the car engine was starting up and he was off – and who can blame him!

After a sudden and unexpected illness, he died of cancer of the throat, aged 64, and left a devastated Grace behind. Indeed, she was so upset by the loss that several days later, in a state of shock, she began to burn much of Ken's original artwork, sketches and his autobiography draft until a friendly neighbour realised Grace's shocked condition and retrieved the remaining works. Grace went to live in New Zealand for six years after her husband's death, returning to England in 1976. I acknowledge my debt to her for much of the above information and the kindness with which it was given.

Chapter 3
A carriage seat tour of Britain

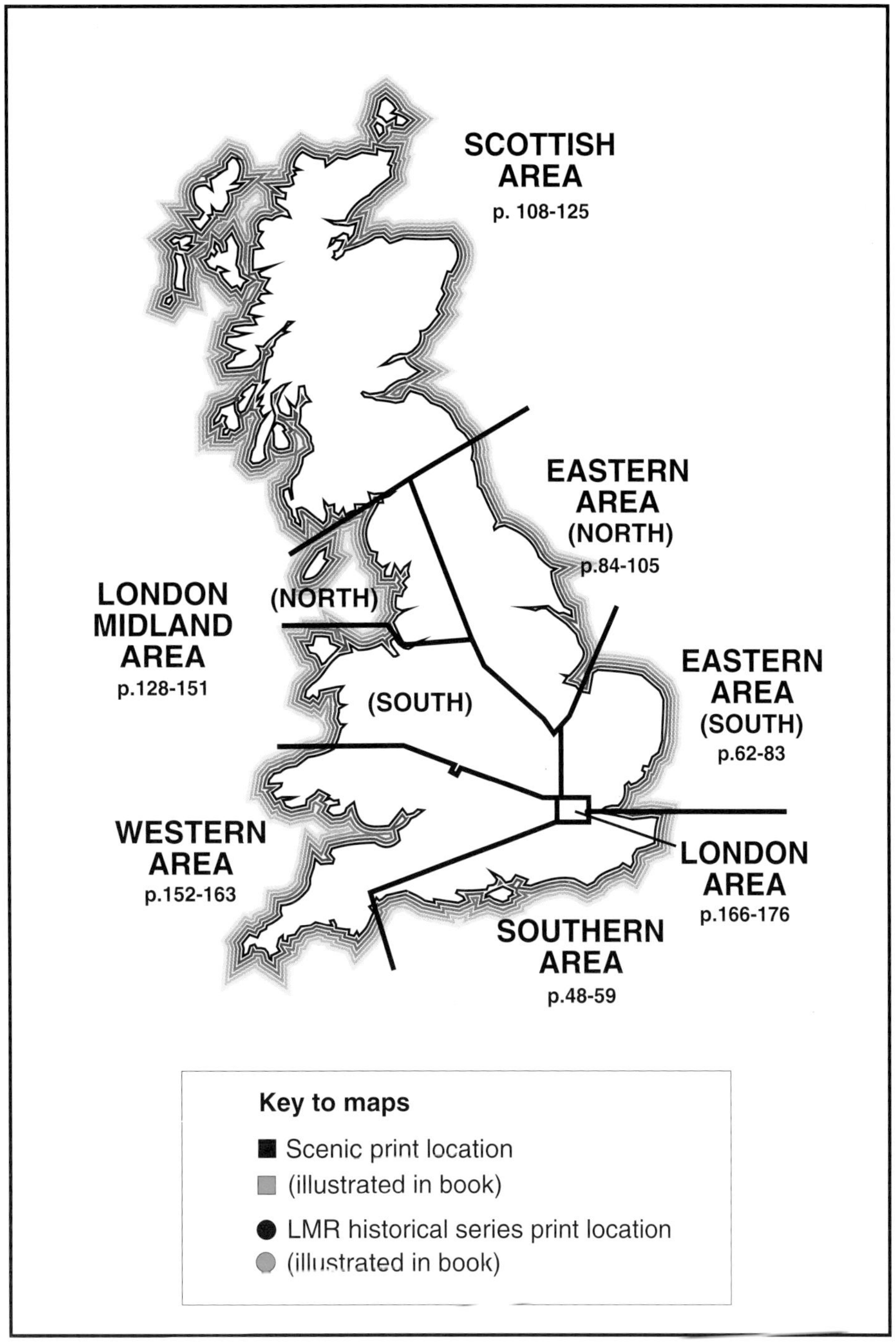

SCOTTISH
AREA
p. 108-125

EASTERN
AREA
(NORTH)
p.84-105

LONDON
MIDLAND
AREA
p.128-151

(NORTH)

(SOUTH)

EASTERN
AREA
(SOUTH)
p.62-83

WESTERN
AREA
p.152-163

LONDON
AREA
p.166-176

SOUTHERN
AREA
p.48-59

Key to maps

■ Scenic print location
■ (illustrated in book)

● LMR historical series print location
● (illustrated in book)

The maps for each area show all of the *standard format* colour prints issued by the railways between 1937 and 1957. Those highlighted are illustrated in the book.

N.B. The date following the artist's name in each caption refers to the approximate year of issue by the railways.

Introduction to the Southern Area

'The Sunshine Railway' . . . 'Summer comes soonest in the south' . . . 'The sun shines most on the southern coast' . . .

As these old and famous slogans show, the Southern Railway seemed to enjoy selling its weather attractions to the public. Ever since the London, Brighton & South Coast Railway had called itself 'The Sunshine Line', posters of beaches basking in blazing sunshine and baked, bathing beauties in their 'baiting' suits left you with the impression that Brighton was only two degrees from the equator. If you've lived in southern England at all, you'll find it difficult to believe that the climate is that different from, say, Watford, but, as the sales marketeers tell us, make sure you promote any positive difference between you and your competitors – no matter how small it may be.

Apart from its climate, the Southern also had a long stretch of coastline in its territory, including part of the Devon area, and the advertising department were obviously keen to promote the 'holiday' image that sun and sea afforded. John Betjeman, in his poem *Beside the Seaside* expressed this summer migratory approach to the coast quite graphically as a time when . . . 'England leaves her centre for her tide line'. In as early as 1841, the London & South Western Railway was organising combined rail and sea excursions to the Isle of Wight from their Nine Elms terminus in London; a bargain 220 miles for £1. Some of the south's seaside resorts, however, were not too keen at first to be visited by the 'dreaded excursionists'. At a meeting to consider the coming of the railway to the town of Bournemouth, a man had leapt to his feet and read the following poem:

Tis well from far to hear the railway scream;
And watch the curling, lingering clouds of steam;
But let not Bournemouth – Health's approved abode,
Court the near presence of the iron road

It was another 27 years after the railway had appeared that the invalid and retired (and, it must be said, somewhat aloof) residents of Bournemouth at last welcomed the traffic.

A similar, somewhat prejudiced, attitude prevailed at Brighton where the 'affluent season' operated in July and the 'tradesmen's season' in August and September. Railway excursions had certainly transformed this resort

on the south coast. The first 'cheap day' excursion train to Brighton was rather overcrowded. 48 carriages and four engines left London and as it picked up at stations en route, increased to *60 coaches* and *six engines*. It was so delayed that, at Brighton, a director and locomotive were sent to look for it! It finally appeared safely at 1.30pm. By 1860 the London Brighton & South Coast Railway were running 36 excursions from London every Sunday and the slogan 'To Brighton and back for 3s 6d' was born. No wonder the resort attracted some topical rhymes during this period i.e. . . . .

I took the train to Brighton,
I walked beside the sea,
And 30,000 Londoners
Were there along with me.

The other member of the Southern pre–grouping trio, the South Eastern & Chatham Railway had the privilege of being the closest railway company in Britain to France, and its channel ferries from the coastal towns of Dover and Folkestone brought a steady flow of traffic to and from the continent. By 1958, 3,503,000 passengers were using these cross–channel ferries, and by 1966, over five million. So from the earliest railway days, whether poor or rich, whether taking a day trip or a 'grand tour' of Europe, an excursion in the south by train awaited you.

Although the Southern area only had a small percentage of the route mileage of the country, much of it lay within or around the London area and most of the region was heavily influenced by the capital's proximity. Hence they had the highest passenger receipts per mile due to their heavy suburban commuter, coastal resort excursion, and London to channel port traffics. They often took the lead in their pioneering of new dock facilities and short–sea crossing services. The above factors and the density of the population in the south east made the Southern's network one of the most complex in Europe and, in the early 1930s, at a time of declining passenger numbers, an electrification programme was started by the Southern's chairman Sir Herbert Walker.

By the end of 1939 over 30 per cent of the route mileage had been electrified, accounting for a huge 60 per cent of the trains operated. The electrics were soon recognised as being frequent and reliable, were cheaper to operate than steam, and traffic increased greatly. By 1957, the Region was carrying as many passengers on its trains as the whole of the Class 1 railways in the USA put together! Carriage panels proliferated in these new units, advertising the companies services and its scenic views.

After the Second World War the company's photographic panels and Hesketh Hubbard and Adrian Allinson's carriage prints mainly concentrated on coastal resorts and their surrounding landscapes. This emphasis continued when other artists were commissioned to paint landscapes when the Southern Region came into being in 1948. Merriott's *Cinque Ports* carried the coastal flavour and added a historical seasoning, too. Frank Sherwin's south coast and Channel Island resorts continued the pattern – blue skies, piers, promenades, beaches etc – all sought to coax the bored London commuters, sitting in their electric units from Kingston and Bromley, down to the seaside and lure them with the thought of basking out in the heat all day... ah sunbathing, where ignorance is blister.

It is surprising that only relatively few standard-format prints were issued by the Southern Region, considering the large number of holiday resorts in the area. Even the Isle of Wight and the Devon coast were ignored. It can only be assumed that the advertising department was aiming at impression rather than detail.

The wooing of passengers to the Southern's coastline (which, in Brighton's case, is a mere 60 miles from London) meant that it was not worthwhile trying to promote the lovely countryside of the Surrey heaths, the North Downs and the Kent Weald which lay in between. After all, why encourage short journeys, with little potential revenue, when longer ones were more profitable and passed through most of these areas anyway. Thus the quaint villages and towns inland were largely overlooked except, indirectly, by D W Burley's sketches in the Southern Railway's *Hovis* adverts depicting quiet spots such as Cranbrook, Westerham and Rotherfield.

If the Southern had largely forgotten it had a countryside, however, it certainly remembered its cathedrals inland and the strong tourist attraction that they possessed, hence a series of four by Claude Buckle. These magnificent buildings attracted many sightseers and it must be remembered that their structural vastness must have appeared even more impressive to the public in the days when skyscrapers were still only a twinkle in an architect's eye.

Considering the small area in which the Region had to prove itself (with the exception of the North Devon runs), the Southern gained a fine reputation for its express trains and, particularly, for its titled Pullman services. The *Bournemouth Belle, Brighton Belle* (formerly the *Southern Belle*), *Golden Arrow,* and *Atlantic Coast Express* soon

became household names. Richard Ward's paintings of *Merchant Navy* and *West Country* pacific locomotives operating in the south coastal counties intended to show that the Region could compete with the best of the country's trains and was also a picturesque way of selling its services, in much the same way as Buckle's paintings of Channel Island shipping in the same series.

When the Beeching axe finally struck in the early 1960s, the Southern fared better than the other regions, losing lines around the West Country, Isle of Wight and Sussex areas, but relatively few others. Interestingly enough, these closed lines tended to be in the areas avoided in their carriage print subjects.

A lack of geographical spread and the comparatively few prints produced are the chief criticisms of the Southern Region's carriage panel views, but a few imaginative attempts to sell itself perhaps made up for these weaknesses. In what was a densely populated commuter area with an obvious logical bias towards commercial advertisements in carriages, perhaps we should be grateful that any scenic prints of the Region appeared at all.

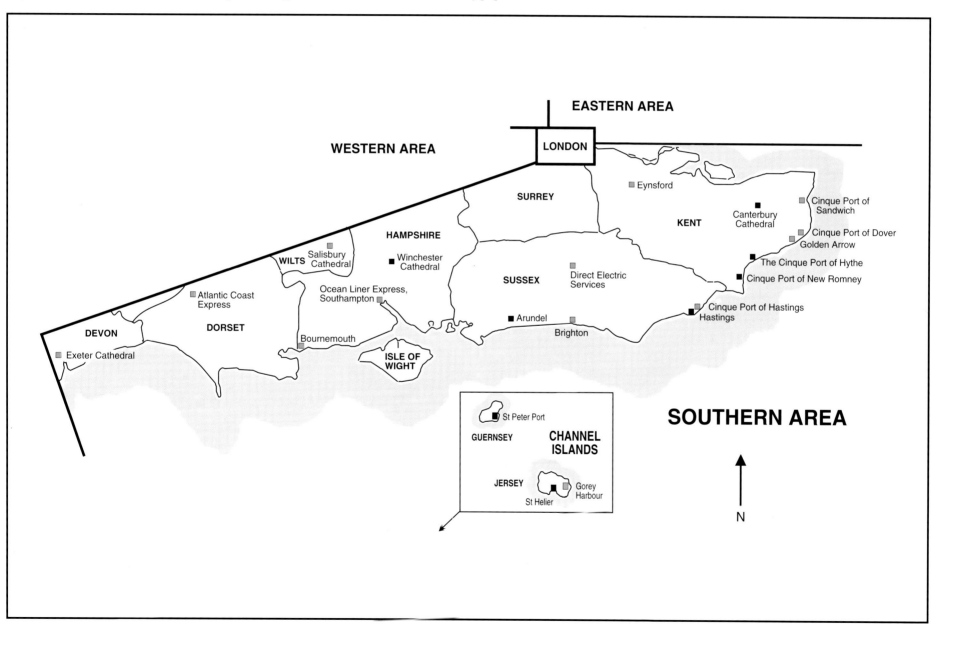

Bournemouth, Hampshire
from a watercolour by
Frank Sherwin RI (1956) *(top)*

Until 1811, Bournemouth (which now lies in Dorset) was
nothing more than commonland, through which the stream
of Bourne ran, en-route to the sea. Dr Granville, a famous
physician, recommended its mild, sunny climate to the masses
for health purposes, and wealthy investors did the rest: from
1850 to 1900 the population grew from just 695 to 59,000!
Due to local opposition the town was by-passed by the
LSWR and it was not until 1870 that it was connected to
the main line via a spur. A further 18 years elapsed before it
became part of the Waterloo main line direct and the
current Bournemouth Central Station was opened in 1885.
Bournemouth West (ex LSWR, closed), was the terminus of
the former Somerset & Dorset line to Bath and provided a
direct route for holidaymakers from the north west. From
the start of its operations at least two of its four daily trains
provided through coaches from Birmingham and in later days
many holidaymakers will remember The *Pines Express* which
traversed this lovely route until 1967. Sherwin hints here at
parks, pavilion, pier, people, sea, sand and sun, capturing
some of the characteristics of the town — but where is all
the traffic you get caught up in when you visit?

Brighton, Sussex
from a watercolour by
Frank Sherwin RI (1956)   *(top facing)*

Beginning life as Brighthelmstone, a small fishing village,
Brighton began to grow in 1754 when a Dr Richard Russell
moved there and prescribed sea bathing and sea air as the
cure for all ills. When the railways came, London flocked to
the town and elegant terraces and squares were constructed
for the patrons. The population grew from 46,661 in 1841
to 147,427 in 1931 and Brighton became the south coast's
most popular resort. Even though Sherwin has made the
beach appear to be sand instead of shingle, the holidaymakers still prefer to walk the Palace Pier rather than brave the
sea, and this view has changed little over the years. Regular
express trains from London have been bringing passengers
down to this resort in a little under an hour for many years
now — the most famous of these undoubtedly being the
Brighton Belle. This train was steam hauled until the end of
1932, when a new pullman electric service was introduced.
The train was finally withdrawn in 1972, in spite of a public
outcry supported by celebrity figures.

*Brighton is the former LBSCR terminus of the main line from
London and the coastal lines from Hastings and Worthing*

Gorey Harbour, Jersey
from a watercolour by
Frank Sherwin RI (1956)   *(bottom facing)*

The sky and the sea say it all in this view of Gorey Harbour
in the Channel Island of Jersey. Sherwin says come and sail
away south for some peace and quiet, where the phone
won't ring and the problems will all disappear (or, more
realistically, be postponed). Jersey's chief fortress, the 14th
century Gorey Castle, otherwise named Mont Orgeuil
(Mount Pride), adds a little cultural interest too.

*Gorey Harbour is situated on the eastern coastline of Jersey and
because of its close proximity to the French coast, serves as the
port for two ferry services to France. The island was originally
served by ferries to St Helier from Southampton (LSWR) and
Weymouth GWR)*

Cinque Port of Dover, Kent
from a watercolour by
Jack Merriott RI (1952) *(⇦ overleaf)*

Merriott in a somewhat subdued mood. The famous white cliffs at the end of the North Downs appear grey and the Norman castle atop them seems to want to withdraw from the town rather than to dominate it. However, the sun at last appears to be breaking through onto this ancient Roman town of 'Dubris', chief of the Cinque Ports. Dover was first reached by rail in 1844 and, with its close proximity to France, proved to be the major ferry terminal for the continent and a fine source of revenue to the railways. By 1966, almost four million passengers were using the shipping service and British Rail was, then, the largest operator of short-sea ferry crossings in the world.

Dover had two stations, Marine (closed 1991) and Priory, both formerly SECR

Eynsford, Kent
from a watercolour by
Alan Gray (1956) *(top)*

Served by the regular Victoria to Sevenoaks trains, Eynsford village, on the North Downs, is a typical London commuter belt location, and a somewhat, surprising choice for the carriage panel pictures. It is blessed with a Roman villa, a ruined castle and also the intact, 12th century Lullingstone Castle, yet Alan Gray with his strong charcoal style, has chosen the more classic trio of public house, church and quaint 15th century bridge over the meandering River Darent to illustrate the location. Very peaceful and perfectly English.

Eynsford is a former SECR station on the line between Swanley and Sevenoaks/Maidstone

Cinque Port of Sandwich, Kent
from a watercolour by
Jack Merriott RI (1952) *(top facing)*

Cinque Ports were granted special privileges by the king on the condition that they supplied ships for the royal fleet. Sandwich was once an important naval base and smuggling haven, but is now two miles from the sea due to a changing coastline, It is certainly an attractive town with its narrow streets and fine buildings. Although Henry VIII's castle has long since gone, the town still displays evidence of its important heritage and Merriott's view of the bridge over the River Stour and the surrounding buildings blend well together. Shortly after the coming of the railway, two famous golf courses were built on the sand dunes nearby which finally put an end to the town's maritime trade.

Sandwich is a former SECR station on the line between Ramsgate and Dover

Exeter Cathedral, Devon
from a watercolour by
Claude Buckle (1952) *(bottom facing)*

Claude Buckle seemed to enjoy painting cathedrals as much as marine subjects, and here he portrays Exeter, one of four he painted for the Southern Region. Although this structure does not have the soaring spire of Salisbury Cathedral, he captures Exeter's lofty grandeur adequately enough. The cathedral, having survived the bombing of the Second World War, dates from the early medieval period, although its two towers are Norman and its 300 ft long nave is the longest span of unbroken gothic rib–vaulting in the world. Exeter is a historic railway junction on the route to the West Country and was a source of much company rivalry in the days before BR.

Exeter's main stations are (i) St. David's (ex GWR) on the main line from Paddington and (ii) Central (formerly Queen Street) (ex LSWR) on the line from Waterloo

Direct Electric Services, London – Brighton
from a watercolour by
Richard Ward (1956) *(top)*

Electrification revolutionised rail travel on the Southern. Whilst journey times showed little improvement over steam hauled trains under the new scheme, frequency, reliability and reduced costs quickly meant an increased revenue for the Southern. The London to Brighton main line electrification was completed in 1932 and the first services ran on January 1 1933 – the expresses leaving London 'every hour on the hour'. Here we see Richard Ward's painting of two six–car electric units crossing the 37–arched, Ouse Viaduct between Balcombe and Hayward's Heath. Designed by J. Rastrick and D. Mocatta, it was completed in 1841. The first unit shown here was designated *6–PUL,* due to the inclusion of a pullman car in the formation.

The London – Brighton main line was part of the LBSCR network

Golden Arrow, Continental Express
from a watercolour by
Richard Ward (1956) *(top, facing)*

Richard Ward shows the famous Southern Express emerging from the unusually shaped portals of Shakespeare Tunnel, between Dover and Folkestone. The locomotive is a BR standard *Britannia,* class 7. The 1100 hours departure from Victoria to Paris had operated for years before gaining the title *Golden Arrow* in 1929. It originally consisted of luxurious, first class pullmans only, but second class facilities were introduced, too, in 1931. The French section from Calais was, like- wise, named the *Fleche d'Or* and the total journey originally took six hours, 52 minutes, including the Channel crossing by the steamer *Canterbury,* which was specially designed for the service. The train was withdrawn during the war years and was reinstated in 1946. The days of the named, luxurious, continental rail expresses were drawing to a close, however, and the train ran for the last time in 1972.

Atlantic Coast Express, London & The West Country
from a watercolour by
Richard Ward (1956) *(bottom, facing)*

This painting should bring back some holiday memories! Introduced in 1936, (although the 1100 hours Waterloo to the West Country service had been running for a long time beforehand), the *Atlantic Coast Express* was the most multi-portioned train in the country. It had *nine* different sections – Ilfracombe, Torrington, Padstow, Bude, Plymouth, Exmouth, Sidmouth, Seaton and Exeter! After a quick, non–stop run to Salisbury, the next section of line involved some of the most exciting, fast–running in the country and, consequently, beat the 11.00 hours GWR departure from Paddington to Exeter by a full half hour. The A.C.E. also had the rather unusual experience of passing the GWR expresses, bound for the *same* cities, *twice,* in the *opposite* direction – at Exeter, St. David's and Plymouth, North Road! Ward portrays a stream-lined, 'Merchant Navy' 4–6–2 locomotive No 35013, *Blue Funnel* in BR livery at the head of the train at Tisbury. These locomotives were affectionately known as 'spam cans' due to their rectangular, streamlined shape. The service ended in 1964, when the WR took over the lines west of Salisbury and much of the ex LSWR network in Devon and Cornwall was then closed.

Ocean Liner Express, Southampton Docks – London
from a watercolour by
Richard Ward (1956) *(overleaf ⇨)*

In 1911, the White Star Line shipping company moved its base from the great port of Liverpool to Southampton and other companies then followed suit. With its unique four high tides every 24 hours, Southampton Docks became the place to see the huge ocean liners come and go until international air travel took over, half a century later. Special boat trains ran from Waterloo to Southampton to serve these sailing's and, pictured here, is *The Cunarder* pullman train hauled by 'West Country' locomotive No. 34095 *Brentor* as it connects with the famous ship the *Queen Mary* on the left. By 1952, 13,480 vessels were carrying 650,000 passengers and 12 million tons of cargo yearly. Now these days are gone and most vessels visiting the port are container ships conveying freight traffic. The Southampton Ocean Terminal which opened in July 1950, is no longer in use, and Tite's Southampton Terminus station which lay close to the Eastern Docks at the end of a short branch from Northam Junction was closed in 1966.

Holiday Haunts 1947

GWR

SIXPENCE

Carriage panels, *clockwise from top left:*
Padstow, Cornwall by Hubbard (SR post–war series);
Bridlington, Yorks by Blake (LNER); Gorleston, Norfolk by Blake (LNER);
North Cornwall by Allinson (SR post–war) [who added detergent to the surf?];
Robin Hood's Bay, Yorks by Sherwin (LNER); Holiday Runabout Ticket by Mills (WR);
Westcliff, Essex by King (LNER); *Centre:* South Sands, Tenby, Pembroke (GWR panel);
Background: The Beach, Aberdeen (LMS panel)

L. M. & S. R.

This ticket entitles the holder of a
ordinary rail ticket to travel from

9243

BLACKPOOL

127

ON THE DATE AND BY T
TRAIN WHICH IS INDIC
BY THE SCHEDULED NUM
PRINTED HEREON.

To be given up at Platform Barrier Starting Station
which point the Rail ticket must also be produce

THE BEACH, ABERDEEN

TRAIN
SERVICES
and FARES

LONDON EUSTON
and
SOUTHPORT
LYTHAM
ST. ANNES
SQUIRES GATE
BLACKPOOL
FLEETWOOD

12th September, 1960 to 11th June, 1961
(or until further Notice)

SUBJECT TO ALTERATION

Engineering work in connection with
modernisation may cause delay to trains on Sundays

NORTH CORNWALL

Beside the seaside

During the first half of the 20th century, a trip to the seaside was synonymous with a ride in a railway carriage. Before the upsurge of modern road transport chaos, huge numbers of scheduled and excursion trains were arriving at resorts around the country's coastline, disgorging holiday–makers in their thousands. Railway advertising departments grasped the sales opportunities, and publications, posters and carriage prints of British resorts proliferated.

Explore the district of your choice with a
HOLIDAY RUNABOUT TICKET

UNLIMITED RAIL TRAVEL IN HOLIDAY AREAS AT EXCEPTIONALLY CHEAP RATES. AVAILABLE FOR SEVEN DAYS MAY 10 OCTOBER INCLUSIVE

ASK THE LOCAL STATIONMASTER FOR FULL PARTICULARS

HOLIDAY HAUNTS
SIXPENCE

2nd · SINGLE   SINGLE · 2nd
Margate
Ramsgate   Margate to   Margate
Ramsgate
RAMSGATE
61 84   61 84
(S)   1/8 Fare 1/8   (S)
Forconditionssecover...Forcondit secover

Introduction to the Eastern area

It may appear to some readers of this book that the London & North Eastern Railway captures more than its fair share of the coverage of the history of this subject. This is not due to any particular bias of the author towards this company, but simply because the pioneering work in its advertising department and, in particular, the sheer volume of artwork produced, rather overwhelmed that of the other companies. For example, if an award had been given to the railway company that had the most pride in its own area, in terms of the variety of subjects and the geographical spread covered in its carriage prints, then it is certain that the LNER would have won comfortably. Following on closely from its success with the originality of its fine posters, the LNER was keen to advertise as many of the places of interest in its territory as possible and this regional pride meant that they were not ashamed of scenes that other railway companies would never have considered – who else, but the LNER, would have gloried in atmospheric views of Hull and Grimsby Docks!

Scenes, especially of villages, cities and towns, were often realistically portrayed in great detail, with little of the pretentiousness sometimes displayed by their rivals. The LNER felt that this honest approach would be appreciated by the travelling public. It certainly brought a breath of fresh air to the normal range of scenic views.

Because of this attitude an excellent locational coverage of views was commissioned by the advertising department and then executed by the fine artists concerned. These ranged from viaducts, castles and bridges in Durham and Northumberland to seaside towns, ruined abbeys, rivers and country hamlets in Yorkshire and from village landscapes in moors, dales, wolds and fens to town and city scenes all over the area including London itself. East Anglia alone had over 80 paintings commissioned for use in the production of prints in LNER/ER days and these, in themselves, could well illustrate a historical guide book for that period.

This wide geographical coverage was part of an attempt to draw passengers from the railway's main line arteries into the smaller capillary and lesser–used branch lines. Whether this intention actually worked is questionable but it was a bold and determined effort to encourage the use of their full system. The network of railways on the eastern side of the country had a relatively easy terrain to negotiate when they were originally constructed. The

East Anglia and Lincolnshire routes radiated out from the London termini of Liverpool Street, Kings Cross and Fenchurch Street over flat countryside with a network of connecting lines in between. Unlike other parts of the country, the railways in the southern half of this region were not built to supply industrial areas but agricultural locations, North Sea ports, holiday resorts and ecclesiastical and university towns. The railways themselves were often the only industrial element in the area.

The north east with its many moors, is more undulating, but not mountainous, and the main problems that tested the skills of the early railway engineers were spanning rivers such as the Tyne, Tees, Wear and Tweed. Heavy industry in this area, however, provided the eastern railways with much of their freight traffic – coal from Northumberland, Durham and South Yorkshire; steel and manufacturing products from Sheffield, Teeside and Leeds etc. Coastal ports at Hull, Grimsby, Hartlepool, Sunderland and Tyneside helped to give this area much of its character too and provided a steady freight revenue – a factor the LNER advertising department were keen to publicise in their panels.

The East Coast Main Line has witnessed much railway history through the years ever since Darlington saw the world's first steam operated public railway service in 1825. The Great Northern Railway opened the line from Kings Cross to York in 1852 and this route has since seen some fierce competition for the fastest journey time from England to Scotland, initially with the LNWR and, latterly, witnessing the famous LNER versus LMS 'races' between the wars. *The Flying Scotsman* and the new streamlined *Coronation* and *Silver Jubilee* expresses operating on this line caught the public's imagination and Mallard's 126 mph world steam speed record was the final triumph for the company. The LNER's pioneering carriage prints were initially conceived to enhance the interiors of these new luxury trains. After this first set of 16 etchings appeared in 1936, a continuous stream of prints was issued, including many of Scotland and also some of locations on the old Great Central main line during the LNER period. Commissionings ceased in the mid–1950s by which time over 200 different prints had been issued – the series had lasted almost as long as the television programme *Coronation Street!*

Over 40 artists contributed paintings to it, many of whom were well respected nationally. In the LNER days particularly, many gifted artists (Badmin, Byatt, Causer, Hilder, Holding, Rushbury and Taylor to name but a few) produced much 'fine art' and certain of these paintings

were well worth viewing just in terms of sheer quality and style alone.

The Eastern area also had its fair share of 'bracing' holiday resorts including Southend, Great Yarmouth, Skegness, Cleethorpes and Scarborough and, naturally enough, the railway carriage panels sought to interest the vast numbers of factory workers and city dwellers in a trip down to the coast. One resident of Scarborough in a letter to the local paper saw this excursion traffic in a rather more negative light. He noted that the railways had . . . 'brought a new host of invaders who were the pale, emaciated inhabitants of mirky and densely populated cities, seeking to restore their sickly frames to health and vigour by frequent immersion in the sea'. The correspondent obviously wasn't a member of the coastal swimming association.

During the BR period the high standard of carriage print artwork dropped, although some artists, including local ones, still seemed to be capable of quality work. It must also be said that many of the prints really deserved a better gallery for their viewers than the simple mount–less, narrow frames enclosing them in the carriages.

The Eastern Region suffered badly when the railway network declined in the middle of the century. It had an elaborate web of little–used rural lines which was a prime target for closure. Much of the East Anglian and North Eastern 'capillary' network, for example, disappeared and the quaint carriage pictures of stranded railway–linked towns such as Lavenham, Saffron Walden and Cavendish; Coxwold, Tattershall and Alnwick no longer wooed their viewers away from the main arteries.

When these rural lines closed, many people felt that not only had the railways lost their 'capillary' routes, but they had had the very 'heart' knocked out of them, too. We can at least be glad that the Eastern left a veritable feast of down–to–earth, historical railway art behind for future generations.

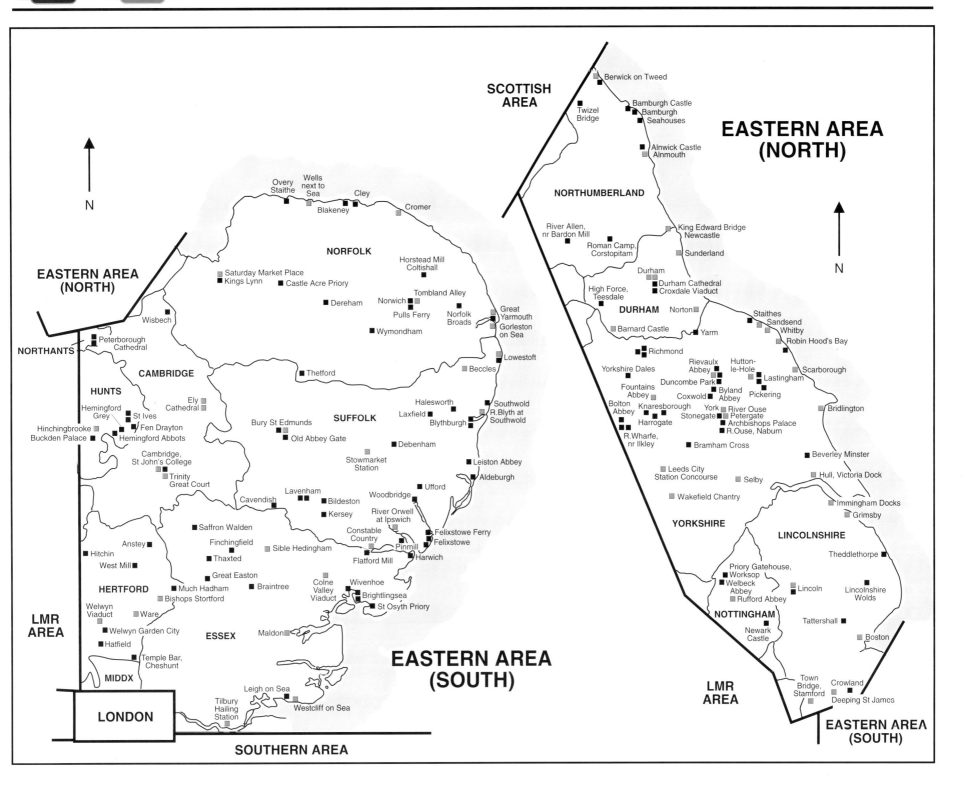

SCOTTISH
AREA

EASTERN AREA
(NORTH)

N

Berwick on Tweed

Twizel
Bridge

Bamburgh Castle
Bamburgh
Seahouses

Alnwick Castle
Alnmouth

NORTHUMBERLAND

River Allen,
nr Bardon Mill

King Edward Bridge
Newcastle

Roman Camp,
Corstopitam

Sunderland

Durham

High Force,
Teesdale

Durham Cathedral
Croxdale Viaduct

Norton

DURHAM

Barnard Castle

Yarm

Staithes
Sandsend
Whitby

Robin Hood's Bay

Richmond

Yorkshire Dales

Rievaulx
Abbey

Hutton-
le-Hole

Scarborough

Fountains
Abbey

Duncombe Park

Lastingham

Bolton
Abbey

Coxwold

Byland
Abbey

Pickering

Knaresborough

York

River Ouse

Stonegate

Petergate

Archbishops Palace

R.Ouse, Naburn

Bridlington

Harrogate

R.Wharfe,
nr Ilkley

Bramham Cross

Beverley Minster

Leeds City
Station Concourse

Selby

Hull, Victoria Dock

Wakefield Chantry

YORKSHIRE

Immingham Docks

Grimsby

LINCOLNSHIRE

Theddlethorpe

Priory Gatehouse,
Worksop

Welbeck
Abbey

Lincoln

Lincolnshire
Wolds

Rufford Abbey

NOTTINGHAM

Newark
Castle

Tattershall

Boston

LMR
AREA

Town
Bridge,
Stamford

Crowland

Deeping St James

EASTERN AREA
(SOUTH)

EASTERN AREA
(NORTH)

N

Overy
Staithe

Wells
next to
Sea

Cley

Blakeney

Cromer

NORFOLK

Horstead Mill
Coltishall

Saturday Market Place

Kings Lynn

Castle Acre Priory

Dereham

Norwich

Tombland Alley

Pulls Ferry

Norfolk
Broads

Great
Yarmouth

Gorleston
on Sea

EASTERN AREA
(NORTH)

Wisbech

Wymondham

NORTHANTS

Peterborough
Cathedral

Thetford

Lowestoft

Beccles

CAMBRIDGE

HUNTS

Ely
Cathedral

Halesworth

Laxfield

Southwold
R.Blyth at
Southwold

Hemingford
Grey

St Ives

SUFFOLK

Blythburgh

Hinchingbrooke

Fen Drayton

Bury St Edmunds

Buckden Palace

Hemingford Abbots

Old Abbey Gate

Debenham

Cambridge,
St John's College

Stowmarket
Station

Leiston Abbey

Trinity
Great Court

Aldeburgh

Cavendish

Lavenham

Ufford

Bildeston

Woodbridge

Saffron Walden

Kersey

River Orwell
at Ipswich

Anstey

Finchingfield

Constable
Country

Felixstowe Ferry

Hitchin

Sible Hedingham

Pinmill

Felixstowe

West Mill

Thaxted

Flatford Mill

Harwich

Great Easton

Wivenhoe

HERTFORD

Much Hadham

Braintree

Colne
Valley
Viaduct

Bishops Stortford

Brightlingsea

Welwyn
Viaduct

Ware

St Osyth Priory

LMR
AREA

Welwyn Garden City

ESSEX

Maldon

Hatfield

Temple Bar,
Cheshunt

MIDDX

Leigh on Sea

LONDON

Tilbury
Hailing
Station

Westcliff on Sea

EASTERN AREA
(SOUTH)

SOUTHERN AREA

River Blyth at Southwold, Suffolk
from a watercolour by
Eric Scott (1945–55) (⇐ overleaf)

A favourite landscape painting of mine but, sadly, I can find little information about the artist. Scott's treatment of the River Blyth and its reflections is superb and the whole scene brings an atmosphere of peace, beauty and solitude – qualities somewhat unobtainable in a railway compartment. The quaint and notorious, 8½ mile long, 3 ft gauge, Southwold Light Railway ran across the river not far from here, between Walberswick and its terminus at Southwold, a pleasant seaside town. The line opened in 1879 but its equipment was never sufficient for the loads it was called upon to carry and trains could barely reach 20 mph! The railway became the butt of many humorous postcards issued at the time. It suddenly announced one Friday in April 1929, that it was going to close, and did so – the following day! A bus service was operating the former route when this print appeared.

The Southwold Railway (closed) ran between Halesworth and Southwold. Halesworth is a former GER station on the Ipswich to Lowestoft line

Welwyn Viaduct, Hertfordshire
from a watercolour by
S R Badmin RWS (1945–7) *(bottom)*

The first of Badmin's marvellous detailed and illustrative, paintings of railway architecture on the LNER is that of Welwyn Viaduct on the east coast main line. It is also known as the Digswell Viaduct, (the name of the village it overlooks) and is 22 miles north of London. It was designed by Lewis Cubitt for the Great Northern Railway and construction was completed in 1850 at a total cost of £69,397. The viaduct comprises 40 x 30 ft span brick arches, reaching up to a height of 98ft above ground level, and is 1,560 ft long. The structure was originally faced with red bricks which proved to be porous. An outer shield of harder blue facing bricks was added in October 1935 at a cost of £25,000. An engine can just be seen with a goods train at Welwyn North (formerly Welwyn) station, to the centre left of the picture, whilst a passenger train steams over the last few arches of the viaduct, heading north.

Welwyn was an ex GNR station on the main line between Kings Cross and Peterborough

Ware, Hertfordshire

from a watercolour by
Claud Muncaster RWS (1945–7) *(top)*

As Lady Jane Grey was crowned Queen here in 1553, Ware does have an interesting past, yet Muncaster chooses here to reveal a little of the town's river history in his painting of Ware, otherwise known as 'the granary of London'. The River Lee navigation bisects the town and once saw a very heavy traffic of boats bringing products for the local malting industry, and Claud portrays some of this heritage here with his picture of the fine riverside buildings and barges. The navigation is now almost solely used by pleasure boats and anglers, who take advantage of the pleasant surroundings the river affords. The railway line here was originally built to a five foot gauge and electrification took place in 1960.

Ware is a former GER station on the Liverpool Street to Hertford line

Lowestoft, Suffolk

from a watercolour by
E T Holding RWS (1945–7) *(overleaf ⇨)*

Just after the war, the LNER commissioned five paintings of old docks and ports on their coastline and they couldn't have chosen a better artist than Edgar Holding to undertake them. His paintings mix detail with plenty of atmosphere and here he shows part of the port of Lowestoft during some of its more prosperous years before the fishing fleets diminished. The town thrived when the Dogger Bank fishing ground opened up and the west country fleet moved round to the east coast. It was quicker to fish from Lowestoft, Grimsby and Hull and then rail the catches to London, than to sail from London itself. However these boom years have since gone. Herrings were cured in 'fish houses' which used to stand along the shore on the right. The river on the left runs on toward Oulton Broad and Beccles, and part of South Town is just visible on the left hand bank. With its easy rail access from Ipswich and Norwich, the town also became a tourist gateway to the Norfolk Broads.

Lowestoft station (ex Central) is an ex GER terminus on the lines from Norwich, Yarmouth and Ipswich

Maldon, Essex
from a watercolour by
Henry J Denham SMA SGA (1948-55)   *(top)*

It is possible that the marine artist, Frank Mason had some influence over the advertising departments of the LNER and ER as they seemed particularly keen on boats and ships. Henry Denham was also a marine artist and uses the boats and the gently ambling, riverside walkers to achieve an atmosphere of tranquillity – far from the madding crowd of commuters in a railway carriage. Maldon is an attractive town, with a harbour situated on the River Blackwater – the original reason for building the railway in 1848.

Maldon had two stations, both ex GER and now closed.
(i) Maldon East and Heybridge on the branch from Witham and
(ii) Maldon West on the line to Woodham Ferrers

Tilbury Hailing Station, Essex
from a watercolour by
Francis R Flint ROI SMA (1948–55)   *(top, facing)*

'Come in Number Five, your time is up!', the man appears to be saying from his cabin (which looks remarkably like an old railway signal box). An unusual subject to choose, although this ancient port in the industrialised Essex marshlands is the first real outpost of the Port of London. Tilbury was once a great passenger port and special boat trains from St Pancras were still connecting with the liners at Tilbury when this print was issued in the early 1950s. The only human cargo it now carries are those who travel on the local ferry across to Gravesend. The docks are now mainly used for container traffic. Flint was the son of the famous artist William Russell Flint.

Tilbury Riverside is a former LTS station between London and Southend

Ely, Cambridgeshire
from a watercolour by
R E Jordan (1948–55)   *(bottom, facing)*

In a totally different style from Hilder's treatment of Ely, Jordan's softer approach produces a pleasing view of the location. Here the interest is more focused on the activity (or to be precise, non–activity) in the area around the riverside pub, yet the cathedral still dominates the scene. According to the Venerable Bede, in the 9th century, the fenland waters were populated by countless eels and these formed an important part of the diet of the Saxon population – hence the town's name. In 1845 the station was built and, because of the marshy swampland, proved to be an expensive building to construct – costing a huge £81,500. R. Jordan, incidentally, is the artist and not the river – which happens to be the Great Ouse!

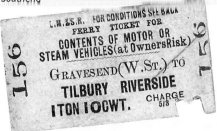

L·R·Squirrell—

Saturday Market Place, Kings Lynn, Norfolk
from a watercolour by
Leonard Squirrell RWS RE (1945–7)   (⇐ ⇐ pages 72–3)

Squirrell's wonderful artistic flair comes to the fore here, with this very dramatic view of the Saturday Market Place and St. Margaret's Church – a scene of activity since the 12th century. Painted just after the war, shoppers with their ration books make their way home along the street before the storm clouds break overhead. Most locals call the town 'Lynn', although is was Bishop's Lynn until the 16th century, but was appropriated to King Henry VIII at the dissolution of the monasteries. The few old cars remind us that street parking in those days was not the problem that it is today.

Kings Lynn is the former GER terminus station of the lines from London, Norwich (closed) Peterborough (closed) and Hunstanton (closed)

Sible Hedingham, Essex
from a watercolour by
Leonard Squirrell RWS RE (1945–7)   (⇐ overleaf)

Squirrell's confident use of pencil, ink and watercolour washes capture the essence of the Essex rural village in his painting of Sible Hedingham. A tradesman at work with his horse and cart does little to detract from the serenity of the scene, whilst the long shadows in the foreground give the painting depth and contrast.

Sible and Castle Hedingham station (closed) was situated on the Colne Valley & Halstead Railway between Haverhill and Chappel & Wakes Colne

Bishops Stortford, Hertfordshire
from a watercolour by
Leonard Squirrell RWS RE (1948–55)   (top)

A typical English street scene of the period. Although cars and bus are evident on the wide street on this summer's day, the only activity revolves around the pedestrians and the horses and cart. The main focal point of the attractive town of Bishops Stortford is the spire of the church of St Michael which dates back to the 15th century. Its old vicarage was the birthplace of Cecil Rhodes and is now a museum devoted to his memory. The town was well situated to benefit from the steady growth of rail commuter traffic over the years.

Bishops Stortford is an ex GER station on the Liverpool St to Cambridge line and a junction for the branch to Witham (closed)

Norwich, Tombland Alley
from a watercolour by
J Fletcher Watson (1945–7) *(top)*

An unusual view of part of one of England's most attractive, provincial capitals. Norwich. Tombland Alley is situated in the heart of Old Norwich between the castle and the cathedral spire, *(centre top)* and is one of many similar alleys and arcades in this part of the city, which lie near Tombland, the old market place. James Fletcher Watson, who has painted widely in Norfolk, follows in the tradition of the old Norwich School of Artists, who painted scenes of the city and surrounding East Anglia. Note how the artist draws the inquisitive viewer's eyes along the end of the alley to the lone figure at the end. Norwich has always been an important railway town and in 1937, the LNER acknowledged the importance of the passenger traffic patronage by introducing *The East Anglian*, a streamline six coach express.

Norwich had three terminus stations
(i) Thorpe (ex GER, open) – lines to Ely, London and Yarmouth
(ii) Victoria (ex GER, closed) – line to Ipswich
(iii) City (ex M&GN Joint, closed) – line to Melton Constable

Bury St. Edmunds, Suffolk
from a watercolour by
F W Baldwin (1948-55) *(overleaf ⇨)*

A typical Baldwin town scene, so suited to his draughtsman-like, pen and wash style. Bury St. Edmunds is the county town of West Suffolk and is named after the lst King of East Anglia who was tortured, scourged, shot with arrows and, as if this wasn't enough, finally beheaded in A.D. 870, by the Danes. He refused to renounce his Christian faith. Ironically, it was a Dane, Canute, who founded a monastery in honour of Edmund, where his remains were interred. The church of St Mary is a great 15th century church and is reputed to have the longest aisle of any church in the country.

Bury St. Edmunds is a former GER station on the Ipswich to Cambridge line, and was once an important junction for the lines to Thetford and Colchester (now closed)

F.W.Baldwin

Cromer, Norfolk
from a watercolour by
F W Baldwin (1948–55) *(top facing)*

Like so many other Victorian seaside towns, Cromer was a product of the railway boom of the 19th century – once a small fishing village and now a busy summer holiday resort. The view is a classic example of unashamed LNER realism. Baldwin shows a heavy overcast sky, a few people braving the water, the rather unattractive seafront buildings and a couple of old boats drawn up on the beach. The pier on the right is almost omitted – so different from so many seaside posters with their sand, sun and syrupy smiles. Note the 160 ft tower of St. Paul's church in the background – the highest in the county.

Cromer had two stations: (i) the former GER terminus (open) on the line from Norwich and (ii) Cromer Beach, the former M&GN Joint terminus (closed)

Great Yarmouth, Norfolk
from a watercolour by
F W Baldwin (1948–55) *(bottom, facing)*

Great Yarmouth is now one of Britain's most popular seaside resorts. It has five miles of sandy beach, two piers, safe bathing, theatres and, more importantly in Baldwin's eyes, a quayside freight line with fish wagons and factory smoke – just the sort of landscape to entice the travelling public to have a quick bathe! To be fair to the artist, this was painted just after the war when the town had been very badly bombed and suitable locations to paint were hard to come by. Yarmouth was, for centuries, a centre of the herring fishing industry and the freight line ran for over a mile alongside the River Yare quayside to the Vauxhall Fishmarket – a great source of revenue for the railways. South Town lies on the opposite bank. From 30th June 1846, when 6,000 excursionists from Norwich arrived by train, Yarmouth has been a favourite destination for holidaymakers. Fares were a little cheaper on that occasion – one shilling for adults and three pence return for Nonconformist children!

Yarmouth had two stations: (i) Vauxhall (open), the former GER terminus from Norwich and (ii) Beach (closed) the former M&GN Joint terminus from Lowestoft and North Walsham

Beccles, Suffolk
from a watercolour by
F W Baldwin (1948–55) *(top)*

Beccles was almost a seaport centuries ago, when the Broadland area was largely flooded, and it was still a flourishing port in the heyday of the Norfolk Wherry, as there are no locks between here and the sea. Several fires destroyed most of the Tudor buildings in the town, but the impressive church remains, built, like so many churches in this area, close to navigable waters where stone could be shipped in. Nowadays the Beccles waterfront has a well–to–do Edwardian air about it, with gardens running down to private jetties and large pleasure boats cruising past. With the ever growing popularity of overseas package holidays and much wider car ownership, the days of the numerous summer Saturday 'specials' heading to this corner of the country and the Norfolk Broads has, sadly, ended.

Beccles is a former GER station on the Ipswich to Lowestoft line, and a junction for the Tivetshall and Yarmouth lines (both closed)

Ely Cathedral
from a watercolour by
Rowland Hilder RI (1937–9) *(bottom)*

Hilder's dark foreground emphasises the brighter cathedral's grandeur, exaggerating its height above its surroundings. Begun in 1083 on the site of a 7th century monastery, the building dominates the Fenland around it. Oliver Cromwell inhabited the old vicarage for ten years when he was a tithe collector for the cathedral. At one time Ely was an island and it was here that Hereward the Wake held out against the Normans until they bridged it in 1071. Ely continues to enjoy regular passenger services to a number of destinations, including recently–introduced through trains from Stansted Airport. A classic Hilder–style painting.

Ely is a former GER station and a junction for several East Anglian lines

Trinity Great Court, Cambridge
from a watercolour by
R T Cowern RWS (1948–55) *(top, facing)*

Great use was made by the LNER of the cathedrals and colleges within their area in their advertising propaganda – you sometimes got the impression that they owned the places. Cowern uses the long perspective of the carriage prints to full effect here, in depicting the Great Court built in 1610. It is longer than any other at either Oxford or Cambridge and the magnificent renaissance fountain stands in the centre of it. When Henry VIII came to the throne there were already four other foundations on the site of Trinity College. In 1546 he amalgamated them, adding fresh buildings and making Trinity the largest of the colleges. Little has changed since then.

Cambridge has one large junction station – the former GER

Hinchingbrooke, Huntingdonshire
from a watercolour by
Edward Walker ARCA (1945–7) *(bottom, facing)*

Edward Walker, the Headmaster of the Scarborough School of Art, contributed two paintings to the LNER series and these were both stately homes within half a mile of each other. The 13th century Buckden Palace, belonging to the Bishops of Lincoln was one and Hinchingbrooke House, shown here, was the other. Huntingdon's most famous son, Oliver Cromwell, was born in the High Street in 1599 and Hinchingbrooke then became the family home, later purchased by the Montagu family. The house is an early 13th century nunnery converted in the 16th century into a Tudor mansion and Walker's view of it, on this bright day, is very satisfying.

Hinchingbrooke House is close to Huntingdon station (ex GNR) on the Kings Cross main line. Huntingdon also had a MR station on the Northampton to St. Ives line (closed)

R.T.Cowern

Hinchingbrooke

Edward Walker

Durham

from a watercolour by
John C Moody RE RI (1937–9)   (top, facing)

Another fine example of Moody's etching style. Here he views Durham from the north, alongside the River Wear, next to the Northern Electric building. The cathedral and castle, tower over the area on their wooded hill of sandstone rock and are surrounded on three sides by the river – one of the most superbly sited cities in Britain. The cathedral was built between 1093 and 1133 on a site once colonised by Saxon monks. The Normans then built the castle next to the cathedral and it was the only northern castle never to fall to the Scots. Note the foundations of the ice rink pad (extreme left) which date the picture at 1938/39. The rink was completed in 1942 and now spoils the view! The sights of Durham have attracted many rail passengers to its station over the years, and saw a vast flood of people in 1950 during the Durham miners' gala which recorded a staggering 250,000 visitors, involving 90 special trains.

Durham is a former NER junction station on the London to Newcastle main line

Scarborough, Yorkshire

from a watercolour by
Henry Rushbury RA (1937–9)   (bottom, facing)

An interesting panorama of Scarborough by Henry Rushbury, drawing on some of his skills as a former draughtsman for his topographical detail. Another popular seaside resort on the Yorkshire coast, with a mixture of history and entertainments, Scarborough has a harbour, fishing village, stately hotels (when they're not falling off the edge of cliffs) and, of course, the dreaded 'amusement' arcades. The Norman castle overhanging the town on its 300 ft headland, was formerly a Roman signal station. It was reduced to rubble by Roundhead artillery in the Civil War, yet the large square keep survives. I love the free and easy traffic system (or lack of it) along the sea front – these were days when there were more pedestrians than parking meters. Like Bridlington, Scarborough was host to many excursions, including specials to the nearby Butlin's holiday camp at Filey.

Scarborough is a former NER terminus station with lines to York, Hull (open) and Whitby (closed)

Durham

from a watercolour by
Sidney Causer RI (1945–7)   (top)

Another fine view of Durham this time from the towpath at Old Elvet.

Barnard Castle, Co. Durham

from a watercolour by
John C Moody RE RI (1937–9)   (overleaf ⇨)

What an amazing amount of detail went into John Moody's landscapes! Almost every dwelling has been faithfully drawn in, although the artist does appear to have omitted the River House to improve the composition. From a view point near Startforth Church, Moody looks along the River Tees towards the castle ruins standing on its cliff top 80 ft high. The castle was built by Bernard Balliol in the 12th century (hence originally Bernard's castle) on the site of a family stronghold and John Balliol became King of Scotland a century later. Painted just before the war – a marvellous example of early LNER topographical artwork.

Barnard Castle was an NER junction station on the Kirkby Stephen to Bishop Aukland/Darlington lines (all closed)

Deeping St. James, Lincolnshire
from a watercolour by
Freda Marston ROI (1945–7)   *(top)*

Here we have another English village with a train service of only five or six trains a day to its small station – an attempt by the railways to advertise locations away from their main lines. Freda Marston was the only woman artist commissioned to paint carriage print scenes and her paintings have a marvellous translucent quality about them – one of the signs of a great watercolour artist. This is a timeless English village scene – warm stone cottages and a quaint bridge, blending in with nature's surroundings. A lazy River Welland flows past, watched by an equally lazy countryman over the parapet. Beautiful.

Deeping St. James Station (closed) was a former GNR station on the Peterborough to Spalding line (open)

Rievaulx Abbey, Yorkshire
from a watercolour by
Edwin Byatt (1937–9)   *(top, facing)*

Scenes of abbeys and cathedrals proliferated in carriage panels and it would give an unbalanced treatment of the subject if one of these was not included. The sunlight cleverly highlights the stonework ruins of Rievaulx Abbey, which once housed a thriving Cistercian Christian community of 150 monks and over 500 lay brothers. Founded in 1132, it became prosperous through its flocks of sheep but like so many similar movements in the past, prosperity in the church often sounded the death knell of spiritual life. Here it lies in its beautifully secluded site in the Rye valley, nestled beneath the North York Moors.

The nearest station to Rievaulx was Helmsley, a former NER station on the Pickering to Gilling line (closed)

Hutton–Le–Hole near Pickering, Yorkshire
from a watercolour by
L J Wood FRIBA (1954)   *(bottom, facing)*

Without doubt, Hutton Le Hole is one of the prettiest villages in the North York Moors. It is the meeting place of two becks, and the stone cottages, with their red roofs, cluster around the green, producing a scene which is every tourist's idea of an archetypal moors village. In spring the surrounding dales are brightened by thousands of daffodils. John Wood was an architect but also painted, and this was one of the last pictures commissioned by the Eastern Region for carriage prints. It shows the date next to his signature. Although the nearest station, with its five trains a day each way, has long since closed, the village is still kept neat and tidy as a tourist attraction and contains the Ryedale Folk Museum, but has consequently lost some of its country feeling.

Hutton-Le-Hole was a few miles from Kirkbymoorside, the former NER station on the Pickering–Gilling line (closed)

E.T.HOLDING

Sunderland, Co. Durham

from a watercolour by

E T Holding RWS (1945–7)　(⇦ overleaf)

The final panel in Holding's series is this painting of Wearmouth Bridge in Sunderland. Whilst it demonstrates his artistic skill, this masterpiece of industrial ambience throws up a question or two. The first bridge across the River Wear was built in 1796 and was one of the first cast iron bridges in the country. The designer was Thomas Paine, better known for his book *The Rights of Man*. It was rebuilt in 1858 under the supervision of Robert Stephenson and this is the bridge seen here. The railway bridge can be seen behind it. However, a new road bridge was built in 1929 by Sir W Arrol & Co Ltd, which dates the painting to the late 1920s (the paddle steamers confirm this). Holding's prints were introduced around 1947, which is something of a mystery. Sunderland's name derived from the fact that it was 'sundered' from a monastery founded near the river in 674. It was once a large coal port but was better known for its shipbuilding industry which has since declined. Ships, smog, steam, and steel spans – lovely!

Sunderland is the ex NER station (formerly Central) on the Newcastle to Hartlepool line

Berwick on Tweed, Northumberland

from a watercolour by

S R Badmin RWS (1945–7)　(top)

Another detailed view from Badmin – this time of the Royal Border Bridges from Tweedmouth. The nearest bridge is the 15 arch, Berwick Road Bridge which was built between 1611 and 1624. Behind this is the concrete, four arched, Royal Tweed Road Bridge built in 1928 and, finally, carrying an A4 locomotive with teak coaches, is the Royal Border Bridge built by Robert Stephenson in 1850 for only £120,000. It has 28 arches, is 120 ft high and 2160 ft long. Berwick is the most northerly town in England, having changed hands 13 times in the border clashes between England and Scotland, before capitulating to the English Crown in 1482. Many sightseers arrived in Berwick by train over the years, although things got off to a bad start in the early days when 7,000 North British Railway workers from Cowlairs Works descended on the town. Apart from overcrowding the streets, two workers fell to their deaths over the castle ramparts – not the most successful awayday trip!

Berwick is a former joint NBR/NER station on the East Coast line between Newcastle and Edinburgh

Alnmouth, Northumberland
from a watercolour by
S R Badmin RWS (1945–7)   *(bottom)*

A marvellously detailed composition by the illustrator, Stanley Badmin, of the Aln railway viaduct at Lesbury, which was built by the Newcastle and Berwick Railway in 1847. Alnmouth *(in the left background)* prospered as a port and shipbuilding centre until the River Aln changed its course in a gale in 1806. Alnmouth station is just visible south of the viaduct, near the disappearing steam train, and the signals which are in an impossible position! Badmin painted the scene from Hawkhill and must have hired a helicopter to have been able to get this particular perspective of sea and estuary. Note also the haycocks and bus which help date the painting.

Alnmouth is a former NER station on the main Newcastle to Edinburgh line and was once a junction for the Alnwick branch line

Boston, Lincolnshire
from a watercolour by
Freda Marston ROI (1945–7)   *(overleaf ⇨)*

Another lovely, bright and colourful view by Marston of Boston, from the South Quay on the Haven side of the town. Before the silting up of the river and the change in world trade patterns, Boston was an immensely prosperous port – second only to London in the 14th century. It was from here that the Pilgrim Fathers first tried to flee in 1607 from religious persecution before being imprisoned. The town became a popular destination for rail travellers, and paddle steamers to Skegness were operated specially for the day trippers. The famous 'Boston Stump' – the 272 ft octagonal tower of St. Botolph's church and one of the tallest in the country – is also included in the picture and gives spectacular views for miles around from the top . The name Boston is thought to derive from a corruption of 'Botolph's Town'.

Boston was a former GNR station on the main line to Grimsby (now a branch line to Skegness)

Whitby, Yorkshire
from a watercolour by
Rowland Hilder RI (1937–9)   *(pages 96–7 ⇨⇨)*

Hilder makes excellent use of contrasting tonal values in this painting of Whitby as the sun catches the roofs and walls of the many terraced fishermen's cottages nestling below East Cliff. The town is attractively located at the mouth of the River Esk and has been associated with fishing for centuries and was once a whaling port. The navigator, Captain Cook, also lived here as a lad. The remains of Whitby Abbey lie close to the Norman church of St Mary's which can be seen towering above the cottages at the top of the picture.

Whitby is an ex NER terminus station on the branch (open) and coastal (closed) lines from Middlesbrough

Immingham Docks, Lincolnshire
from a watercolour by
Frank H Mason RI (1945–7) *(top, facing)*

An error by the printer, causing a slight overlap of the original colour separations, has caused some loss of definition and detail to this view of Immingham Docks by the marine artist, Frank Mason. This is a modern, deep water port, handling oil, coal and iron ore and is capable of taking today's modern ships which Grimsby, five miles down the coast, cannot handle. It became a fine source of revenue for the LNER who didn't mind advertising it in this fashion even though it is not the most beautiful of locations. The steam locomotive shed at Immingham was sited close to the docks and was blessed with a large allocation of engines of various classes.

Immingham has always been a freight location, served by ex GCR lines, and is a bus ride from Grimsby

King Edward Bridge, Newcastle on Tyne
from a watercolour by
Kenneth Steel RBA SGA (1948–55) *(bottom, facing)*

Kenneth Steel enjoyed painting railway architecture and the commissioners recognised his ability in this field and often allocated these subjects to him. He was certainly consistent in producing some fine artwork. Here we see the King

Edward Bridge, Newcastle viewed from Redheugh Incline, near Redheugh Bridge, looking north east along the Tyne towards the High Level and Tyne Bridges in the distance, before the new 'Metro' (QE2) Bridge was built in between. The King Edward Bridge has four tracks and carries the trains 112 ft above the river. It was built for the North Eastern Railway in 1906 and designed by C Harrison. Gateshead loco depot and works were located at the south approach to the bridge and could be viewed from the train. Note the colour of the coaches on the train – this, almost certainly, dates the painting to 1952 and this artwork was used in Jenkin Jones' book *100 years of the NER* in 1954. The Normans built a 'new castle' on the site of an old Roman fort in this city – hence its name.

Sandsend, near Whitby, Yorkshire
from a watercolour by
Jack Merriott RI (1945–55) *(top)*

One of the few prints to appear on a glossy paper – and one of the many scenic railway vistas of this era which, alas, no longer remains. Sandsend station boasted several holiday camping coaches and was located on a winding coastal line between Middlesbrough and Whitby and saw a regular train service. The track ran across the trestle viaduct here which was constructed from tubular metal columns. It was very similar to the one at Staithes which carried its own wind

gauge for safety reasons. Jack is looking from the tidal line towards the station, as an A6 or A8 locomotive is about to cross the frail–looking structure. The sea wall has now been rebuilt, the road realigned and the viaduct and line have long since disappeared.

Sandsend (closed) was a former NER station

Wakefield Chantry, Yorkshire
from a watercolour by
Sidney Causer RI (1945–7) *(overleaf ⇨)*

I love Causer's eye for detail and his use of subtle colours which give an atmospheric effect to his townscapes. Wakefield Chantry standing alongside the River Calder, is the most attractive of the four surviving bridge chapels in England. The parish church of All Saints which became a cathedral in 1888 can also be seen on the right with its 247 ft spire – the tallest in Yorkshire. Causer here depicts the industrial north at its best – a realistic blend of solid architecture and smoke.

Wakefield still has two stations (i) Kirkgate (nearest to the Chantry) and (ii) Westgate. Both were ex GNR & L&Y Joint stations

Town Bridge, Stamford, Lincolnshire
from a watercolour by
John Bee (1945–7) *(top, facing)*

One of only two of John Bee's paintings to appear as carriage prints (his Western Region artwork was unfortunately commissioned in the wrong size [*see Appendix C*]). A beautiful study of the water reflections of the old stone bridge in what is considered by many to be England's most beautiful stone-built town. Stamford was at one time the fenland capital and also a wealthy wool town. The River Welland runs through the town here, only a short distance from the ex MR railway station.

Stamford had two stations: (i) Midland (open), a former MR station on the Leicester to Peterborough line and (ii) the ex GNR terminus (closed) on the lines from Wansford and Essendine

The River Ouse, York
from a watercolour by
Gyrth Russell RI SMA (1948–55) *(bottom, facing)*

Resisting the temptation to paint a commercial view of York Minster, Gyrth Russell has located himself on the Ouse Bridge, only a brisk five minutes walk from the station close to York City centre. He is looking north–westwards, upstream toward the Lendal Road Bridge, with the Guildhall visible on the right before the bridge. The sightseers on the passing launch are gazing at the right hand bank which is giving its best impersonation of Venice, whilst the left hand side is more akin to the South Yorkshire Navigation at Doncaster! The river nowadays sees mainly pleasure craft and this view has changed considerably over the years. The city was originally the Roman capital of Britain in AD 71 and, after it had declined, the Danes built it up as Yorvik – hence its name.

York is a former NER junction station on the main East Coast Main Line. It was opened in 1877 and, at one time, was thought to be the largest in the world

Lincoln
from a watercolour by
Fred Taylor RI (1937–9) *(bottom)*

This was one of the first standard format prints to be produced and is a classic Taylor interpretation of Lincoln, using the poster–style technique of bright, flat, contrasting colours and a dark foreground in ink. This style was rare for carriage prints as they were too small to show this approach off to best effect. Set upon the site of the celtic hill fort of Lindon, Lincoln Cathedral rises majestically to the sky and is visible for miles around. The Romans called it 'Lindum Colonia' from which we get our word Lincoln. It was the first cathedral the Normans built, yet much of it dates from the 13th century. Fred Taylor is looking northwards at the cathedral, across Brayford Pool, which links the River Witham with the Fosse Dyke Canal and is close to both stations. The castle, to the left of the huge church, is not quite so easy to see.

Lincoln had two stations (i) Central (ex GNR) (open) and (ii) St Marks (ex MR) (closed in 1984)

Grimsby, Lincolnshire
from a watecolour by
E T Holding RWS (1945–7) *(overleaf ⇨)*

What marvellous atmosphere this picture has! A superbly painted sky overhead frames all the bustle of the busy docks scene with its numerous fishing boats. At this time, Grimsby was one of the great fishing ports of the world and provided a large quantity of freight traffic for the railways – 3,000 different stations all over Britain received daily consignments from Grimsby's quays and 4,000 tons of fish a week left the docks all the year round. The port has since declined, however, due to the Icelandic Cod war in the 1970s and other factors. It was named after the legendary Danish fisherman Grim and it is interesting that this location was preferred by the company as a scenic view, to the seaside resort of Cleethorpes just down the road – LNER realism at its best.

Grimsby had three stations – (i) Town (open); (ii) Docks (open) and (iii) Pier (closed); all on the ex GCR line to Cleethorpes

E.T. HOLDING

THE CROWN JEWELS OF ENGLAND WERE STOLEN BY "COLONEL" BLOOD, AN IRISH ADVENTURER, IN 1671. HE WAS TAKEN, BUT CHARLES II PARDONED HIM, AND RESTORED HIS IRISH ESTATES. HE DIED IN 1680

Carriage panels, *clockwise from top left:*
St John's College, Cambridge by Taylor (LNER); Crown Jewels . . . by Winslade (LMR History); Petergate, York by Tittensor (LNER); Melrose Abbey, Roxburghshire by Squirrell (LNER); Selby, Yorks by Steel (LNER); Ely, Cambridgeshire by Barraud (LNER Intermediate); Salisbury Cathedral, Wilts by Buckle (S. Region [A]); Stokesay Castle, Salop by Sherwin (WR);
Background: Conway Castle (LMS panel)

CONWAY CASTLE

Castles, Cathedrals, Colleges & Churches

Views of castles, cathedrals and churches abounded in carriages before the Second World War. These huge and ancient buildings survive as monuments to an older Britain and, before the advent of modern leisure pursuits, drew many pilgrims by rail to pay respect to the country's Christian (and not so Christian) heritage.

Introduction to the Scottish Area

It could be said that Scotland is best known for what rises above it in the same way, perhaps, that Wales can be remembered for the slate caverns, coal mines and quarries that lie beneath it.

Paintings of Scottish landscapes with deep blue lochs lying at the feet of magnificent rugged mountain scenery; majestic castles rising above rushing streams and thick forests, and ferries chugging across the waters to distant hilly islands, all help to bring back memories of past holidays or journeys through this spectacular country. After viewing all the Scottish carriage prints the tourist could be forgiven if he thought that Scotland had little else to offer apart from the mountain scenery, for most of the painted views were commissioned to project this highland image.

Scotland's railway development was largely influenced by the terrain it had to negotiate. The country can neatly be divided into three regions: the Highlands, a mountainous and sparsely populated area to the north; the Central Lowlands, the main urban, industrial and agricultural belt; and the Southern Uplands, the hilly and, again, under-populated area to the south. Until the closure in 1965 of the, fondly remembered, ex-North British Railway, 'Waverley' route via Hawick, this last area had four main line routes running through it to England: the former NBR East Coast Main Line from Berwick to Edinburgh, the ex Caledonian Railway West Coast Main Line via Beattock, and the former Glasgow & South Western Railway line via Dumfries being the other three. These routes saw the regular passage of many famous expresses, including *The Aberdonian, Royal* and *Coronation Scots, Thames–Clyde Express,* and, of course, *The Flying Scotsman* too.

Most of the early railway expansion took place around the two large cities of Glasgow and Edinburgh, and the former dominated the Scottish scene in much the same way that London did for the English network. Glasgow even had its own underground system, completed in 1896. The city originally had four main line termini: Central (ex CR), Queen Street (ex NBR), St Enoch (ex GSWR) and Buchanan Street (ex CR). Only the first two have survived. The Scottish carriage panels, however, tended to avoid focusing on Glasgow, preferring the charm and the history of Edinburgh.

The highland region was the last area to feel the impact

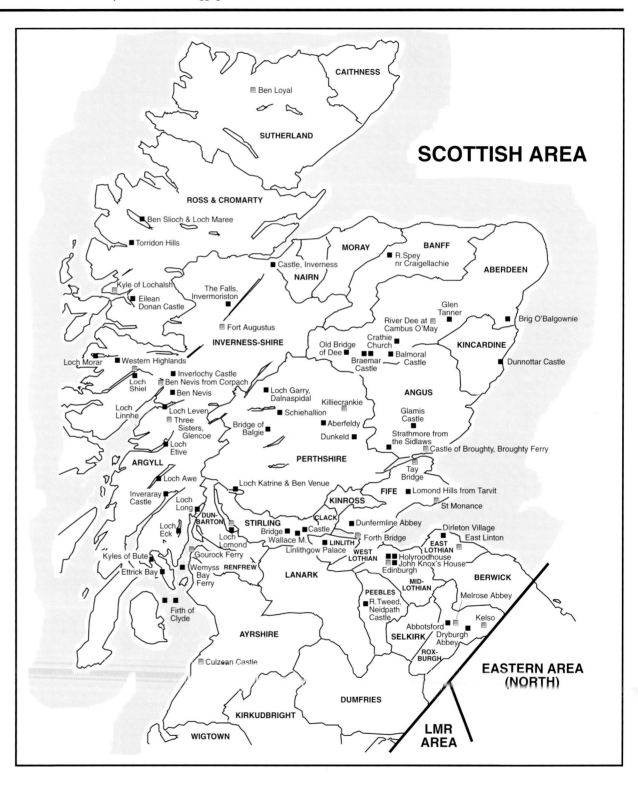

of 'railway mania' and the end of the 19th century saw the network spread as far away as Mallaig, the Kyle of Lochalsh, Thurso and Fraserburgh – often through superb scenery. Many of the isolated towns and villages in these areas came to depend on the railway for their contact with the more populous areas.

The London & North Eastern Railway, which included parts of Scotland in its area, did, initially, achieve a variety of different views in its carriage prints and commissioned some fine paintings of *Edinburgh* by prominent artists Fred Taylor, Sidney Causer, Edwin Byatt and Henry Rushbury in addition to the standard fare of mountain scenery and castles. After the war the Eastern Region of BR also added a few Scottish views (for travellers on its East Coast Main Line) and these prints of the *Forth Bridge* and *Abbotsford* and small villages such as *Dirleton* and *East Linton* continued the trend of variety. However, around 1956, when the Scottish Region commissioned its own series of over 40 paintings, it produced a rather unimaginative selection of prints, ignoring village, city or townscapes and mainly featuring mountain landscapes and views of castles. It could be argued, of course, that with so much of Scotland being blessed with the striking scenery so often visible from its railway carriages, why bother to promote anything else? People travelling in the confines of a stuffy compartment would have been more encouraged to travel by scenes of open-air grandeur than by an atmospheric view of Glasgow Docks. By the time these prints were issued it was planned to use them in other Regions' coaching stock as well as their own, so, knowing that many of their viewers would be travelling through Brixton and Bethnal Green, we can't exactly criticise them for promoting their region in this way.

After the Scottish series was issued there was certainly a good geographical spread of views of the country with the exception of the south western (ex LMS) area, even if the landscapes often looked rather similar. Unfortunately, the narrow widths and long lengths of artwork imposed by the carriage panels made it difficult for the artists to achieve the effects of mountainous heights and the series was not quite up to the high standards of artwork of previous LNER panels.

The rugged terrain and geography of the country necessitated some spectacular bridges and viaducts and, although the Forth and Tay bridges were included in the series, it is surprising that little attempt was made to capture some of the area's other engineering accomplishments in picture form as the London Midland Region had done in their Railway Architecture set of prints. We shall just have to imagine a picture of a Kenneth Steel rendition of the Glenfinnan Viaduct. However, the Scottish did take the opportunity to include some pictures of island ferries by poster artist Alasdair Macfarlane and thus promote their shipping services. Any view of a man-made vessel had one drawback of course – it soon became outdated, especially if it included any cars. At least the Scottish Region didn't have to worry about their mountain scenery going out of date!

The lines in the south west and the north east of Scotland suffered badly when the railway system declined after the war. Almost all of the old Great North of Scotland Railway lines disappeared and Edinburgh lost much of its suburban network. Many scenic branch lines were closed too, including a number of those indirectly advertised in the carriage prints. Mercifully, the Mallaig, Kyle of Lochalsh, Oban and Thurso lines survived.

Over 70 prints of the area were finally produced, so at least Scotland provided plenty of work for the artists – and, no doubt, some pleasant journeys for them on these scenic branch lines, too.

Castle of Broughty, Broughty Ferry, Angus
from a watercolour by
Edward Lawson (1956)   *(bottom)*

A kilted lad and his Scottish terrier add a nice finishing touch to Lawson's Scottish landscape. Broughty Ferry is now a suburb of Dundee and became a thriving fishing community when the harbour was built in 1872. Ten years later, the new steam trawlers couldn't get into the harbour and trade declined. The castle itself was built in 1498 on the crag which thrust itself into the Firth of Tay. It was occupied by the English between 1547–50 and then by French mercenaries employed by the Scots. It is now a museum devoted to the fishing and whaling industries. All that appear to be missing from this bonny scene are the empty whisky bottles on the quayside.

Broughty Ferry Pier was an ex Dundee & Arbroath Joint Railway station (closed) at the end of a short branch from the main Dundee to Aberdeen line. A ferry ran from here to Tayport across the Firth of Tay

Loch Lomond
from a watercolour by
Frank H Mason RI (1945–7) *(top)*

Frank Mason was a superbly consistent marine artist and knew his subject well, having spent much of his life at sea or associated with shipping in one capacity or another. His masterful use of different shades of blue in his treatment of water is particularly pleasing. Loch Lomond is the largest lake in Britain, being 23 miles long from Balloch in the South to Ardlui in the north. Its width varies from five miles to just ³/₄ mile at its narrowest point. Mason illustrates one of the various pleasure boats which operate along its length and around its 30 islands. The service consisted of three boats in each direction between Balloch Pier and Ardlui with a journey time of two hours and 10 minutes. Classic Scottish scenery from a classic artist.

Loch Lomond has three stations along its course: (i) Balloch at the south. The terminus of the former Dumbarton and Balloch Joint line from Dumbarton. (ii) Arrochar & Tarbet (middle) and (iii) Ardlui (north end) – both ex NBR stations on the Glasgow to Fort William line. (All are still open)

Ben Nevis from Corpach, West Highlands
from a watercolour by
F Donald Blake (1956) *(top, facing)*

Compare this 'final' painting with Blake's 'rough' on p.40, and you can see what a difference an interesting foreground makes to the overall picture. The signal box at the one–platform station of Corpach, highlights the important commercial fact that some of the best mountain views in Scotland can be seen whilst relaxing in a railway carriage. The dark foreground gives depth to the distant mountains lying behind the sunlit Loch Eil, and the beginning of the town of Fort William can just be seen towards the right hand corner of the landscape. Ben Nevis, at 4,406 ft is the highest mountain in Britain but its southern slopes have been negotiated by car several times this century. However, the A.A. do not appear to recommend this route in their guide books.

Corpach is a former NBR station on the Fort William to Mallaig line

Three Sisters, Glencoe, Argyll
from a watercolour by
Frank Sherwin RI (1956) *(bottom, facing)*

There can be few locations in Britain more famous for their beauty, yet at the same time, so symbolising mans' inhumanity to man, than the Pass of Glencoe. The lovely rugged glen ascends 1,100 feet in ten miles to the bleak and vast expanse of Rannoch Moor, and is known as the 'Glen of Weeping' due to the infamous massacre of 38 men from the MacDonald clan in 1692. It was then that the Campbell troops who were stationed in the glen turned on their hosts because of their failure to forswear the Jacobite cause. When Sherwin painted this picture of *The Three Sisters* (Faith, Hope and Charity) the branch line to Ballachulish, a few miles from Glencoe, was still open and saw a handful of trains a day. The road through the pass was then, relatively, empty. Today's massacre, as some would point out, has been that of rail by road.

Ballachulish station, the former CR terminus of the branch line from Oban (closed) is two miles from the village of Glencoe

The Tay Bridge, Scotland
from a watercolour by
J McIntosh Patrick ARSA ROI (1956)

In the early days, travellers on the Edinburgh, Perth &
Dundee Railway had to cross the Firth's of Forth and Tay by
ferry – and this was not always the smoothest of journeys.
The first Tay Bridge was completed in 1878 to the design of
Thomas Bouch, to connect the NBR route from Edinburgh
to Dundee, which lies on the north side of the bridge across
the River Tay (left). Tragedy struck on the night of 28
December 1879 when the central spans (the high girders)
collapsed in a strong gale, as a train carrying 73 passengers
was crossing. All occupants of the train including the locomotive crew were killed in this accident. Bouch later suffered a nervous collapse and died soon after the enquiry.
The second Tay Bridge was one of the last great structures
to be built in wrought iron and was designed by W. H. Barlow
and his son and opened in 1887. It was built alongside the
original structure, the piers of which can still be seen. Its
overall length of 3,509 yards makes it the longest railway
bridge in the U.K. It has 85 spans, and still serves as the rail
link from Edinburgh to Aberdeen. Two steam trains can be
seen crossing the long bridge in this painting by McIntosh
Patrick – a renowned artist who lived locally.

Kelso, Roxburghshire
from a watercolour by
S R Badmin RWS (1945–7) *(overleaf ⇨)*

Described by Scott as 'the most beautiful, if not the most romantic village in Scotland', Kelso is a small market town on the River Tweed. The 12th century abbey was virtually destroyed in the 16th century and the remains can be seen in the top right corner of the picture. Badmin loved his bridges and viaducts and has faithfully captured John Rennie's five arch road bridge built in 1799. Each of the arches is 72 ft wide and it is thought that this was the prototype for the London Bridge built in 1811. Passenger train traffic ceased to Kelso in 1964 and the line was closed in 1968 with the demise of the fondly–remembered, 'Waverley route'. Note the *Badmin Circus* lorry on the bridge!

*Kelso was a former NBR station on the Tweedmouth to
St. Boswells line (closed)*

Loch Shiel, Inverness–shire
from a watercolour by
E W Haslehust RI (1937–9) *(pages 116–7 ⇨⇨)*

A marvellous blend of sunset colours light the hills surrounding one of the finest, freshwater lochs in the Highlands in this painting by Haslehust. No more than a mile wide from end to end and having no roads along its shores, it is a rare, unspoilt location. The Glenfinnan monument, depicting a kilted highlander, can be seen as you pass by in one of the few trains which run beside the head of the loch. It marks the spot where Bonnie Prince Charlie unfurled his father's standard in 1745 at the start of his doomed campaign to regain the throne for his father, the Old Pretender. It was erected in 1815 by Alexander MacDonald as a tribute to the Highlanders. The nearby Glenfinnan viaduct is a spectacular crescent shaped structure built of concrete and spanning the Finnan valley.

*Glenfinnan is a former NBR station and passing loop on the
Fort William to Mallaig line, just a short distance from
the monument*

E·W·HASLEHUST.

The Forth Bridge, Scotland
from a watercolour by
Kenneth Steel (1948–54)   *(top)*

Kenneth Steel didn't have the problem of the new Forth Road bridge spoiling his view when he painted the mighty railway bridge, although he did have to travel a fair distance in order to include the whole of this magnificent and elegant structure in his painting. Designed by John Fowler and Benjamin Baker, the bridge was opened in 1890 and was a true climax in the history of bridge building in Britain. Completion of the bridge resulted in an 'unbroken' East Coast railway route all the way from London to Aberdeen. It comprises three main cantilever sections supporting two suspended spans with approach viaducts on the south and north, giving an overall length from end to end of over 1½ miles. The bridge deck level is 157 ft above the high water mark and the superstructure of the bridge comprises over 50,000 tons of steel connected by around 6½ million rivets! The rock of Inchgarvie Island, where the centre cantilever stands, is supporting a total weight of 18,700 tons of mild steel. The bridge celebrated its 100th birthday in 1990 and, once again, saw a steam–hauled train crossing its rails.

Kyle of Lochalsh–Kyleakin Ferry, Western Highlands
from a watercolour by
Kenneth Steel (1956)   *(top, facing)*

The establishment of a rail link to 'The Isles' was first envisaged by the Dingwall and Skye Railway which was later incorporated into the Highland Railway. The original link was via the Strome Ferry (which sailed from Loch Carron), further inland. Extension of the line westwards to 'the Kyle' required blasting a cutting through solid rock to the new pierhead, but added the dimension of a quick five minute ferry crossing to Kyleakin, on the Isle of Skye. Kenneth Steel shows this ferry, chugging across the short stretch of water to the beautiful island, whilst the former HR Kyle of Lochalsh Hotel is seen behind the ferry ramp. In its earlier days, the hotel was notorious for its lack of modern facilities. Even well into LMS days the hotel residents still went to bed carrying candles as there was no electric or gas supplies! The Kyle line from Inverness is a beautiful scenic route in a remote area and, having survived various attempts to close it, is well worth a journey. A road bridge has now destroyed the atmosphere of the island crossing.

Kyle of Lochalsh is the terminus station at the end of the ex HR line from Dingwall

Culzean Castle, near Maybole, Ayrshire
from a watercolour by
Kenneth Steel RBA SGA (1956)   *(bottom, facing)*

The sole example of a carriage print location in the south west is Culzean (pronounced Culane) Castle. Overlooking Culzean Bay, and set in a 565 acre park, it was built in the 1780s by Robert Adam for the 10th Earl of Cassillis. The surrounding area saw its first rail excursion – to Ayr and the 'land of Burns' – in 1846 and the old Glasgow and South Western route, with its resorts and golf courses, was a popular one. The railways were also well aware of the potential revenue from the American tourist market and any place that had a connection with the States was often heavily promoted. Here it is the fact that General Dwight D Eisenhower was presented with a suite in the castle in 1945 by the people of Scotland in gratitude for the role he played as Commander of the Allied Forces. He made several stays during his presidency.

The nearest station to Culzean is Maybole, an ex GSWR station on the Stranraer to Ayr line (open)

Ben Loyal, Sutherland

from a watercolour by
W Douglas Macleod (1956) *(top)*

Here we have ample proof that carriage prints in British Rail days, were not designed solely to attract passengers to beauty spots on the railway system, but were often used to project a generalised image of the country for tourism, bringing in more travel revenue. Ben Loyal is a shapely granite mountain rising to 2,504 ft and situated in the far north of Scotland, 30 miles away from the nearest station! Surrounded by moors, it is of little interest to climbers, although the nearby Loch Loyal is a favourite spot for trout and salmon fishing.

Ben Loyal is approximately 30 miles north of Lairg station (open) on the former HR Inverness to Thurso line

East Linton, East Lothian

from a watercolour by
John E Aitken RSW (1948–54) *(top facing)*

The ER produced four Scottish prints, for use on the East Coast Main Line services. One of these is a fine painting by John Aitken, capturing some of the character of eastern Scotland as the River Tyne flows under the fine stone bridge with the 'kirk' to the right and the clouds scud away above. John Rennie, the famous engineer was born nearby. East Coast Main Line trains pass through Linton on their way to Edinburgh, although at present day speeds, there is little opportunity to see the town in the same detail as you can here. Local stopping trains did call at the small station, however.

East Linton was a former NBR station (closed) on the Berwick to Edinburgh main line

Gourock–Dunoon Car Ferry, Firth of Clyde

from a watercolour by
Alasdair Macfarlane (1956) *(bottom, facing)*

In 1866 the Caledonian Railway purchased the existing jetty at Gourock Bay and plans were formulated to extend the existing line between Glasgow and Greenock onward towards Gourock. After a long delay the CR steamers started their sailing's in 1889. *Cowal* was built for BR in 1954 by the Ailsa Ship Building Co. at Troon. She was the first Clyde steamer to be fitted with radar and also worked the Wemyss Bay to Rothesay ferry service. This is an interesting period painting by Macfarlane, drawing attention to the many ferry services to the islands of Scotland.

Gourock is the terminus station on the ex CR line from Glasgow

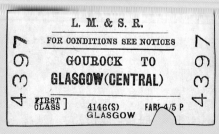

Fort Augustus, Inverness–shire

From a watercolour by
Henry Rushbury RA (1937–9)   *(bottom)*

Satisfying all the classic requirements for a Scottish carriage print, Rushbury's painting has mountains, loch, and towering fort. Until 1933, it even had its own branch line terminus yet, by the time the print emerged, an LMS motor omnibus was conveying the passengers along its 24 mile route instead of a train. Fort Augustus lies about half way along the Caledonian Canal – the superbly attractive stretch of natural lochs and man-made canals between Fort William and Inverness which divides Scotland into two. The fort is situated just at the start of Loch Ness and was built after the 1715 Jacobite rising and named after the Duke of Sutherland. It shares the site with a 19th century Benedictine abbey and a Roman Catholic school.

Fort Augustus was a former NBR terminus station on the branch line from Spean Bridge (closed)

River Dee at Cambus O'May, Aberdeenshire

From a watercolour by
Lance Cattermole ROI (1956)   *(top, facing)*

One of the few carriage print pictures attempted in an impressionist style. Royal Deeside was always an area given a high profile in the advertising literature of the LNER and, in latter days, the Scottish Region of BR. This involved a journey on a branch line from Aberdeen past Cambus O'May pictured here, to Ballater, the terminus station where passengers changed and continued their journeys a little further to Balmoral and Braemar castles in the Grampian mountains. Balmoral was a favourite residence of Queen Victoria and when it was proposed to extend the line through to the locality she was 'not amused'! Now the line is closed and the track–bed between here and Ballater is a public footpath.

Cambus O'May was a former GNSR station on the Ballater branch (closed)

Killiecrankie, Perthshire

from a watercolour by
Jack Merriott RI (1945–7)   *(bottom, facing)*

This painting, with its use of fast washes of watercolour, is very similar to another of Jack's paintings of nearby Aberfeldy (not shown), and it is probable that he painted them both on the same day. The 'Pass of Killiecrankie', where the River Garry flows through the Grampian mountain scenery between Pitlochry and Blair Atholl, is best known for the battle fought at its head in 1689 when Viscount Dundee (the 'Bonnie Dundee' of Scott's ballad) won a victory for the Jacobites, losing his life in the process. Nice to see Jack showing a bit of railway interest too, with the Highland line running through the pass over the ten span masonry viaduct, 54 ft above the ravine.

Killiecrankie station (closed) was on the Highland Railway line between Perth and Inverness

Edinburgh
from a watercolour by
Sidney Causer RI (1945–7) *(overleaf ⇨)*

An excellent, atmospheric, early morning panorama of the city by one of my favourite artists. Edinburgh got its name from the king of Northumbria, Edwin, who built its earliest fortress in the 7th century, hence 'Edwin's Burgh'. This view looks from Calton Hill past the Stewart monument, centre right, across to the castle on its volcanic rock base, centre left. The tall clock tower belongs to the old North British Hotel close to the National Gallery, and to the right of this can be seen the Scott Monument on Princes Street. Waverley Station lies hidden in the dip towards the bottom left of the picture. The line was extended here in 1846 by the Edinburgh & Glasgow Railway, after a legal wrangle with the owners of Princes Street, who insisted that the railway be tunnelled below the adjacent park.

Edinburgh Waverley is the main station in the city and formerly belonged to the NBR. The former CR station (Princes Street) is now closed

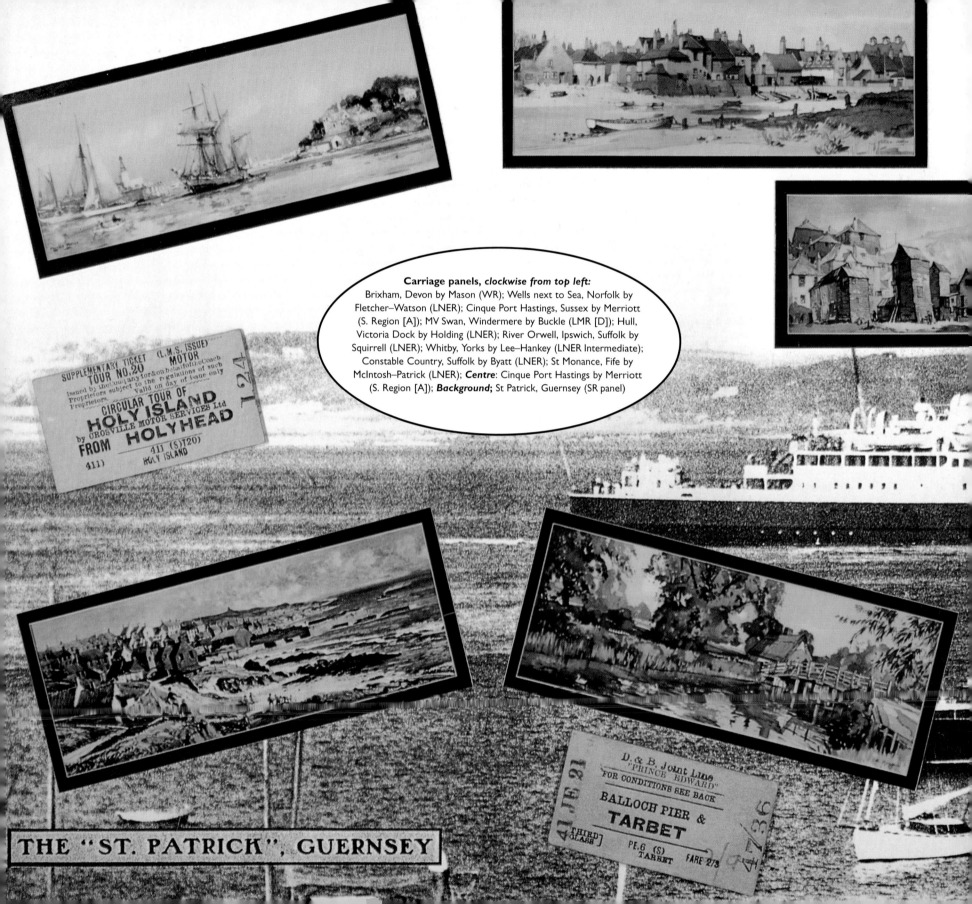

Carriage panels, *clockwise from top left:*
Brixham, Devon by Mason (WR); Wells next to Sea, Norfolk by Fletcher–Watson (LNER); Cinque Port Hastings, Sussex by Merriott (S. Region [A]); MV Swan, Windermere by Buckle (LMR [D]); Hull, Victoria Dock by Holding (LNER); River Orwell, Ipswich, Suffolk by Squirrell (LNER); Whitby, Yorks by Lee–Hankey (LNER Intermediate); Constable Country, Suffolk by Byatt (LNER); St Monance, Fife by McIntosh–Patrick (LNER); *Centre*: Cinque Port Hastings by Merriott (S. Region [A]); *Background*; St Patrick, Guernsey (SR panel)

SUPPLEMENTARY TICKET (L.M.S. ISSUE) MOTOR TOUR NO.20
Issued by the Company for & on behalf of the Coach Proprietors subject to the regulations of such Proprietors. Valid on day of issue only
CIRCULAR TOUR OF HOLY ISLAND
by CROSVILLE MOTOR SERVICES Ltd
FROM HOLYHEAD
411) HOLY ISLAND
411 (S)120

D. & B. Joint Line "PRINCE EDWARD"
FOR CONDITIONS SEE BACK
BALLOCH PIER & TARBET
41 JE 21
[THIRD CLASS]
PE.6 (S) TARBET
FARE 2/3

THE "ST. PATRICK", GUERNSEY

Water & Waves

Britain has a coastline of almost 8,000 miles, so it is not surprising that many of the carriage panels featured rivers, harbours, ships and ferries. Much of Britain's history, heritage and industry is closely linked with the sea and the railways have played a large part in the transportation of goods and passengers from ports all around the coast.

SOUTHERN RLY, GOV'S STEAMERS.
This ticket is issued subject to the Bye-laws,
Regulations and Conditions stated in the
Company's Time Tables, Bills and Notices.
BOAT No. 2.
PORTSMOUTH to
RYDE
Excess to First Class.   Fare 6d.
To be given up on landing.
20
3644

Introduction to the London Midland Area

The London & North Eastern Railway had been producing a steady flow of scenic prints for 13 years before the London Midland Region of British Rail began to adopt the same policy in 1949. After viewing the rather dreary sepia photographs in ex London Midland & Scottish stock, it is easy to understand why George Dow, the public relations and publicity officer, decided that a more innovative and colourful policy was needed.

Like the eastern side of the country, the LMR had a heritage of historic railway events in their area too. The Liverpool and Manchester Railway became the first regular passenger carrying line in the world in 1830 and the London & Birmingham Railway was the world's first trunk route, completed in 1838, so, to his credit, Dow decided to stir public interest by projecting and promoting this fine heritage, rather than simply duplicating a quantity of photo views in print form by using artists' landscapes. This was not altogether surprising considering that Dow was a railway historian himself. Hence the LMR passengers were treated at an early stage to two fine series of paintings in their coaches.

One of these series contained 24 oil paintings by the railway historian and artist Cuthbert Hamilton Ellis and depicted brightly coloured transport scenes of some of the pre-grouping railway undertakings which later went to form the LMS in 1923. Covering the period 1835 to 1920 and containing some quaint and evocative views of trains and boats, these tended to capture the attention of the public eye and, particularly, the railway enthusiasts amongst them! The second railway-related series was of 16 views of railway architecture by poster artists Claude Buckle and Kenneth Steel. Again this achieved a good geographical coverage – from the Doric Arch at the entrance to Euston station to Carlisle Citadel station and the Britannia tubular bridge in North Wales, and so encouraged travel to the LMR's farthest boundaries. This included a large area and it is worthwhile having a brief look at the region in a little more detail.

Just before the turn of the century there were three main lines from London competing for traffic to the Midlands – the London & North Western Railway (LNWR), the Great Central (GCR) and the Midland (MR) with their termini situated relatively close to one another on the Euston Road at Euston, Marylebone and St Pancras, respectively. Many famous trains over the years have departed from these stations, heading northwards, including the various Scots, *The Irish Mail, Thames–Clyde Express, Master Cutler* and *The Liverpool Pullman* and *Manchester Pullman*.

The GCR, completed in 1899, was the last main line to be built in the country and was also the first to close. It was a superbly–engineered line, yet the upward trend in the numbers of passengers carried in Victorian times failed to continue for long into the 20th century and the competition proved too strong. It was later taken over by the LNER and several views of locations on this line appeared in their carriage print series.

The MR had set the pace for carriage improvements and instituted the abolition of second class in the late 19th century. It had its headquarters and works at Derby. Also located just within the Midlands area was the Crewe works of the LNWR – the largest undertaking in the world at the beginning of the 20th century

As well as the larger industrial cities in the Midlands including Birmingham, Nottingham and Leicester, the area also contained part of the Peak District – a popular tourist spot and a favourite subject for the carriage panels.

North Wales is a sparsely populated area, possessing the ex LNWR coast line to Holyhead (a port for ferry crossings to Ireland) and connecting branches which reached out into the more mountainous areas of Snowdonia. The North Wales coast developed as a holiday centre with Llandudno as its chief resort. It catered largely for the industrial population of Cheshire and Lancashire and the area was an obvious choice for various carriage panel views.

The north west of England was one of the cradles of the industrial revolution and, consequently, a vital source of freight traffic to the railways. Liverpool was once the foremost port in Britain, handling much of the railways shipping cargo. The area also possesses some of the railways' great engineering achievements with its viaducts and bridges; several appearing in the *Railway Architecture* series. The most popular resort on this coast was undoubtedly Blackpool, yet it is surprising that no colour print of the famous town ever appeared in coaching stock although several views appeared in the photograph panel days.

A rather different tourist area was the Lake District which, like Snowdonia and the Peaks, attracted excursion traffic. It is difficult to resist quoting another rather hysterical piece of early written public opinion towards railway excursionists here, this time from James Payne, a friend of Harriet Martineau – the writer of *A Guide to the Lakes* . . . 'Our inns are filled to bursting point, our private houses broken into by parties desperate for lodgings . . . a great steam monster ploughs up our lake and disgorges multitudes upon the pier; the excursion trains bring thousands of curious, vulgar people . . . the donkeys in our streets increase and multiply a hundredfold, tottering under the weight of enormous females visiting our waterfalls from morn to eve . . . ' Beautiful!

The LMR interspersed their historical railway pictures with several series of landscapes in their area but these tended to be fairly conservative in terms of the locations chosen compared to the LNER subjects. They clung mainly to views of the main tourist areas already mentioned, and few towns or cities were included. As the Region was fortunate enough to have all these mountainous beauty spots in its territory, it is not too surprising that they failed to promote too enthusiastically other less glamorous areas such as Birkenhead Docks or the Black Country.

Locations in the ex Great Western parts of the LMR seemed to be omitted too, especially around Shropshire, but perhaps this was coincidental rather than a continuance of former company feuds!

Some fine artists were commissioned, including Charles Knight, Ronald Maddox and Edward Mortelmans, but it can be safely said that the overall high standards of consistency and detail achieved by the LNER were never attained by the LMR.

In 1954, just when it appeared that the LMR were conforming regarding scenic views, they issued the large set of 48 prints depicting historical events in their area. All of a sudden, the travelling public were treated to scenes of medieval knights jousting at Ashby–de–la–Zouch; John Bunyan in jail in Bedford Prison and Ann Boleyn at Dunstable with Henry VIII as he considered whether to chop and change his wife. Lady Godiva in full transparent battle–dress, riding through the streets of Coventry was certainly a little different from views of Curzon Street Goods Depot and the Ribblehead Viaduct – but full marks for imagination! These prints included the only Northern Ireland and Isle of Man locations in any series (these areas were well covered by photographs in LMS days) and definitely tried to break out of the 'scenic' mold, but never seemed to catch the public's imagination in quite the same way that the the earlier LMR series had.

It was back to the earlier theme of boats and trains when the final set appeared in the late 1950s. This included

views of shipping services to Ireland by Claude Buckle and diesel trains running through valleys by John Greene – a foretaste of the impending changes to come on Britain's railways.

A very short space of time after this, many routes had been closed on the LMR, including the old GCR main line. Electrification of the West Coast Main Line to Birmingham, Liverpool and Manchester was beginning and the issuing of carriage prints on the Region was an event of the past.

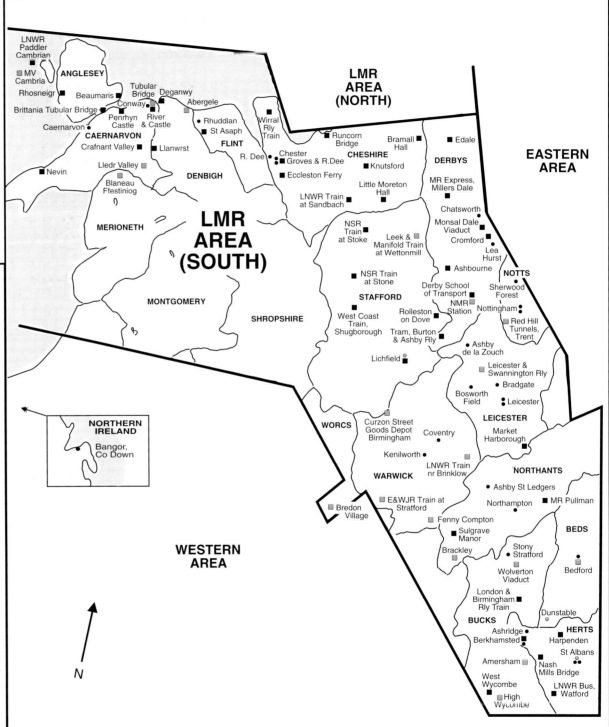

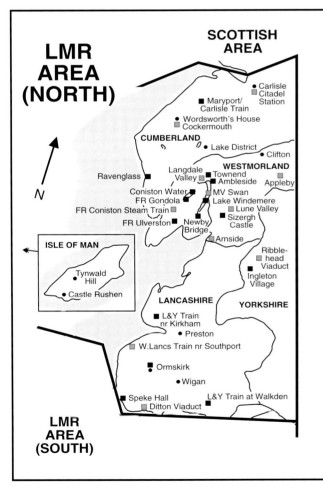

Bedford
from a watercolour by
Claude Buckle (1950) *(bottom)*

Buckle gives this beautiful, tranquil scene a slightly misty atmosphere as if the memory is recalling some long forgotten location. The River Ouse flows gently under the town bridge and the spire of St Paul's church near the town centre is visible above the trees. The county town of Bedford has existed since Saxon times and nowadays likes to be associated with John Bunyan, the humble and brave Christian pioneer who wrote *Pilgrims Progress* and *The Holy War*. When he was alive, however, the town authorities persecuted and jailed him for 14 years, for his refusal to submit to the dead religious traditions of his day.

Bedford has two stations i) Midland (ex MR) on the St Pancras to Sheffield main line and ii) St John's (ex LNWR) on the Cambridge to Bletchley line (closed between Cambridge and Bedford)

Lune Valley, near Tebay, Westmorland
from a gouache painting by
John Greene (1957) *(top, facing)*

Look out – the diesels are coming! . . . The Lune Gorge formed part of the selected route adopted by the Lancaster & Carlisle Railway and constitutes one of the most scenic sections of the West Coast Main Line, with the Borrowdale Fells on one side of the line and the Howgill peaks on the other. Being close to Shap and Dillicar water troughs, it shared with these two locations as a popular spot for the steam railway photographer. However, John Greene chooses to reveal a Class 40 English Electric here, in this gouache painting. The M6 motorway now runs alongside this lovely stretch and, as if this wasn't ugly enough, the railway now adorns itself with overhead electric gantries and wires too.

The Lune Valley is situated between Tebay and Low Gill stations (both closed), on the ex LNWR main line to Carlisle

Blaneau Ffestiniog, Merioneth
from a watercolour by
Montague B Black (1950) *(bottom, facing)*

Dwarfed by the Snowdon mountain range and the excavations for its slate quarries and caverns, the town of Blaneau Ffestiniog, with its rows of old workers' cottages, lies spread out below. Slate quarrying began in 1818 on the Oakley's Estate and the caverns once produced much of the world's supply of roofing slates. The quarries now exist as an excellent tourist attraction, and still give the town a really unique character. The standard gauge branch line from Llandudno arrived in 1879 and the 1 ft 11½ inch, narrow gauge, steam operated, (though once horse–drawn). Ffestiniog Railway also runs from here to Porthmadog (Maddock's Port), which was once a prosperous slate exporting centre. The route was opened in 1836, and steam was first used in 1863, but the line became derelict in 1946. It was reopened in 1954 and is, once again, the premier narrow gauge line in Britain. Note the distant steam train approaching in the centre of the picture.

Blaneau Ffestiniog once had three stations: (i) LNWR (open) at the end of the branch line from Llandudno Junction; (ii) Ffestiniog Railway station (now uses the LNWR station); (iii) ex GWR (closed)

Amersham, Buckinghamshire
from a watercolour by
Horace Wright (1945–7)   (top, facing)

I'm quite fond of Horace Wright's quaint old street scenes. Although his occupation was that of a chemist, he enjoyed painting some of England's street heritage before the motor vehicle finally took over and destroyed much of a town's character. The attractive market town of Amersham is situated in the Misbourne Valley, and showed no real expansion until the railway arrived in 1892. Rapid residential development followed. It still retains its spacious main street lined with old inns (the old timbered *Kings Head* is on the right) and houses. The old Market Hall shown here was built at the expense of William Duke in 1682. The commuter line to London was electrified by London Transport in 1961.

Amersham is an ex Metropolitan/Great Central Joint Railway station on the London to Aylesbury line

Bredon Village, Worcestershire
from an oil painting by
Ronald Lampitt (1952)   (bottom, facing)

An interesting location for an LMR print, as it was well into Western Region territory when published. Although it was located on the south west – north east main line, it was only served by local stopping services. This timeless view of the village might well have been painted 200 years ago. Lampitt has had to lop off the top of the 60 ft, 14th century spire of St Giles church, which contains the fine canopied remains of St Giles Reed whose family built the almshouses in the main street. Bredon Hill is located only three miles away and is said to offer views of 14 counties on a very clear day. The *Rose and Hounds* pub, the horse and cart and the mad dog and Englishman out in the midday sun all make this composition so perfectly English, what!

Bredon station (closed) was on the former MR main line between Bristol and Birmingham

Fenny Compton, Warwickshire
from a watercolour by
Jack Merriott (1950)   (bottom)

With it's blend of old stone and brick cottages and close by the Dassett Hills, Fenny Compton presents a peaceful and timeless vista of the immortal small English country village to the speeding railway traveller. Merriott uses simple, yet effective, mellow washes of colour to achieve his aim, and the low spire of the 14th century church helps to hold the elements in the landscape together. Fenny Compton is still a pleasant village not far from the lovely Oxford canal and close to the massive ammunition depot at Kineton. This depot is still served by a freight line which connects with the main line at Fenny Compton.

Fenny Compton once had two stations i) ex GWR (closed) on the Paddington to Birmingham main line and ii) ex S&MJ (closed) on the Stratford to Towcester line

Montague B. Black.

Abergele, Denbighshire
from a watercolour by
Montague B Black (1950) (⇦ overleaf)

The poster artist, Montague Black, captures a lovely sunset panorama of this North Wales coastal town and seaside resort, using a lavish amount of viridian green. The fading sun catches the prominent church towers in the days when they were the only tall structures to be seen and high-rise flats weren't even on the drawing board, but Gwrych Castle on the hillside is barely visible. The distant Cambrian mountains and sea add their own beauty and, just in case we forget that this is a railway print, two plumes of smoke can be seen along the coastline indicating steam trains hard at work serving the locality.

Abergele is the former LNWR station on the North Wales, Chester to Holyhead main line

NORTH WALES

Holiday Pleasure Travel

Croeso i Gymru!
Welcome to Wales!

1962

ABERGELE	LLANDUDNO JUNCTION
BANGOR	LLANFAIRFECHAN
COLWYN BAY	PENMAENMAWR
CONWAY	PRESTATYN
DEGANWY	RHYL
LLANDUDNO	

BRITISH RAILWAYS

Ditton Viaduct, Lancashire
from a watercolour by
Claude Buckle (1952)

Buckle and boats were always a great double act, and here Claude manages to include some river craft in the West Bank Dock of the River Mersey in his painting of Ditton Viaduct on the Liverpool approach to the Runcorn Bridge. The coal wagons on the quayside and the smoking factory chimney and workers cottages in Widnes complete this atmospheric view of the north west's industrial heritage. Even though the railway sidings are now lifted and the docks have been filled in, the area is still, unmistakably, industrialised.

Ditton Viaduct is sited between Ditton Junction and Runcorn on the ex LNWR Liverpool to Crewe main line

Conway Tubular Bridge, North Wales
from a watercolour by
Claude Buckle (1952)

A Holyhead–bound express is about to traverse Robert Stephenson's Conway tubular bridge, which spans the 400ft width of the River Conway. The masonry work on the bridge was begun in early 1846 to the design of Francis Thompson to harmonise with the stonework of the adjacent Conway Castle. The castle was the third of Edward I's mighty strongholds and, with its huge battlemented walls and eight tall drum towers, is one of the best preserved medieval castles in the U.K. The two rectangular tubes carrying the bridge across the river were assembled on–site in 1848, and were then raised to the required level by powerful hydraulic presses. Passenger and freight traffic between Chester and Bangor commenced later that year. Unlike Stephenson's bridge over the River Dee, near Chester, which collapsed with a crossing train in 1847, the Conway bridge has proved very successful and the original design survives to the present day. It was a favourite spot for the railway photographer – especially when *The Irish Mail* was crossing the bridge.

Conway is situated on the ex LNWR main line between Rhyl and Bangor

MV Cambria, B.R. Holyhead–Dun Laoghaire Service
from a watercolour by
Claude Buckle (1957) *(top)*

Buckle shows a slightly choppy sea and a marvellous, unpredictable sky here, reminding passengers that the crossing to Ireland is not always that smooth! Before the days of cheap domestic flights, Holyhead was the normal choice of route for travellers to Ireland from England and most arrived by train along the North Wales coast main line. The M.V. Cambria was a steamer, ordered by the LMS and built by Harland and Wolff, Belfast in 1949 for the Holyhead – Dun Laoghaire passenger/mail ferry service. She was 396 ft long, had a 54 ft breadth, and a gross tonnage of 4,972 tons. Her speed was 21 knots and she could accommodate 750 first class and 1,250 third class passengers. On top of running a railway, BR was also the largest operator of short–sea ferry crossings in the world at this time, and many of the ports situated at the extremities of the British coastline were a welcome source of passenger revenue. The crossing time on the 58 mile trip across the Irish Sea on this boat was three hours and 15 minutes.

Citadel Station, Carlisle
from a watercolour by
Kenneth Steel (1952) *(top, facing)*

Carlisle's famous station is a fitting subject for Steel's superb pen and wash style and has often been referred to as 'The Gateway to Scotland'. It served more pre-grouping railway companies than any other station in the UK and in its heyday played host to a great variety of locomotives and rolling stock in the numerous pre–grouping liveries. The companies who influenced the siting and construction of the station were the Lancaster & Carlisle Railway and the Maryport & Carlisle Railway. Original ownership was to be vested jointly between these, the Newcastle & Carlisle Railway, and the Caledonian Railway. The construction of the original station building was completed in 1847 and in 1880 was completely rebuilt. From then until 1923, it was the joint property of the LNWR and the 'Caley', with the other pre–grouping railway companies being allowed to use the station by virtue of granted running powers. The cars in the forecourt all look rather similar, but at least they don't have to negotiate the overcrowded station car parks of today.

Curzon Street Goods Depot, Birmingham
from a watercolour by
Claude Buckle (1952) *(bottom, facing)*

This grand building was originally the London and Birmingham Railway terminus near the city centre and served as a crossroads between the lines to Derby, Manchester and London. Built in 1838, it was planned in the classical style by Philip Hardwick and the Ionic gateway, which towered above the squat, red brick houses surrounding it, was designed to complement his Doric arch at Euston Station. Curzon Street station was reduced to goods status when the Birmingham New Street station of the LNWR was built in the 1880s. In later years, the station buildings were allowed to fall into disrepair and by 1980 had become almost derelict. Birmingham City Council then acquired the site as a spearhead for its urban renewal projects and the former station entrance has now been restored to its former glory. It can be glimpsed on the right when approaching Birmingham New Street by train from the south. Whilst Buckle reveals laden lorries coming in and out of the goods depot, it's nice to see him showing a good old horse and cart delivering too!

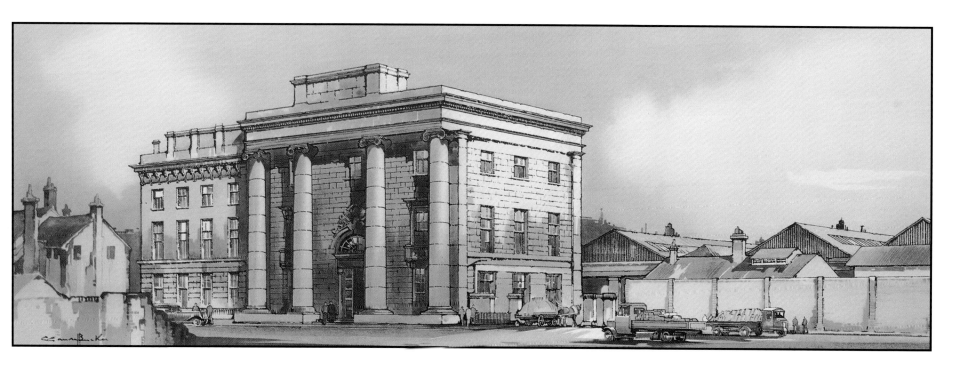

Brackley, Northamptonshire
from a watercolour by
Charles Knight (1952)   (⇐ ⇐ pages 140–1)

We come now to a superb townscape by Charles Knight, an artist once described as the 'modern Cotman'. In this view of the long Brackley High Street he captures the brilliant sunshine on the right hand shops with great effect, whilst those in shadow on the left give the required contrast and depth. As well as having a station on the GCR main line, Brackley also boasted a handful of trains in each direction on the Buckingham line. Alas – all has now gone. The A43 Brackley by–pass has since been built, and the street has fewer cars, but not as few as Knight depicts here – perhaps he rose early one summer morning to paint this almost deserted scene. The 18th century town hall built by the Duke of Bridgewater dominates the street with its high roof and cupola. It was an important town in the middle ages with its castle, but declined in importance and gained a reputation for harbouring vagabonds and felons for miles around. Not really surprising, since the author lives nearby.

Brackley had two stations (both closed) i) ex GCR on the Marylebone to Rugby main line; and ii) ex LNWR on the Banbury to Buckingham line

High Wycombe, Buckinghamshire
from a watercolour by
W Fairclough (1947)   (⇐ overleaf)

Like Amersham, High Wycombe saw particular growth when the railways arrived. In 1910 the GWR main line from Paddington to Birmingham was opened and the town benefited accordingly. Wilfred Fairclough adds the year 1947 to his signature here as he reveals a post war town centre market scene. The Guildhall *(left)* which dates from 1757 and the octagonal Little Market House *(centre right)* are both scheduled as ancient monuments. The 13th century church rises behind the latter. Note the distinct lack of road markings in those days!

High Wycombe is a former GWR/GCR Joint station on the London to Birmingham line, and was a junction for the branch to Maidenhead (closed)

Appleby, Westmorland
from a gouache painting by
Ellis Silas (1950)   (bottom)

Gouache, as a medium, never seemed to work quite as well for the carriage print pictures as did the translucent quality of the watercolours. Ellis Silas, a former president of the London Sketch Club, here creates a slightly sombre feel in his street scene of Appleby – Westmorland's most historic (and England's smallest) county town. We are looking from the bottom of the attractive main street towards the 600 year old St. Lawrence church, twice burned by the Scots and twice rebuilt. The entrance to it can be seen through an iron gate in the central archway of the cloisters. The tall black and white pillar with the sundial is called 'the Low Cross' (the High Cross is at the top of the street). The LMR were keen to show here, that they were, like the LNER, not deficient in their cultural history. Steam hauled special trains still call at Appleby – a convenient point for watering the locomotives.

Appleby had two stations: (i) ex MR (open) on the Settle to Carlisle line and (ii) ex NER (closed) on the Penrith to Kirkby Stephen line

Arnside, Westmorland
from an oil painting by
David Cobb (1952)   *(top)*

A good example of the LMR's aim at effect, compared to the LNER's more realistic approach. David Cobb, currently the president of the Royal Society of Marine Artists, here reveals a sunset over Arnside, the only location where Westmorland comes down to the sea. His buildings, for example, are suggested rather than painted in detail and this helps to produce the mellow and tranquil atmosphere that exudes from this landscape. The fading sun reflecting on the calm water of the River Kent estuary in Morecambe Bay and on the broad sands with a lone (and rather brave) woman who is paddling at this late hour, bids the train passenger to come and escape from the rush of life. Even the 50 arch railway bridge across the estuary just around the corner is ignored.

Arnside is a former FR station between Barrow and Carnforth (open) and a junction with the former FR line to Oxenholme (closed)

Travel in 1875 – LNWR Northbound Tourist Express near Brinklow (Warwicks)
From an oil painting by
C Hamilton Ellis (1951)   *(overleaf ⇨)*

The Grand Union Canal follows the Euston main line for much of its route, and the two highways, with a dark menacing sky overhead, make a colourful combination. LNWR 2–4–0 locomotive No. 2175 *Precedent,* designed by F. W. Webb, speeds its 16 – coach train past *Sarah,* a colourful narrow boat heading towards Braunston at a far more sedate four m.p.h. In these days, canal boats were often owned by the families who operated them and were commonly referred to as 'Number Ones'. By 1875, the railways were taking much of the freight traffic from the canals and often ended up buying out the canal companies in the process.

Brinklow was an ex LNWR station (closed) on the West Coast Main Line, between Rugby and Nuneaton

C. Hamilton Ellis

Travel in 1840 – Old Derby station, North Midland Railway
from an oil painting by
C Hamilton Ellis (1951) *(top)*

The site for a joint station was selected to the south east of the town centre at a place then known as Castle Fields. The station was designed by the famous railway architect Francis Thompson and built between 1839 and 1841. It was a 'trijunct' station, where the North Midland, Midland Counties and Birmingham and Derby Junction Railways all met and was a vital junction, as almost all of the traffic between the north east and London passed through it. It saw some real cut–throat competition between companies, too! The Midland Railway's headquarters and works were also sited here. In these early days, larger stations were often built as 'sheds' to house the freight and rolling stock. At Derby, the light iron roof of the station covered 140 ft in three spans and there was originally only one, 1,050 ft long, platform, with a continuous brick frontage onto the street. Note the small turntable being used to turn the coach just to the centre right of Hamilton Ellis's colourful painting.

Derby (Midland) is still a major junction station for routes around the Midlands

Travel in 1905 – Leek & Manifold Railway train at Wettonmill
from an oil painting by
C Hamilton Ellis (1951) *(top, facing)*

Another colourful view by Hamilton Ellis showing the rocky limestone outcrops, so common in this part of the Peak District. The Leek and Manifold Valley Light Railway was first proposed in 1895 as a means of opening up the isolated moorland villages in the area and facilitating local trade with Leek. The relevant Railway Act was passed in 1896 and the proposed railway between Hulme End and Waterhouses was 8 miles 11 chains long, with 2' 6" gauge. Connection from Waterhouses to Leek was to be made by a standard gauge branch of the North Staffordshire Railway. The line opened in 1904 and the L & M was later absorbed by the LMS. The two Leek and Manifold locomotives were built by Kitson and Co., Leeds, in 1904. They were powerful 2–6–4s and were the first to run in Britain, although they never had much to pull – the railway only ever had four coaches! Unfortunately, although the line ran through spectacular scenery, the railway was rarely discovered by tourists except during the 'Wakes Week' – the Potteries' annual factory holiday. It sometimes earned half of its annual revenue in this week! The last passenger train ran in 1935 and the last section of the line closed in 1941. Most of the old trackbed is now a pleasant public footpath.

Travel in 1890 – West Lancs train 'Blackburn', near Southport
from an oil painting by
C Hamilton Ellis (1951) *(bottom, facing)*

People either seem to love Hamilton Ellis's simple style of artwork or find it rather overpowering. I confess to being one of the former. The West Lancashire Railway was incorporated in 1871 with the objective of operating a train service between Southport and Preston. Construction was completed in 1882, and Hamilton Ellis shows one of its, rather quaint, 2–4–0 locomotives hauling some colourful, four-wheeled, clerestory coaches along the line. It is watched with interest by a train–spotting bird of prey.

The WLR line was later taken over by the L&Y and has since closed

ALBANUS, A ROMAN OFFICER, BECAME OUR FIRST MARTYR WHEN HE WAS BEHEADED NEAR VERULAMIUM IN AD. 303 FOR HELPING A CHRISTIAN PRIEST. ST. ALBAN'S ABBEY STANDS ON THE SITE OF THE MARTYRDOM.

THE FAMOUS SAMUEL JOHNSON WAS BORN IN LICHFIELD IN 1709. HERE HE IS SEEN REVISITING THAT CITY IN LATER YEARS WITH JAMES BOSWELL, WHO WROTE THE GREAT LIFE OF JOHNSON.

— RONALD A MADDOX —

Albanus at St Albans
from a gouache painting by
A R Whitear (1954) *(top, facing)*

Unashamedly my favourite carriage print! Albanus, following in the footsteps of Stephen and the early disciples, awaits the blow which will terminate his brief life on earth and start his new life in a nobler place. Verulanium, from which St Albans grew, was the only British city important enough in Roman days to be accorded the status of municipium, which meant that its inhabitants had the right to a Roman citizenship. The abbey dates from the 11th century and attracted a steady trickle of pilgrims via its nearby railway stations. Was this print issued specially by BR for football supporter's trains?

St Albans had three stations i) ex MR (open) on the St Pancras to Sheffield line; ii) ex LNWR (open) at the end of the branch line from Watford and iii) ex GNR (closed) on the branch line from Hatfield

Samuel Johnson at Lichfield
from a gouache painting by
Edward Mortelmans (1954) *(bottom, facing)*

An interesting painting of the dynamic duo by Edward Mortelmans. Lichfield's cathedral spires (known locally as the 'Ladies of the Vale') appear in the background – the only English cathedral with three of them. The central spire was destroyed by Cromwellian troops and was later rebuilt. Before the development of the large office blocks in the city centre it was possible to obtain a good view of the cathedral from the train window. No doubt Johnson is about to come up with some rather witty remark to Boswell about the unfortunate lady walking past the carriage who appears to be missing half of her head.

Lichfield has two stations, both ex LNWR (i) Trent Valley station on the Euston to Preston main line and (ii) City station on the Burton to Birmingham line

Wordsworth's House, Cockermouth, Cumberland
from a watercolour by
Ronald A Maddox (1957) *(top)*

One of the four paintings executed during Ronald's outing to National Trust properties in the Lake District (see p.7). A colourful view of the 18th century house in the main street of the old town of Cockermouth, where William Wordsworth the poet was born in 1770. It is now a museum devoted to his life and works. Wordsworth was a fierce critic of the intrusion of railway lines into the Lake District and wrote poetry deriding the railway architecture of the time, which he considered was destroying the landscape. Nowadays, he would find few to support this view – most people now see the viaducts and architectural works as complementing creation rather than destroying it. A railway carriage was therefore an ironic setting for this attractive painting in memory of Wordsworth!

Cockermouth was a station on the scenic, ex Cockermouth, Keswick and Penrith Railway. It was a line which saw much cattle traffic and was closed in 1966 despite strong local opposition

Introduction to the Western area

Many people have memories of distant summer holidays whenever the 'Western' is mentioned – the long hot days spent on sandy beaches are easily recalled even if the rainy ones seem to have been forgotten. The holiday image, like that of the Southern, was a logical target for the Great Western's advertising department, especially when the popularity for Devon and Cornwall as tourist centres increased in the early 1900s. Not surprisingly, the GWR slogan in pre–grouping days was *The Holiday Line*. The vast coastline in its territory and the numerous, well–advertised, seaside towns in the GWR *Holiday Haunts* guidebook, beckoned countless thousands of holiday-makers in the summer months and kept the company tills ringing merrily. Nowadays the best guidebook for holiday locations tends to be your chequebook.

Honeypot resorts such as Torquay, Newquay and Pembroke were prime subjects in the GWR's photographic panels and posters up until the late 1940s and were often given a more middle class emphasis than the Southern's more 'bucket and spade brigade' appeal. The names of Teignmouth, Tenby and Torquay do leave a slightly different impression when compared with those of Brighton, Bexhill and Bognor, after all! *The Railway Magazine* in June 1898 summed up the difference in holidaymakers in its own inimitable fashion when it reported that . . . 'Tenby, like Newquay, has never catered for the rowdy "half a crown there and back" picnickers, with their accompaniments of ginger beer and sandwiches. Its clientele has always been of the respectable debonaire class who, satisfied with their treatment and the very moderate tariff, return year after year . . . ' How frightfully spiffing.

Although the Southern Region operated lines into Devon and Cornwall until the mid–1960s, they never produced any standard–format carriage prints of locations in the area apart from the borderless *Atlantic Coast* by Langhammer. Therefore, for the sake of simplicity, the whole of this area is shown on the map as being under Western control, which tended to be how the Western viewed this part of the country anyway!

Summer Saturdays would see thousands of holidaymakers journeying by train to this part of Britain and the names of the *Cornish Riviera Express*, The *Cornishman*, *Cambrian Coast Express*, *Bristolian*, *Cathedrals Express* and the *Torbay Express* were synonymous with the excitement of journeys to the west. The GWR, of course, offered more main lines than just the west country route. Operating

from the great terminus at Paddington, built by Brunel in 1854 and originally housing his seven foot 'broad gauge' track, the GWR ran expresses via Swindon to Bristol and to South Wales, via Newport and Cardiff. This included the company's greatest industrial area and gave them its largest source of freight traffic, particularly coal. The GWR also operated expresses as far north as Birkenhead via Oxford, Birmingham, Wolverhampton and Chester, providing them with a vital link to the north west and into North Wales. The company was not partic-ularly noted for its suburban services but more for the main lines and its many rural branches.

By 1893, the broad gauge had been lifted in order to bring the GWR into line with the country's other railway companies and, through the acquisition of other smaller railways, the company now had the largest route mileage in Britain. It retained its identity during the amalgamation of 1923 and largely escaped all the reorganisations that the other companies were forced to implement. There was thus little need for any changes in the company's advertising policy and carriage panel propaganda during its latter years. Nationalisation, however, with its altered geographical boundaries, and the need for standardisation, presented a different proposition.

In 1949 the newly–formed Western Region was instructed to implement colour prints to replace the old photographic panels, many of which showed seaside resorts that, by this time, were in a state of flux. There was also the pos-sibility that the Western hills and moorlands and Welsh mountains, which had not shown up well in the photographs, might now become suitable subjects in print form, given some artistic licence by the painters. However, this process of changeover turned out to be something of a protracted farce. Possible locations were gleaned from the GWR *Holiday Haunts* booklet and a short list of 60 subjects were chosen. The prevailing accent of those actually planned tended more towards the picturesque, rather than the outwardly commercial destination, towards aesthetic appeal and enlightenment rather than popular travel. Whereas posters continued to illustrate seaside resorts and main revenue–earning areas, the carriage prints often looked to the more obscure locations, not necessarily on the railways.

At this juncture, either the Western suffered amnesia about the new BR, standard format 20 inch x 10 inch frame size or possibly, following in GWR tradition, decided to paddle its own canoe. The Region sent its artists off to paint pictures based on its old frame dimensions – in

three different sizes. The artists were commissioned on an area basis in the summer of 1949. Frank Sherwin, covering the Worcestershire/Shropshire area, was com-missioned to paint his on 1 July 1949 and returned with them just two weeks later – the fastest 'draw' in the west! Perhaps he enjoyed a good holiday in the process too.

However, after a selection of the paintings had been received the project seems to have ground to a halt. At that time the bulk of the Western Region stock was anti-quated and due to be scrapped as soon as replacements could be constructed and the policy makers no doubt questioned the wisdom of replacing most of the panels in the soon to be condemned old GWR carriages. In all events, the commitment shown by the WR to what was originally an LNER inspired idea, can be questioned. The artist Francis Flint (son of Sir William Russell Flint), commissioned to paint subjects in South Wales did not, for some reason, carry out the task and whilst, presumably, another could have carried it through to completion, this was not done – hence the reason for the complete lack of coverage of South Wales locations.

The BR standard corridor stock was finally introduced in 1951, yet it was not until 1954, five years after the commissioning, that the WR seriously looked at the reproduction of watercolours in carriage panels. By this time anyway, much of the artwork produced would have been useless. For example, John Bee's hard work in Devon was all to no avail as his paintings were all to the wrong dimensions for the production of standard sized prints!

Only 24 designs were submitted to the general manager of the day, K W C Grand, and 18 were selected for printing plus a couple of commercials. [A complete list of the proposed WR prints appears in Appendix C]. As it turned out, the non-corridor stock had a very short life–span on the WR and most of the prints disappeared when the diesel multiple units had arrived, in strength, on the scene by 1960. Much of the old GWR stock was sent to the breakers' yards at this time too, still displaying their maps and aged photographs. The closure of many of the ex GWR branch and rural lines followed shortly afterwards in the early 1960s.

After this great or, more appropriately, 'Grand', comedy of errors, we can only salvage some consolation that the Western did, at least, produce a token offering of views for posterity. A pity really, as the area had so much to offer. To have let Jack Merriott wander around amongst

the Cornish coastal villages with his palette and Rowland Hilder spend a time in the South Wales valleys would, no doubt, have resulted in some marvellous landscape paintings, but unfortunately, it was not to be.

St. Mawes, near Falmouth, Cornwall
from a watercolour by
Gyrth Russell RI (1954)

A fine effort by Gyrth Russell of this unspoilt Cornish location on the Roseland peninsula. The empty sand, the boats and harbour wall and the distant sight of Pendennis Castle on the other side of the, ferry – connected, 'Carrick Roads', all help to give a more upmarket appeal to the joys of holidaying.

St Mawes was not near a railway line! The nearest station was Falmouth, the terminus of the former GWR Truro branch, which was a ferry journey away

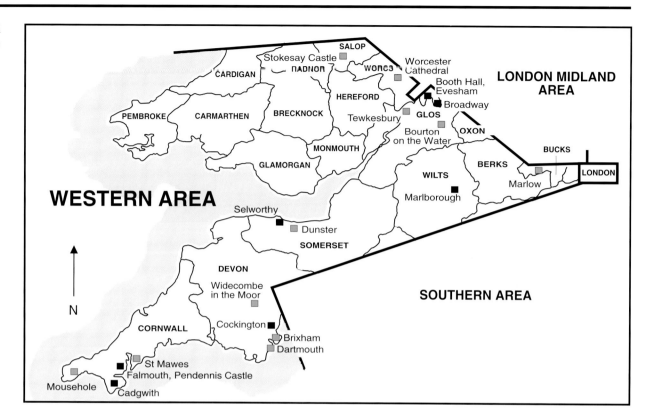

JACK MERRIOTT

Mousehole, near Penzance, Cornwall
from a watercolour by
Jack Merriott RI (1954)   (⇐ overleaf)

Pronounced 'Moozle', this is a pretty little Cornish village
which used to thrive off its pilchard harvest. Four Spanish
galleys escaped our Elizabethan warships in 1595, landing 200
Spaniards who burnt the village to the ground. Only the pub
survived so perhaps the invaders had a copy of the *Good
Beer Guide* with them. Dolly Pentreath, the last person to
speak Cornish as her native tongue, died here in 1777. An
excellent watercolour by Merriott, who lived in Cornwall –
full of colour and Cornish characters – and not a holiday-
maker in sight.

Mousehole is about four miles by road, south of Penzance – the
terminus of the GWR's main line to the west country and once
the haunt of many express steam locomotives.

Something different!
**CAMP COACH
HOLIDAYS**
FURTHER INFORMATION FROM THE COMMERCIAL
SUPERINTENDENT, PADDINGTON STATION, W.2.

Dunster, Somerset
from a watercolour by
R Lander (1954)   *(top, facing)*

A typical Lander painting of the village using his poster style of flat, bright, contrasting hues – a technique which tended to make some of his paintings look like pictures to test colour blindness. The focal point in the view is the, eight–sided, Yarn Market in the middle of the medieval timbered village. Many of Dunster's buildings' architectural styles span the 12th and 18th centuries and include a castle on a wooded hill (not shown). The village lies just outside Minehead on the ex GWR branch from Taunton.

Although closed in BR days, Dunster station once again enjoys the sound of steam trains passing through, as the line has now been preserved and is called the West Somerset Railway

Camping Coach Holidays
from a watercolour by
Arthur G Mills (1954)   *(bottom, facing)*

Camping coaches were old refurbished and equipped railway carriages, located at out of the way country locations and hired out by the railway companies for the use of holiday-makers. They were very successful around the middle of the century, but declined in popularity afterwards. This print was unusual, in that it was one of two commercial adverts, included in the WR series. Here we see typical, Arthur G Mills, poster–style characters, who appear to have the world to themselves. It also appears as though the muscle–bound, Brylcreamed, macho, teenage lad on the right is wearing lipstick.

Worcester Cathedral
from a watercolour by
Frank Sherwin RI (1954)   *(top)*

I have never been the greatest admirer of Frank Sherwin's work – but I find this painting quite pleasing. One of the most common views of Worcester – looking across to the cathedral from a bend in the Severn – a pleasant river, but one which is notorious for flooding the area. The cathedral in this county town is mostly early English in style although parts were built in the 11th century. It holds the tombs of King John and Arthur, the elder brother of Henry VIII. In Sherwin's day, the town still had its fine steam depot with its allocation of named engines.

Worcester has two stations (i) Foregate Street (ex GWR) and (ii) Shrub Hill (ex GWR & MR Joint)

Dartmouth, Devon
from a watercolour by
Frank H Mason RI (1954)   (⇐ *overleaf*)

A beautiful view up the River Dart by the marine artist. Dartmouth, to the left of the picture, has been an important harbour since Roman days. Edward III's fleet sailed from here to assist in the siege of Calais in 1347 and the Britannia Naval College, built in 1905 (not shown), now overlooks the town. The church near the riverside is St. Petrox church, rebuilt in 1644, and alongside are the remains of Dartmouth Castle – a 15th century, cliff castle which faces Kingswear Castle on the other side. A thick chain once reached across the estuary from these two buildings to hold off enemy ships.

Kingswear, opposite Dartmouth, was the end of the former GWR branch line from Newton Abbot and once the destination point of The Torbay Express. The Paignton to Kingswear section of this is now owned by the steam-operated, Torbay Steam Railway

Widecombe–in–the–Moor, near Ashburton, Devon
from a watercolour by
Jack Merriott RI (1954)

It almost seemed that the railways, in their later series of prints, seemed to have capitulated to the road lobbyists, and decided to illustrate locations which were easier to reach by car than by train! This view should certainly appeal to those who like to get away from it all. Standing at 800 ft, this old village is surrounded by the hills of Dartmoor on all sides. It is famed, of course, for its fair, which is held every second Tuesday in September, and by the song which is commemorated by a sign on the village green. The tower of the large 14th century church of St. Pancras (often referred to as the 'Cathedral of Dartmoor') was struck by lightning in 1638, killing several people in the process. The Bishop of Durham was not in the area at the time.

Widecombe was not served directly by rail – its nearest stations were Ashburton and Princetown, both termini of GWR branch lines into Dartmoor

Tewkesbury, Gloucestershire
from a watercolour by
Claude Buckle (1954) *(top)*

The view across the River Avon towards the fine Norman tower of St. Mary's church, achieves a pleasing composition and captures the town's flavour of river, medieval timbered houses and Christian heritage. Tewkesbury avoided the probable destruction of its church during the dissolution of the monasteries by, somehow, buying it from Henry VIII – a very public spirited action. It is situated at the confluence of the Severn and Avon rivers but, like so many other British towns, is now devoid of any railway.

Tewkesbury station was on the old MR line between Ashchurch and Malvern (closed)

Marlow, Buckinghamshire
from a watercolour by
Claude Buckle (1954) *(top facing)*

The rivers of Britain have always attracted artists since Constable's day and Claude Buckle was never happier than when he had a waterway in front of him. Here he is situated by the beech trees of Quarry Wood looking across an idyllically calm, Thames towards All Saints church across the river. The elegant suspension bridge, begun in 1829, and later renovated in 1966, is just out of view around the corner to the left. Marlow still enjoys a fairly regular branch line service, mainly for the use of London commuter traffic. It even boasted a small steam sub–shed once, providing the motive power for the branch.

Marlow station is the terminus of the former GWR branch from Maidenhead

Bourton on the Water, Gloucestershire
from a watercolour by
Claude Buckle (1954) *(bottom, facing)*

Set on the eastern edge of the Cotswold hills, and once served by a handful of trains in each direction, Bourton on the Water is an archetypal Cotswold village with its beautiful stone cottages and little peaceful stream. Quiet, mellow, attractive, tranquil and almost devoid of people – painted, no doubt, very early in the morning before the thousands of tourists arrived from all directions. Buckle's granddad lived nearby and Claude used to play in the little river Windrush here, as a boy.

Bourton on the Water was a station on the former GWR line from Kingham to Cheltenham – now closed

Carriage panels, *clockwise from top left:*
Stowmarket Station, Suffolk by Squirrell (LNER); Leeds City Station, Yorks by Buckle (LMR Rly Arch); Ribblehead Viaduct, Yorks by Steel (LMR Rly Arch); Red Hill Tunnels, Notts by Steel (LMR Rly Arch); East & West Jct Train at Stratford on Avon by Ellis (LMR Travel–In); FR Coniston Steam train by Ellis (LMR Travel–In); Lledr Valley, North Wales by Lander (LMR [C]); Leicester & Swannington Train by Ellis (LMR Travel–In); **Background:** Colne Valley Viaduct, Essex by Squirrell (LNER)

Picture rail

Britain, of course, was the world's pioneer in the use of railways so it was only natural for the railway companies to extol their own history. The many structures involved in the building of the lines were looked on in awe by a people at the start of the industrial revolution. Viaducts, bridges and preserved trains still testify to the leading role Britain played. Let's hope the current railways system enjoys a successful future too.

Introduction to the London area

What travelogue of yesteryear Britain would be complete without a special look at the city of London?

Apart from the fact that so many rail passengers visit the capital (as many trains start or terminate in London as the rest of England's major cities put together), the centre of London, with its colourful history, possesses a huge tourist potential in its own relatively small area. Overseas tourists flock to London in vast numbers and a visitor to the capital arriving at Cannon Street, Charing Cross, Euston, Fenchurch Street, Holborn Viaduct, Kings Cross, Liverpool Street, London Bridge, Marylebone, Paddington, St Pancras, Victoria or Waterloo stations can often get the impression that there are more railway termini in central London than there are English residents living there.

It may seem surprising to us in these times of tourism and modern communications, to realise that London was visited by very few people in the days before the railways arrived. When the major companies built their city stations in the mid–19th century they were constructed on a magnificent scale to command the awe, respect and confidence of the new travelling public. John Betjeman rightly described these railway buildings as the cathedrals of the era.

When these stations were built, the Marylebone Road, where several of the main lines terminated, became heavily congested. In order to alleviate this problem the Metropolitan Railway was built in 1863 from Paddington to Farringdon via Euston and Kings Cross and was the first 'underground' railway in the world although, strictly speaking, the line lay in a 'trench' rather than a tunnel.

This line was extended into a complete circuit in 1884 and became known as the 'Inner Circle'. The construction of 'tube' lines, built deep underground, soon followed – the Central London opened in 1900 and the Bakerloo in 1906 and these lines became amalgamated into a company called the 'Underground Electric Railways of London'. The capital and its railway network began to spread quickly.

A massive population drift to the suburbs occurred after World War I, almost doubling the built up areas in the country. 'Suburbia' was a truly railway-influenced phenomenon. Wembley alone, for example, had increased its population from 10,277 in 1881 to 124,000 in 1961.

Vast numbers of passengers now travelled by train to work in the capital. In 1921 the Metropolitan Railway was the second largest passenger carrying railway in the country after the GWR, yet it only had a minuscule route mileage in comparison. Carriage panel views and adverts therefore thrived in the railway carriages around London, as more and more people began to commute.

The heart of the City and the main tourist area lay between most of the companies' or Regions' major rail termini, so the possible choices of locations for carriage print subjects were in a sort of 'no man's land'. The London & North Eastern Railway however, had already begun commissioning artists to capture the area in paint at an early stage, and pictures of *Kensington Palace, Lambeth Bridge* and the *River Thames (King's Reach)* were appearing in carriages not long after the 1939–45 war. When the LNER largely became the Eastern Region of British Rail in 1948 the commissionings continued and further obvious locations appeared – *Tower Bridge,*

Horse Guards Whitehall, Marble Arch but, surprisingly, no Buckingham Palace or Trafalgar Square.

By the time the Southern and Western Regions began issuing their own series, there was little point in duplicating the Eastern's work and these regions simply put the ER prints in their own carriage panels. These pictures were to the normal high standard of LNER artwork and captured the tourist image adequately enough.

Many views of London's famous buildings and landmarks can be seen from its river and the Eastern were quick to capitalise on this – seven views of *Old Father Thames* appeared in this series; from *Tilbury Hailing Station* all the way up to Putney – not the most breathtaking locations imaginable!

The London Midland adopted a different strategy from that of the Southern and Western Regions as far as London was concerned. Instead of showing the white flag they strayed away from scenic prints and tried the 'historical' approach. When commissioning their various series they included a smattering of locations in the London area. *The Railway Architecture* set, for example, included views of the famous, and now sadly demolished, Doric arch at the entrance to Euston Station, the Gothic frontage of Scott's St Pancras station, and the entrance to Primrose Hill tunnels, whilst their unique *History* series particularly took advantage of the rich heritage of England's capital. Nine pictures appeared in this latter set, based on 'happenings' in London – some serious and some almost comical!

Even the Hamilton Ellis, *Travel–In* series made an appearance with a view of a North London Railway train

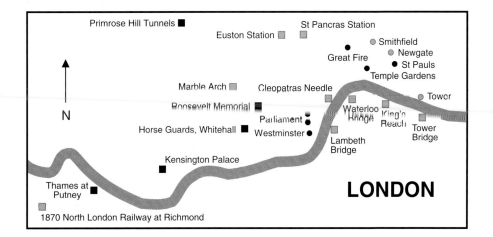

1870 North London Railway at Richmond

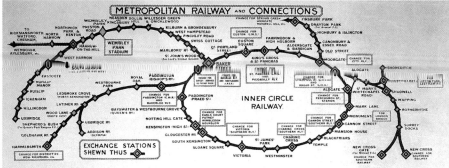

An early Metropolitan Railway map of 1912 showing the Circle Line and branches around London.

at Richmond, a location most people tend to associate with the Southern.

With the exception of Broad Street station, which was once the third busiest terminus in the capital, London has managed to escape the mass closure of lines which affected most of the country and, fortunately, still sees most of its vast railway network in operation.

Even if the tourists in London failed to glance at the carriage panel views in the railway carriages, British Rail still gained some revenue from them. Copies were sold from the Regent Street Travel Centre in London. Situated close to many foreign travel offices, the Centre attracted plenty of wallet–waving tourists. The prints sold well – especially to American visitors, who were keen to take these colourful reminders of their own visit to Britain back home with them.

London, Waterloo Bridge

from a watercolour by
Kenneth Steel RBA SGA (1948–55)   *(bottom)*

Kenneth Steel painted this in a similar style to his view of Lambeth Bridge and probably situated himself on the Hungerford Bridge near the Festival Hall. Cleopatra's Needle can be seen on the opposite bank towards the left, and the large white building on the same bank behind Waterloo Bridge is Somerset House which dates from 1776. A palace for Elizabeth I once stood on this site. The dark shape of St Paul's is to the right of the bridge. I particularly like the realistic overcast sky – a familiar feature of London to many commuters.

The nearest station to the viewpoint is Waterloo (ex LSWR)

London, Lambeth Bridge

from a watercolour by
Kenneth Steel RBA SGA (1948–55)   *(overleaf ⇨)*

Kenneth Steel uses a pleasing blend of blues and greys here to help highlight the stonework of Lambeth Bridge, with the Houses of Parliament situated behind it. Monarchs have lived here from Edward the Confessor to Henry VIII but the Court moved to St. James in 1515 after a fire. In 1834 most of the old Houses of Parliament also burnt down and Charles Barry designed the present gothic structure, entrusting most of its intricate decoration to Augustus Pugin. It has 1,100 apartments and two miles of corridors. The Victoria Tower at this end of the building, although more imposing, is lesser known than the clock tower at the north end which houses 'Big Ben'.

The nearest station is Vauxhall (ex LSWR)

London, Tower Bridge

from a watercolour by
John L Baker (1948–54) *(top)*

A pleasant pen and wash painting of a familiar and spectacular landmark of London. Tower Bridge was designed in the
late 19th century by Sir John Wolfe–Barry and pedestrians
can cross the bridge using the high–level walkway. The roadway
between the gothic towers can be raised and lowered to
allow boats to enter the Pool of London. Originally worked
by steam power, the machinery is now worked electrically.
A late–running bus once jumped the gap between the rising
roadway ends, but this exciting possibility has since been
frustrated by the use of gates. With the decline of the port
of London however, the raising bascules are now seldom used.

Tower Bridge's nearest station is Tower Hill LT

Entrance to Euston Station, London

from a watercolour by
Claude Buckle (1952) *(top facing)*

What memories this typical, 1950s painting by Claude
Buckle brings back! In 1835, an Act of Parliament authorised
the extension of the London & Birmingham Railway southwards to Euston in London. This station became their
London terminus and was constructed in 1837 amongst
open fields. Here we see the famous triumphal arch, with its
four Doric columns supporting the portico which rose to a
height of 72 ft. It was designed by Philip Hardwick and built
at a cost of £35,000. Ten years later Hardwick's son was
commissioned to design the Great Hall of the station and
this was erected in 1849. With its enormous dimensions, it
was the largest station waiting-room in Britain. During the
period 1960-63 both the Doric arch and the Great Hall and
much of the old station infrastructure were savagely levelled
for the rebuilding and modernisation of Euston Station,
ahead of the electrification of the West Coast Main Line.
The demolition contractor offered to build it elsewhere but
BR stubbornly declined the offer. The only remains are the
two side lodges, although other stonework has recently
been discovered in the garden of the contractor and alongside the bank of a river!

Euston is a former LNWR station

Entrance to St. Pancras Station, London

From a watercolour by
Claude Buckle (1952) *(bottom, facing)*

A fine painting by Buckle of the marvellous frontage of St
Pancras, although it is a pity that the narrow height of the
artwork has meant that he has had to omit the top of the
building. Designed by the famous architect and Midland engineer, W H Barlow, this station is complemented by the magnificent, Victorian secular gothic style, Midland Hotel which
was designed by Sir George Gilbert Scott and opened in 1873.
It is one of the ultimate monuments of the railway age and,
with its 400 beds, had little problem in accommodating
travellers. The station itself was opened in October 1868
and the platforms lay under a vast, arched roof with a single
span of 240 ft – the widest in the world at the time. The
station was bombed during the blitz in May 1941, but despite
severe damage to several of the platforms and rolling stock,
the fine roof survived virtually intact. The great building was
threatened with demolition in a 1960s improvement scheme
but, unlike Euston, was mercifully spared. Considering that
King Cross and St Pancras stations were built within 15
years of each other, there is an amazing difference in styles.
The name "St. Pancras" honours a boy martyr in Asia Minor,
killed for his faith by the emperor Diocletian.

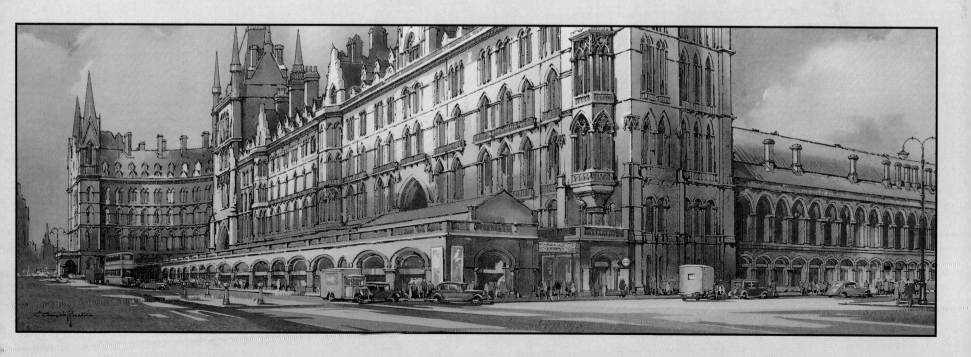

ELIZABETH FRY AT NEWGATE PRISON IN 1813. SHE WAS MOVED SO MUCH BY THE SAD SCENES OF HORROR SHE SAW THERE THAT SHE DEVOTED THE REST OF HER LIFE TO THE IMPROVEMENT OF CONDITIONS IN OUR PRISONS.

Elizabeth Fry in Newgate Prison
from a gouache painting by
Edward Mortelmans (1954) *(top)*

Sometimes the quality of the print reproduction didn't quite do justice to the fine original artwork – this print has lost some of its definition in the process. Here we have a portrait of a Christian who was willing to put her faith into practice. Newgate prison was the scene of public executions until 1868. It was later demolished and the Central Criminal Courts, better known as the 'Old Bailey' now stand in its place.

Newgate's nearest station is now City Thameslink BR

Peasants Revolt against the Poll Tax
From a gouache painting by
Edward Mortelmans (1954) *(bottom)*

It didn't quite come to this state of affairs when Margaret Thatcher tried to apply a poll tax in 1990, although feelings did run high for a while! This is another fine painting by Mortelmans from the LMR *Historical* series. It encouraged no one to travel by rail of course, but brought a little history lesson into the compartments of our trains – a lesson which was obviously not heeded by those in the highest levels of government – or perhaps they just never travelled by train?

Smithfield's nearest station is Barbican BR/LT

London, Marble Arch
from a watercolour by
A J Wilson (1948–54) *(top, facing)*

The solid, colourful old cars and passing pedestrians help to give a real 1950s feel to Wilson's view of this famous landmark. Marble Arch has always had a controversial love-hate relationship with traffic. Originally built by Nash as a gateway to Buckingham Palace, it immediately became redundant because it was too narrow to let Queen Victoria's state coach through. It was re-erected as the entrance to Hyde Park, but by 1908, the traffic became too great for it and it was removed to its present site, near the spot where the dreaded, 'Tyburn Gallows' once stood. Seeing the way some drivers roar around the arch nowadays, perhaps the gallows might present a better deterrent to road accidents than the arch.

Marble Arch's nearest station is Marble Arch tube station (LT) on the Central Line

Travel in 1870 – North London Railway Train for Broad Street leaving Richmond
from an oil painting by
C Hamilton Ellis (1951) *(bottom, facing)*

Ellis gives this painting the Christmas card treatment here, with his view of one of the large and distinctive, 4–4–0 tank locomotives, No.12, at the head of a train to Broad Street as it passes a LSWR loco at Richmond sidings. These NLR locomotives provided the power for most of the company's trains. The origins of this railway were under the auspices of the East and West India Docks and Birmingham Junction Railway in 1846. The railway became known as the North London Railway in 1853 and was built to cater for the new suburbs in the north and west, where a high proportion of city management were residing. Completion of the line to Richmond was effected in 1858. Between 1900 and 1920 passenger revenues on the North London line decreased dramatically due to increasing competition from the tramways and the new Hampstead Tube.

Richmond is an ex LSWR station on the Waterloo to Reading line, and a junction with the ex NLR line to Willesden

THE PEASANTS' REVOLT, IN 1381, AGAINST THE POLL TAX, WHEN, LED BY WAT TYLER, THEY MARCHED ON LONDON FROM KENT. THEY MET RICHARD II AT SMITHFIELD, WHERE TYLER WAS KILLED IN THE FIGHT

London, River Thames (Kings Reach)
from a watercolour by
Frank H Mason RI (1945–54)   (⇐ *overleaf*)

A magnificent landscape painting by Mason from a point,
slightly downriver from the site of the present National
Theatre, looking towards Blackfriars Bridge. On the left are
moored *Chrysanthemum* and *President* alongside the Victoria
Embankment and the 365 ft dome of Sir Christopher Wren's
St. Pauls Cathedral, rises impressively in the background,
unimpeded by the tall buildings around it which now mar the
view. In spite of all the fine architecture on the skyline,
Mason chooses hard working tugs and barges alongside the
river wharf to dominate the foreground and remind us that
London is also a place of work. Two faces of the capital.
Superb.

The nearest station to this location is Waterloo (ex LSWR)

London, Cleopatra's Needle and Embankment
from a watercolour by
Jack Merriott RI (1945–54)   *(top)*

It appears that all the traffic is kindly waiting for Jack to
complete his painting in the middle of the road before
proceeding towards him! Cleopatra's Needle is situated
alongside the Embankment between Hungerford and
Waterloo Bridges and this view looks toward the latter
with the dome of St. Pauls visible, just above the top of the
bridge. Cleopatra's Needle is a 69 1/2 ft obelisk, given to
Britain in 1819 by the Viceroy of Egypt. It had been created
in Heliopolis in about 1500 B.C., but has no real connection
with Cleopatra. Note the tramlines and tram just to the left
of the Needle – once the most popular form of transport in
urban London.

*Cleopatra's Needle nearest stations are Charing Cross (ex SECR)
and Embankment LT*

Chapter 4
Rediscovering the lost art of the carriage print

The growing interest

Fashion can be defined as . . . 'something which goes in one era and out another' and there is no doubt that public interest in transport art has experienced a dramatic resurrection in recent years. As a reaction to the unimaginative and clinical 'plastic' era of travel decor in the 70s and 80s there has been a surge of interest in the nostalgia market of posters and carriage prints. The press, too, are keen to report on instances when piles of old posters are discovered under beds and in the attics of retired railwaymen. The Independent even printed an article entitled . . . *'Art could take the pain out of public transport'* (14 Jan 1992), which gave details of a commissioned study into the place of art in today's travel and a return to a more 'pleasurable, aesthetic and educational experience'.

As a result of this new wave of popularity, a growing demand for the old framed carriage prints and photographs has emerged. Prints of locations holding nostalgic memories of past holidays and local places of interest are bought for increasingly high prices in auctions and antique shops.

It may come as a surprise to many people, though, to hear that the railways have always sold their carriage prints to the public. From the early days of carriage panels, they were advertised and sold publicly as in the case of the GWR in 1907 who sold their pictures for one shilling each and advertised them in their *Holiday Haunts* booklet of that year. In 1937 the LNER, too, advertised their new mounted prints of etchings in the *Railway Magazine* and offered them at ten shillings and sixpence each, a very large sum of money in those days. After the war the LNER continued to sell their numerous prints, usually in sets of six, stapled together inside covers in booklet form. Later on, BR continued this policy, selling them from various outlets including the Regent Street Travel Centre in London. The issuing of these prints in booklets avoided the problem of 'purchase tax', as books were exempt from this, whereas individual prints were not. Prices varied over the years but I seem to remember that loose prints were available from BR public relations & publicity offices at around five shillings each and the old 'Rail Curios' at York certainly sold prints in original frames at a bargain two pounds ten shillings each! Prices obviously increased over the years, but a few remaining loose prints (ex Wolverton carriage works) could still be purchased from the Collector's Corner at York for reasonable prices as late as 2000.

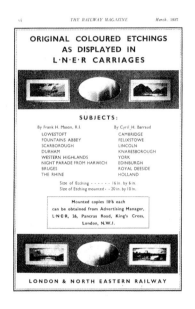

The railways have always sold their carriage panel pictures to the public. This LNER advert listing the Mason/Barraud colour etchings appeared in the March 1937 edition of the *Railway Magazine*. Ten shillings and sixpence was a very expensive purchase in those days.

What has survived?

Prints & photographs All the above data raises the question – what has survived from the countless thousands of panels of photos and prints issued by the railways since the turn of the century?

It is only in recent years that interest in collecting carriage panels has flourished, hence there are relatively few remaining early examples of these in existence. Only a small proportion of the photographic panels have been salvaged, especially from the pre-grouping companies, although it is often surprising how well preserved many of them are considering the effects of temperature changes, smoke, damp and general wear and tear they had been subjected to over the years. The dullness of the black and white and sepia photos probably gave little incentive to anyone to salvage the panels and therefore most were scrapped at the same time as the stock itself. The colour prints were a different proposition, however. Being a more recent implementation in carriages meant that, not only were there some salvaged from the panels in coaching stock, but also that many were still held in store rooms, unused, at the time that BR abandoned the use of carriage panels. Hence, whilst a very small proportion survived from the coaches themselves, many were recovered from the stores – usually in mint condition. Those taken from the carriages in their original frames often carry patches of damp stains on them and have faded due to the sunlight and, in the case of some of the LMR series, were sometimes pasted directly onto the glass itself by the carriage depots.

The number of prints that survived seems to vary enormously in terms of the different series. Whilst, for example, hundreds of certain post war LNER and ER prints were salvaged from York and Liverpool Street stores, far fewer of the Southern, Western and Scottish Regions' ones seem to have survived. The scheduled print run for the WR series alone was 2,000 each (WR use) and 1,000 each (other regions' use) and, apart from a couple of views, they seem far scarcer than the LNER series. We can therefore question whether or not these were actually produced in the end; whether they were all used up, or whether they were destroyed in the stores at a later date.

The prints of etchings and paintings which appeared before the war, including the original LNER etching series by Mason and Barraud, are very scarce and are much sought after. These were all probably taken out of the coaches and disposed of when the wartime adverts replaced them. Certain stocks of other individual print subjects were sometimes used up, too, and hence there appear to be few of these particular ones on the market in good condition. At the moment, though, it seems that enough have survived for most people to be able to acquire the print that they're looking for.

Frames I am not convinced that G.K.Chesterton's opinion that . . . 'art consists of limitation – the most beautiful part of every picture is the frame' really holds true as far

as the later carriage panels were concerned. The frames were mainly designed with function in mind far more than for any aesthetic consideration. A number of these carriage panel frames have survived; either through being sold with the prints 'in situ' via the sales outlets of BR, or as scrap material sold through the carriage depots when the stock was condemned. I have even seen complete sections of LMS hardwood carriage partitions, with the panels set in the middle, on sale in antique shops – a particularly heavy picture to hang on the wall! Frames which survive vary from the older pre–grouping or 'Big Four', more ornate moulding style to the far more numerous and standard, 'screw in the wall' BR type, complete with their recessed brass 'turn buttons' and, in the case of most of the small 20 inches x 10 inches size, their brass corner plates.

Original artwork So much for the prints and frames; what then has happened to the original artwork? BR kept the original paintings after the prints were produced and these seemed to end up in all sorts of places. Some appeared as pictures on office walls or were even given as gifts to staff. A large proportion, however, were simply stacked in piles on the publicity office shelves gathering dust. The Hamilton Ellis *Travel–In* series originals were hung on the office walls of the P.R.& P.O. officer, George Dow at Euston, Birmingham and Stoke on Trent before they found their way to Clapham Museum and, later, to York Museum where they now have a permanent place. Also at York are a sprinkling of other Regions's originals.

The LMR *Historical* gouache paintings are all owned by private collectors, as are most of the Railway Architecture and some of the LNER series. Other originals are sometimes seen in fine art auction houses, such as Sotheby's, and fetch fairly high prices. The listing of all known carriage prints in Appendix B also contains information on the original artwork known to exist and if any readers know of the whereabouts of any more carriage panel artwork, I would be pleased to know of their existence so I can update my records.

Having seen what is available, let's now look at how to go about collecting carriage prints, and the best sources from which to purchase them.

Collecting carriage prints

There seem to be no rigid rules about collecting carriage prints. Some people prefer them framed, others unframed; some collect a series and some acquire the works of a favourite artist or those of a particular area. Unlike many railway relics such as cast iron signs, the prints have an aesthetic quality which will equally appeal to both sexes – no need secretly to smuggle carriage prints into your home past the watchful eye of the lady of the house! They should certainly hold their value too, which makes them a good investment, and they're particularly suitable for gifts – as the sign in the antique shop said – 'There's no present like the past'.

It is not uncommon to see the occasional carriage panel in antique shops, but by far the best way to obtain them is through the railway collectors' market. Thousands of people collect old railway memorabilia and the interest in carriage pictures amongst these collectors has spread rapidly over recent years. A journal is currently published, monthly, called *Railway Collectors Journal*, giving information on all the auctions, swapmeets and other events in the collectors' calendar where carriage panels are likely to be found. Various well–run auction houses hold specialist railway relic sales around the country at regular intervals throughout the year, too – the largest and most well known, being at Sheffield. Many framed carriage prints come up for sale in these auctions.

My many years of collecting have meant that I often have spare prints available too. Information on these and the auctions mentioned above, will gladly be supplied by the author, c/o publisher (address on page 4) on receipt of a stamped addressed envelope or visit my website at www.carriageprints.com on the internet.

Price ranges

It would be unwise to quote likely prices for carriage panels, however approximate, in this book, as these can change considerably, even in a short space of time. The price of prints is largely dependant on condition, rarity, demand for certain areas or locations and whether they are in original style frames or not. Unframed prints are obviously cheaper. I produce a *Price & Rarity Guide to Railway Carriage Prints*, giving full information on prices realised in auctions. The original artwork for the prints are certainly valued highly and quite understandably so, as they are unique records. These, then, can sell for thousands of pounds each and it is worth keeping a look out for them, not only in railway auctions but in art sales generally – you never know, a bargain may turn up!

Reproductions

At present, the only colour prints to have been reproduced over the years are the *Travel–In* series. These were replicated (and clearly marked as such) by the N.R.M. at normal size, and the series was also reproduced in a smaller (21¼ inches x 6¾ inches*) size for an American restaurant chain. The *LNWR Brinklow canal* print in the same series was also reproduced (in 22 inches x 7 inches*) by the British Waterways Board – a slightly smaller size than the original series which was 23 inches x 7½ inches*. Again in the same series, the *Travel in 1865, West Coast Express at Shugborough Tunnel* was also reproduced, full size, for an anniversary of Wolverton Works. *[* picture size, excluding border]*. Various carriage maps have been reproduced over the years, however, and are clearly marked as such.

I am fortunate in having a copy of all the genuine prints and, by comparing the paper, colour, and type of lithographic process used, can differentiate quite easily between an original and a reproduction.

The future

It seems certain that the number of collectors of carriage prints and panels will continue to increase over the years. This observation is based on the growing interest shown in them by many people, including the general public who have little interest normally in old railway items. Whenever I have shown friends or visitors the pictures, I've been surprised at just how many people do have a fondness for them. Constant remarks such as . . . 'Oh I remember those when I used to travel to . . . ' or 'I used to like the one of . . . ' are often heard. I suppose it is not so surprising really – they must have been some of the most 'gazed at' pictures ever – even if they weren't always appreciated at the time.

You may be aware that the railways have, relatively recently, resurrected the idea of pictures in railway carriages, and the decor in many electric units now includes very simple drawings of locations by textile designer, Edward Pond, and other artists, which have been screen printed on to the coaches' veneer bulkheads. Whilst not really in the same category as the steam age, fine art panels, they are, at least, a move in the right direction. Who knows what will follow . . . Lowry's under the luggage racks?

Appendix A
Index of artists

There has only been one attempt at listing carriage panel artists before, and that was, ostensibly, for the Eastern Region series. This appeared in Cyril Bracegirdle's book *Collecting Railway Antiques* and was incorrect. The list omitted many artists, included erroneous ones and produced some interesting names, too – Lawson was shown as Rawson, Stringer became Sturger and poor Roy Badmin, the fine illustrator, became Badman! Much research has been undertaken in compiling the following data and the index should prove both comprehensive and helpful in providing some background information on the people behind the paintings. The years of birth and death of the artists are shown, where known.

Abbreviations used

Prefixes
A   Associate of
F   Fellow of
H   Hon. Member of
P   President of

Art Societies/Academies etc
BA	Bachelor of Arts
BPD	British Society of Poster Designers
BWS	British Water Colour Society
CSD	Chartered Society of Designers
MSIA	Member of the Society of Industrial Artists
NEAC	New English Art Club
NS	National Society
PS	Pastel Society
RA	Royal Academy
RBA	Royal Society of British Artists
RBC	Royal British Colonial Society of Artists
RBSA	Royal Birmingham Society of Artists
RCA	Royal College of Art
RE	Royal Society of Painter-Etchers and Engravers
RI	Royal Institute of Painters in Watercolours
RIBA	Royal Institute of British Architects
ROI	Royal Institute of Oil Painters
RSA	Royal Society of Arts
RSMA	Royal Society of Marine Artists (formerly SMA)
RSW	Royal Scottish Society of Painters in Watercolours
RWA	Royal West of England Academician
RWS	Royal Society of Painters in Watercolours
RWSAC	Royal Society of Alchemists & Chemists ?
SAI	Society of Architectural Illustrators
SMA	Society of Marine Artists (see also RSMA)
SGA	Society of Graphic Art
UA	United Artists
USA	United Society of Artists

Acanthus BA FRIBA 1909–   *Series* LNER
Real name was Frank Hoar. Architect, cartoonist in watercolour, lecturer in architecture. Born India 13/9/1909. Educated Plymouth College and London University. Studied art at Bartlett School of Architecture and Slade School. Lived in Ealing, London.

Aitken, John Earnest RSW RCA ARWA ARBC BWS 1881–1957 *Series* LNER
Painter of landscapes and coastal scenes. Born Liverpool. Son of James Aitken, a marine painter. Studied with his father and at Manchester and Liverpool Schools of Art. Lived many years on the Isle of Man. Painted regularly overseas. Widely exhibited. Died 15/6/57.

Allinson, Adrian Paul ROI RBA PS 1890-1959
Series (Southern Railway Prints)
Landscape painter, sculptor, poster designer. Born London 9/1/1890. Son of a doctor. Educated Wycliffe & Wrekin. Studied art at the Slade School under Tonks, Steer, Brown and Russell 1910–12, and won the Slade scholarship. Worked for a time in Munich and Paris. Teacher of painting and drawing at Westminster School of Art. Lived London. Died 20/2/1959.
Produced posters for GWR, SR & BR

Badmin, Stanley Roy RWS RE ARCA 1906–1989 *Series* LNER
Landscape watercolour artist, lithographer, illustrator & engraver. Born Sydenham, London 18/4/1906, son of a schoolmaster. Studied art at Camberwell School of Art and at RCA. Was art teacher and lecturer at Central School of Arts and Crafts. Elected to RWS in 1939. He illustrated several books including *British Countryside in Colour, The Seasons, Shell Guide to Trees and Shrubs* etc. Very elaborate style. Lived at Bignor, Sussex for some time.
Produced posters for BR

Baker, John L *Series* LNER
Landscape, portrait & equestrian artist in watercolour, illustrator and author. Born Birmingham and trained in art at Birmingham, W. Bromwich and later at the Slade School. Began career as teacher but turned to illustrating and writing, especially for the press. Lectured in architectural development. Wrote and illustrated *A Picture of Surrey* and *A Picture of Hampshire*. Lived Woking, Surrey and Broad Chalke, Wilts.

Baldwin, Frederick William SMA 1899–1980 *Series* LNER
Pencil, pen & watercolour artist. Born 17/3/1899, son of William Baldwin, a builder. Self taught. Draughtsman with 'Brook Marine', Lowestoft and lived at Beccles for many years before moving to Stoven, near Southwold, Suffolk. Was a regular exhibitor at the RA.

Barraud, Cyril H *Series* LNER (Original)/LNER (Intermediate)
Etcher, watercolour & poster artist. Lived Sidcup, Kent and Kensington, London. Exhibited 1912–34 at the RA.

Bee, John Francis 1895–   *Series* LNER/WR
Designer of stage settings, posters and showcards. Born at Wolverhampton. Studied art for four years in Europe and the Near East. Exhibited in Manchester and worked at Loughborough and Liverpool. His work was illustrated in *Commercial Art* and *Posters and Publicity*. His posters bore a distinctive capital 'B' monogram, but his carriage panel artwork carried his normal signature.
Produced posters for LNER & BR

Black, Montague Birrell 1884–19–   *Series* LMR(A)
Poster artist & illustrator. Born Stockwell, London 29/3/1884. Educated Stockwell College. Did military and naval artwork. Was artist war correspondent for *Toronto Star* 1900 40. Lived W.Derby, Liverpool and Harrow, Middx. Was a White Star Line artist and was renowned for his map posters for the railways over many years.
Produced posters for LNWR, M&GN, LNER, LMS, SR & BR

Blake, Frederick Donald RI NEAC 1908–1997 *Series* LNER/ScR
Painter in oils & watercolour, etcher, poster artist. Born 7/6/1908. Studied at Camberwell School of Arts & Goldsmiths College and also at the Brixton School of Building. Worked for International Artists Agency in London. A regular exhibitor at the RI. Lived Wimbledon, London for many years.
Produced posters for BR

Brenet, A *Series:* S. Region (C)
Research has produced no further information on this artist.

Buckle, Claude RI RSMA 1905–1973
Series LMR (Rly Arch)/ LMR(A) & (D)/S.Region (A) & (B)/WR
Painter in oils & watercolour, particularly marine subjects, poster designer. Born London 10/10/1905. Trained as an architect, specialising in industrial drawings., but turned to art in 1928. Was a member of Savages Art Club in Bristol. Produced commissioned artwork for the new nuclear power stations around the country. Achieved a prolific output of artwork for the railways. Painted many of his later subjects in France. Lived near Andover, Hampshire. Died in 1973.
Produced posters for GWR, LMS, SR & BR

Burley, David William MSIA 1901–19–
Series (Southern Rly adverts)
Painter in watercolour and oils of landscapes and seascapes, freelance. Born Greenwich, London 28/4/1901. Studied at Goldsmiths College of Art. Exhibited at various academies etc. Produced advertising artwork for the railways. Lived at Birchington on Sea, Kent.
Produced posters for SR & BR

Byatt, Edwin RI 1888–1948 *Series* LNER
Landscape painter in watercolour. Born 16/12/1888. Educated Wandsworth, London. Apprenticed for seven years to lithographic artist. Later a commercial artist and illustrator for James Haworth photographic studios and printers producing showcards. Lived Ewell, Surrey. Died 6/5/1948.
Produced posters for LNER

Cattermole, Lance Harry Mosse ROI 1898–   *Series* ScR
Painter in oils & watercolour. Born 19/7/1898, son of Sydney Cattermole, an artist, and grandson of George Cattermole (1800–68) – illustrator of *The Old Curiosity Shop* and other Charles Dickens works. Educated Worthing, Sussex and Odiham, Hants. Studied at Central School of Arts & Crafts 1922–23 and at the Slade School 1923-26. Lived near Worthing for many years. Represented in many museums and collections.
Produced posters for BR

Causer, William Sidney RI RBSA NS SMA 1876–1958
Series LNER
Painter of town scenes and landscapes mainly in watercolour. Born Wolverhampton and studied art at Wolverhampton School of Art, and in London and Italy. Held one man shows at the Leger Gallery & Fine Art Society. Painted widely in Spain and had to flee due to Civil War! Widely exhibited. Lived London, Kensington for many years. Died 18/12/1958.

Cobb, Charles David ROI PRSMA 1921– Series : LMR(B)
Marine painter in oils & gouache, writer. Associate Fellow of the Guild of Glass Engravers. Born Bromley, Kent 13/5/1921. Educated Nautical College, Pangbourne. Studied art under R.Borlase Smart. Exhibited widely abroad. Lived Brockenhurst, Hants for some years. President of the RSMA.
Produced posters for BR

Cowern, Raymond Teague RA RWS RE RWA RBSA ARCA 1913–1986 Series LNER
Painter in tempera & watercolour, etcher. Born 12/7/1913 and educated Birmingham. Studied at Central School of Art, Birmingham and RCA 1931-35. Later went to British School 1937-39. Became member of RWS in 1947. Is represented in several public collections. Lived Brighton for many years.

Denham, Henry James SMA SGA 1893– Series LNER
Painter in oil & watercolour of marine and figure subjects, illustrator. Born Bristol and studied at Bristol School of Art 1906-13 under John Fisher and R.E.J.Bush. Was painting and life master at the school 1913–23. Founder member of Wapping Group 1946. Lived at West Wickham, Kent.

Ellis, Cuthbert Hamilton 1909–1987 Series LMR (Travel–In)
Writer and illustrator. Educated Westminster, Munich and Oxford. First wrote for money at the age of 13. Wrote many books on railway subjects including 'British Railway History (1830-1947) in two volumes. Painted for illustration and exhibition and in later years reckons to have painted as much as he had written.

Fairclough, Wilfred RWS RE ARCA 1907–1996 Series LNER
Painter and engraver of landscapes & town scenes. Born 13/6/1907. Educated All Saints, Blackburn. Studied art at Royal College of Art 1931-4, and at British School at Rome 1934-7. Became fellow of RWS in 1967. Was principal of Kingston College of Art 1962-9 and lived at Kingston on Thames, Surrey for many years, producing many etchings in his later life. His works appear in several public collections and he exhibited abroad. Died 8/1/96.

Flint, Francis Murray Russell ROI SMA 1915–1977
Series LNER/WR
Landscape & coastal painter in oils & watercolour. Born 3/6/1915, son of Sir William Russell Flint, the famous artist (who also produced posters for the railways). Educated at Cheltenham College and HMS Conway. Studied art at Grosvenor School of Modern Art, at the RA Schools and in Paris. Was art master at Lancing College. Lived at Burgess Hill in Sussex and Coffinswell, S.Devon and London W8. Was Vice President of RWS. Died accidentally in Spain in 1977.

Gawthorn, Henry George SGA BPD 1879–1941
Series (Sketches for LNER adverts)
Painter, architect, lithographer, portrait painter. Born Northampton. Studied at Regent St Polytechnic and Heatherleys. Began his career as an architect but later turned to pictorial art. Wrote several books on poster design and exhibited from 1917 to 1934. Lived London.
Produced posters for LNER.

Gray, Alan Series S.Region (B)
Lived in Ilford, Essex. Exhibited at RA in 1949.
Research has produced no further information on this artist.

Greene, John A ARCA Series LMR(D)
Artist in oil and watercolour, lecturer. Studied art at the RCA. Lecturer at the Architectural Association School from 1946. Produced work for I.C.I. and the British Transport Commission. Lived at Bordon, Hants.
Produced posters for BR

Haslehust, Ernest William RI RBA RWA RBC 1866–1949
Series LNER
Landscape painter chiefly in watercolour, illustrator. Born Walthamstow 12/11/1866. Educated Manor House, Hastings and Felsted. Studied art at Slade School under Legros. Represented in several public collections. Principal works include *The Bridge nr Arundel* and *A Devon Estuary*. He illustrated the *Beautiful Britain* series of books and produced posters. President of Midland Sketch Club and vice president Kent County Chess Association. Lived in S.London for many years. Died 3/7/1949.
Produced posters for LMS, LNER

Hilder, Rowland PRI RSMA 1905–1993 Series LNER
Landscape & marine painter, illustrator, author. Born 28/6/1905 at Great Neck, Long Island, USA, of British parents. Educated at Morristown, New Jersey. Settled England 1915 and studied at Goldsmiths College School of Art under E.J.Sullivan 1922-25. Work was first selected for RA in 1923 when only 18. Married Edith Blenkiron, also a painter. Represented in several public collections here and abroad and is renowned for his paintings of Kentish oast houses. Was President of RI 1964-74. Illustrated many books incl. *Moby Dick* 1926, *Treasure Island* 1930, *The Shell Guide to Flowers of the Countryside* etc. Designed *National Savings* and *Shell Oil* posters and illustrated the *Army Manual on Camouflage*. Wrote books on watercolour technique and an autobiography *Rowland Hilder, Painter & Illustrator*. Lived in Blackheath, London for many years. Died April 1993.
Produced posters for SR

Hill Adrian RBA RI ROI 1897–1977 Series (LNER adverts)
Painter, etcher, illustrator. Born Charlton, Kent. Studied at St.Johns Wood 1912-14 and RCA 1919-20. Official War artist 1917-19. Elected RBA 1926, RI 1928, ROI 1931. Exhibited at RA and other galleries regularly. Presented BBC TV "Sketch Club". Lived London, Haslemere and Midhurst, Surrey.

Holding, Edgar Thomas RWS 1876–1952 Series LNER
Landscape painter in oils & watercolour. Born 7/3/1876 at Horncastle, Lincs. Spent some years in business then took up painting full time. Became member of RWS in 1929. Represented in several public collections. Was President of the RWS Art Club. His work was illustrated in *English Rivers and Canals* and other publications. Lived for many years at Sutton, nr Pulborough, Sussex. Died 29/7/1952.

Hubbard, Eric Hesketh PRBA ROI RBC ARWA 1892–1957
Series (SR Prints)
Landscape & architectural painter, etcher & furniture designer. Born 16/11/1892 in London. Educated Felsted School. Studied art at Heatherleys, Croydon School of Art and Chelsea Polytechnic. Member of many art societies. Represented in many public collections, home and abroad. Published a number of books including *Colour Block Print Making* and *Architectural Painting in Oils*. Founder and director of Forest Press. Lived Croydon, Surrey; Salisbury, Hants and later in London. Died 16/4/1957.
Produced posters for LMS, GWR & SR

Jordan, Reginald Ernest 1904–1983 Series LNER
Painter in watercolour & oils; photographer. Born 31/3/1904 Queens Park, London. Studied at St. Martin's School of Art, London. Served in the Royal Marines as a photographer and worked as a schoolteacher in Kent. Lived Stourbridge, Worcs. and Chelmsford, Essex. Died 17/10/1983.

King, Charles Series LNER
Landscape painter in oils, poster artist.
Produced posters for LMS & BR
Research has produced no further information on this artist.

King, John W 1893– Series (Sketches for LNER adverts)
Figure & domestic painter. Widely exhibited. Lived Scarborough and St Ives, Hunts. Exhibited at RA.

Knight, Charles RWS ROI 1901–1990 Series LMR(B)
Landscape painter in watercolour & oils. Born Hove 27/8/1901. Father was keen amateur artist and naturalist. Studied Brighton College of Art,(and later lectured there), the RA Schools under Sickert and at the RCA. Represented in many public collections including British Museum. Designed Inn Signs and was asked by Queen Mother to teach Princess Margaret to paint 1944-47. Was elected to RWS in 1935 and was vice president 1961-64. Lived at Ditchling, Sussex for much of his life. Died 15/5/1990.

Lampitt, Ronald Series LMR(C)
Painter of landscapes in oils & watercolour, poster designer. Worked for Artists Partners Agency in London. Lived Hampstead, London.
Produced posters for GWR & BR

Lander, Reginald Montague MSIA 1913– Series LMR(C,D)/WR
Freelance commercial artist in gouache and watercolour, poster designer. Born London 18/8/1913. Educated Clapham Central School and studied art at Hammersmith School of Art. Chief designer and studio manager at Ralph Mott Studio (1930-9). Worked for Government Ministries and British Transport Commission. Lived New Malden, Surrey.
Produced posters for GWR, LNER & BR

Langhammer Series S.Region(C)
Worked for International Artists Agency.
Produced posters for BR
Research has produced no further information on this artist.

Lawson, Edward Series ScR
Landscape artist in watercolour.
Research has produced no further information on this artist.

Lee–Hankey, William RWS RI ROI RE NS 1869–1952
Series LNER(Intermediate)
Painter and etcher of landscapes and portraits. Born 28/3/1869 at Chester. Studied at Chester School of Art under Walter Schroeder, at the RCA and also in Paris. Served with Artist's Rifles 1915–19. Exhibited at most principal London galleries. President of London Sketch Club 1903-4. Represented in many public collections, home and abroad and was a considerable contributor to RWS exhibitions. Won gold medal at Barcelona International Exhibition and bronze medal at Chicago. Lived and worked in France for some time then London. Became member of RWS in 1936, aged 67 and vice president in 1947. Died 10/2/1952.
Produced posters for LNER

Macleod, William Douglas 1892–1963 *Series* ScR
Landscape painter in oils & pastels, etcher & cartoonist. Born Clarkston, Renfrewshire 1/1/1892. Educated Greenock Academy. Worked in bank 1906-15 and was then in Royal Artillery. Took up art and studied at Glasgow School of Art 1919-23 under Griffenhagen. Cartoonist for *Glasgow Evening News* 1920-30. Etched views abroad. Represented in a few public collections. Lived Lenzie, Dunbartonshire.
Produced posters for BR.

Macfarlane, Alasdair 1902–1960 *Series* ScR
Born Tiree 1902; Gaelic speaking, later bilingual. Lived Glasgow. Joined Clyde Navigation Trust in 1929. Exhibited 1932–7. Served with Ministry of War Trasport in London 1940–45. Produced ship drawings for Glasgow 'Evening Times' 1950–60. Produced posters for BR

Macpherson, Alexander RSW 1904–1970 *Series* LNER
Scottish landscape painter in watercolour, especially around Arran, Scotland. Lived Paisley, Glasgow and Wembley, Middx. Exhibited at RA in 1934.

Maddox, Ronald PRI FCSD FSAI 1930– *Series* LMR(C)
Landscape artist, illustrator, designer. Born Purley, Surrey 5/10/1930. Educated Barnsbury Secondary School. Studied art at St Albans School of Art, London College of Printing and Graphic Arts. Freelance from 1962. Designer of British stamps. Represented in many collections. Is currently President of RI. Lives at Welwyn, Herts.
Produced posters for BR

Marston, Freda RBA ROI RBC 1895–1949 *Series* LNER
Painter & etcher of landscapes & figures. Born Hampstead 24/10/1895 (nee Clulow). Educated, Hampstead, London. Studied art at Regent St Polytechnic in Italy and under Terrick Williams 1916-20. Married Reginald St Clair Marston in 1922. Represented in several public collections. She was the only woman artist commissioned by the railway for carriage prints. Lived Amberley, Sussex and later at Robertsbridge. Died 27/3/1949 Produced posters for LMS & BR

Mason, Frank Henry RI RBA 1875–1965
Series LNER (Original) LNER/WR
Marine painter in oil & watercolour, etcher, illustrator, author & poster designer. Born Seaton Carew, Co Durham 1/10/75. Son of a railway clerk. Educated at HMS Conway and followed the sea for a time as a ships engineer. Later engaged in engineering and shipbuilding at Leeds and Hartlepool. Travelled abroad extensively and painted many subjects in watercolour. Served 1914-18 as Lieutenant in the RNVR in N.Sea and Egypt. Studied under Albert Strange at the Scarborough School of Art. Member of RBA 1904, RI 1929. Exhibited at the RA from 1900 and achieved a prolific output of artwork for the railways. Lived at Scarborough, then London. Represented in several public collections.
Produced posters for NER, GNR, LMS, LNER, GWR & BR

Maxwell, Donald 1877–1936 *Series* (SR Prints)
Painter, illustrator & writer. Educated Manor House School, Clapham Common and studied S.Kensington, London and Slade School 1897. Was naval correspondent of the *Graphic* for 20 years. Official artist to the Admiralty, World War One. Accompanied the Prince of Wales on his tour of India and illustrated many guides and books. Lived Twickenham, Middx, Rochester and Maidstone, Kent.
Produced posters for GWR, LMS & SR

Mercer, Sidney Agnew FRSA 19? –1972 *Series:* LNER
Painter of landscapes in watercolour. Elected to Royal Society of Arts in 1936. Lived at Harrogate, Yorkshire.
Produced posters for BR

Merriott, Jack RI ROI PS SMA 1901–1968
Series LNER/LMR(A)/ S.Region(A)/ScR/WR
Landscape & portrait painter in oil & watercolour, poster designer. Born 15/11/1901. Educated Greenwich Central School. Studied at Croydon School of Art and at St Martins School of Art. Lectured in Royal Army Education Corps (1945-6). President of Wapping Group of artists 1947-60. Lived at Shirley in Surrey, Storrington, Sussex and later at Polperro, Cornwall. Lectured widely on watercolour. Was vice president of RI and achieved a prolific output of artwork for the railways.
Produced posters for BR

Mills, Arthur George 1907– *Series* WR
Portrait painter in oil, poster designer. Born 25/5/1907. Educated at Walthamstow Technical School. Studied at Leyton Art School, at the Central School of Arts & Crafts, and at the Camberwell School of Art 1927-29. Produced many posters for the Royal Society for Accident Prevention. Lived London.
Produced posters for BR

Moody, John Charles RI RE PSGA 1884–1962 *Series* LNER
Painter & etcher of landscapes, figures & architectural subjects. Born 21/6/1884 at Walton on Thames, Surrey. Studied art at London, Paris, Antwerp and Italy. Was President of Society of Sussex Artists 1954 and also President of the Society of Graphic Artists. Principal of Hornsey School of Arts & Crafts 1926-47. Lived London then Burpham, nr Arundel, Sussex.
Produced posters for LNER & BR

Mortelmans, Edward Major *Series* LMR(History)
Artist in gouache and watercolour, illustrator. Worked for Artists Partners Ltd at Hyde Park, London. Illustrated books. Exhibited at RA in 1945. Lived at Holloway, London.
Produced posters for London Transport.

Muncaster, Claude Grahame RWS ROI RBA SMA 1903–1974
Series LNER
Painter in oil & watercolour; etcher of landscapes, town scenes & marines, lecturer & writer. Born 4/7/1903 at W.Chiltington, Sussex, son of Oliver Hall (RA). Educated at Queen Elizabeth School, Cranbrook. Elected a member of RWS in 1936. In November 1945 he adopted above name by deed poll but had exhibited under that name from 1923, and previously as Grahame Hall. First one-man show at the Fine Art Society 1926. Wrote book *Rolling round the Horn*, pub.1933 telling of his four month voyage from Australia- Britain. Represented in many public collections. Wrote several books on art. Lived near Pulborough, Sussex.
Produced posters for GWR & LMS

Patrick, James McIntosh RSA ROI ARE 1907–1998
Series LNER/ ScR
Landscape & portrait artist in oil & watercolour, etcher. Born 4/2/1907 in Dundee, son of an architect. Studied at Glasgow School of Art under Griffenhagen (1924-8) and in Paris. Worked for Valentines Cards. Received Guthrie award in 1935. Exhibited at the Fine Art Society and represented in many public collections, including the Tate Gallery. Based in Dundee for many years. Died 7/4/98
Produced posters for LNER & BR

Rushbury, Sir Henry George RA RWS RE 1889–1968
Series LNER(Intermediate)/LNER
Painter in watercolour, etcher & draughtsman of architectural subjects. Born 28/10/1889 at Harborne, Birmingham. Studied stained glass design and mural decoration at Birmingham College of Art 1903-09, later working as assistant to Henry Payne (RWS). Settled London 1912. First one-man show held at Grosvenor Gallery in 1921. Studied Slade School for 6 months under Tonks. Became member of RWS in 1926. Worked home and abroad and represented in many public collections. Created CVO 1955, CBE 1960, KCVO 1964. Lived London, Sussex and Essex.
Produced posters for LMS, LNER & BR

Russell, Gyrth RI ROI SMA 1892–1970 *Series* LNER/WR
Printer, etcher of landscapes & marine subjects. Born Dartmouth, Nova Scotia on 13/4/1892. Son of Benjamin Russell, Judge of Supreme Court, Nova Scotia. Studied art at Boston USA, also Paris at the Academie Julian and Artelier Colarossi 1912-14. Represented in several public collections. Was official war artist with the Canadian Army during World War One. Lived at Topsham, Devon and later at Penarth, Glamorgan and Sussex. Died 8/12/1970.
Produced posters for GWR & BR

Sawyer *Series* LMR(History)
Artist in gouache and watercolour. Worked for Artists Partners Ltd in Hyde Park, London.
Research has produced no further information on this artist.

Scott, Eric Ronald 1904–1960 *Series* LNER
Painter of landscapes in watercolour. Born 12/1/1904, Madras, India. Came to England 1925. Trained as an eletrical engineer Started painting in 1933. Lived Bromley, Kent, and Walberswick Suffolk from 1950. Exhibited at RA 1935, 1949. Full-time artist from 1950. Died 10/7/1960.

Sherwin, Frank RI RSMA BWS 1896–19
Series LNER/LMR (B)/ S.Region(B)/WR/ScR
Marine & landscape painter in oil & watercolour, poster design-er. Born Derby 19/5/1896, son of Samuel Sherwin (painter). Educated Derby and studied at Derby School of Art and at Heatherleys 1920. Exhibited from 1926 to 1940. Lived at Cookham, Berks for many years. Achieved a prolific output of art for the railways.
Produced posters for GWR, LMS, LNER & BR

Silas, Ellis UA 1883–1972 *Series* LMR(A)
Marine & landscape painter in oil & watercolour, poster and stained glass artist. Born London, son of Louis F. Silas, a decorative artist and founder member of the United Artists; and grandson of Edouard Silas, a composer. Studied art under his father and Walter Sickert. He was war artist for the Australian government 1914-18 and spent 3 years in Papua painting and collecting curios which he described in his book *A Primitive Arcadia*. President of the London Sketch Club 1930. Lived in London many years. Exhibited regularly at the RA, ROI and RI. Died in 1972.
Produced posters for BR

Squirrell, Leonard Russell RWS RE RI PS SGA 1893–1979
Series LNER
Painter & etcher of landscapes & architectural subjects, writer. Born Ipswich 30/10/1893. Educated at British School, Ipswich and studied at Ipswich School of Art under G.Rushton and at Slade School. Won British Institution Scholarship in engraving 1915. Received gold medals at the International Print Makers Exhibitions in Los Angeles in 1925 & 1930, and silver in 1923. Represented in many collections, home and abroad. Transferred from the RI to the RWS during his career. Published *Landscape Painting in Pastel* 1938, and *Practice in Watercolour* 1950. Lived near Ipswich and was founder member of the Ipswich Art Club. His son, Martin, was also a painter (1926-50).
Produced posters for BR

Steel, Kenneth RBA SGA 1906–1970
Series: LNER/LMR (Rly Arch.)/ScR
Painter in watercolour, engraver & lithographer of landscapes & street scenes; poster designer. Born Sheffield 9/7/1906, son of G.T.Steel, an artist and silver engraver. Studied at Sheffield College of Art under Anthony Betts. Represented in several public collections. Achieved a prolific output of artwork for the railways. Based in Crookes, Sheffield for years.
Produced posters for LNER & BR

Stringer, Henry *Series* LNER
Landscape artist in watercolour. Lived at Welwyn Garden City, Hertfordshire.
Produced posters for BR
Research has produced no further information on this artist.

Taylor, Fred RI 1875–1963
Series: LNER/ (Sketches for LNER Adverts)
Landscape & architectural painter in watercolour, poster designer. Born London 22/3/1875. Educated at St John the Evangelist. Studied art at Paris at the Academie Julian, at Goldsmiths College School (awarded gold medal for posters) and in Italy. Worked at the Waring and Gillow studio. In 1930 designed four ceiling paintings for the Underwriting Room at Lloyds, London. Worked on naval camouflage during World War II. Renowned for his topographical accuracy and his prolific output, especially for the railways. Represented in several public collections and exhibited at the RA. Lived in London for many years.
Produced posters for MR, GWR, LMS, LNER, BR & London Transport, Empire Marketing Board and several shipping companies.

Tittensor, Harry RI 1887–1942 *Series* LNER
Painter in watercolour of landscapes & figure subjects. Exhibited at RI, RA, and Fine Art Society. Lived at Wolstanton, Stoke on Trent.
Produced posters for LNER

Walker, Edward ARCA 1879–19– *Series* LNER
Painter in watercolour, oil & tempera of landscapes & town scenes. Poster designer, craftworker. Born Bradford 17/1/1879. Studied at Bradford College of Art 1895-1900, and at RCA 1900– 06. Worked widely in Europe. Lived for a time in Scarborough, Yorks. Was head of design department in Sheffield Technical School and was Headmaster of Scarborough School of Art.

Ward, Richard *Series* S.Region(B)
Landscape artist in watercolour. Lived Grantham and Canterbury.
Research has produced no further information on this artist.

Watson, James Fletcher RI RBA 1913– *Series* LNER
Architect; painter in watercolour of landscapes & architectural subjects, author. Born 25/7/1913 at Coulsdon, Surrey. Educated Eastbourne College. Studied at RA School of Architecture where he won a silver medal for design in 1936. Received an Hon. mention at the Paris Salon. Has mainly worked in Norfolk, Gloucestershire, Radnor, Brecon and Cumberland. Has written several popular books on watercolour painting. Represented in several public collections. Lived at Wymondham, Norfolk and then near Burford, Oxon.

Whitear, A R *Series* LMR(History)
Artist in gouache and watercolour. Worked for Artists Partners Ltd in Hyde Park, London. Lived at Tewin, Hertfordshire. Research has produced no further information on this artist.

Wilkinson, Norman [C.B.E.] PRI RBA ROI RSMA HRWS 1878–1971 *Series* (LMS Prints)
Artist in oil, watercolour and dry point, usually of marine subjects but also landscapes, author, illustrator & poster artist. Born Cambridge 24/11/1878 and educated at Berkhamsted School. Studied art at Portsmouth & Southsea School of Art where he later taught. Contributed to *Illustrated London News* from 1898 for a long time. Worked under Louis Grier in Cornwall. Made important contribution in World War One by inventing 'dazzle camouflage'. Travelled extensively by sea. Produced posters for the LNWR from 1905 and later achieved a prolific output for the LMS. Was marine painter to the Royal Yacht Squadron in 1919. Awarded C.B.E. in 1948. Well represented in public collections. Lived London and worked into his nineties. Died 30/5/1971.
Produced posters for LNWR, GER, LMS, LNER, SR & BR

Wilson, A J *Series* LNER
Landscape painter. Exhibited 1924-26. Lived Stapleford, Notts and Nottingham. Worked for Artists Partners Agency in Hyde Park, London.
Produced posters for BR

Winslade *Series* LMR(History)
Painter in gouache and watercolour. Worked for Artists Partners Agency at Hyde Park, London.
Research has produced no further information on this artist.

Wood, Leslie John FRIBA 190?–1971 *Series* LNER
Architect, painter in watercolour of landscapes. Joined RIBA in 1936 and became a Fellow in 1945. Lived Hendon, London.

Wootton, Frank OBE 1914–1998 *Series:* WR
Landscape painter in oil & watercolour, poster designer, author, illustrator. Born Milford, Hants 30/7/1911. Studied at Eastbourne School of Art. Was president of the Guild of Aviation Artists. Author of *How to draw Cars* and *How to draw Aircraft*. Official artist to the R.A.F. 1944-46. Lived in Alciston, Sussex. Founder president of the Guild of Aviation Artists. Died 21/4/98
Produced posters for GWR & BR

Wright, Horace FRSA UOA RWGAC 1888–1960 *Series* LNER
Pharmacist, artist in watercolour, pencil and pen of old street landscapes, illustrator. Born Stamford, Lincs 21/4/1888. Educated at Eversley, Stamford. Studied art at Press Art School. Was a respected chemist and businessman in Edgware, iddlesex. Elected to RSA in 1944. Exhibited at RA. Illustrated books in the *Garden of England* series. Died 12/9/1960.

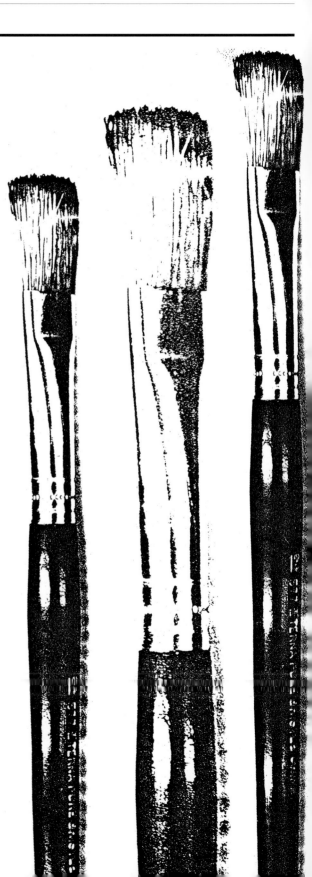

Appendix B
Listing of prints by series

Carriage prints can be divided into two categories:

Standard format – the numerous, unmounted, prints with integral titles and white borders which were issued in the two sizes (A & B) shown below. This design was first used by the LNER and was later adopted by BR.
Non-standard format – any exception to above i.e. early mounted prints etc.

The railways do not appear to have kept records of the prints they issued so the listings have largely been the result of extensive detective work! However, with the possible exception of one or two missing (pre–war) prints in the huge LNER series, I am satisfied that all the standard format series lists are now complete. Incidentally, the titles of the series are purely my own inventions in order to make identification a little easier. The approximate year of issue of each series is shown under the title or, in the case of the long–running LNER series, is shown alongside each individual subject. Each print's full title is shown except in the case of the LMR *Travel-In* and *History* series, where some abridgement was necessary.

Where original paintings are known to exist, these are also indicated after the print subject (see key below).
N.B. No attempt has been made to list the photographic panel views. Countless numbers were issued from pre-grouping days until nationalisation in all shapes and sizes and no official records seem to remain of the subject titles.

Key to listings

Standard format:

A 25" x 10" (panel size) 23" x 7½" (picture image).
B 20" x 10" (panel size) 16" x 6" (picture image).

Non standard format:

C 14" x 9" (size including mount) 11¼" x 7¼" (print size).
D 17½"-16" x 10". Borderless. The S. Region (A) series also appeared in this format occasionally.
E 25" x 10". Borderless. These were often folded or trimmed in order to fit the size B panels.
F 27¼" x 11¾"

Original artwork

▲ Owned by private collectors.
■ Owned by the National Railway Museum, York.

Standard format print series

LMR Travel–in series . . .
Size: A   Issued: 1951
C Hamilton Ellis
1835 Leicester & Swannington Railway Train hauled by 'Samson'. ■
1840 Old Station at Derby, North Midland Railway. ■
1845 Express Mail Train of the London & Birmingham Railway. ■
1850 LNWR Train, Crampton loco "Courier" at Sandbach. ■
1855 Maryport and Carlisle Railway Train, Crampton No 12. ■
1860 LNWR Holyhead-Dun Laoghaire Paddle Steamer 'Cambria'. ■
1865 Blackpool-Manchester Train of the L&Y Railway near Kirkham. ■
1865 West Coast Express, Large Bloomer at Shugborough Tunnel. ■
1870 North London Railway Train for Broad Street at Richmond. ■
1875 LNWR Northbound Tourist Express near Brinklow. ■
1880 MR Express with Pullman Car, on the way to St Pancras. ■
1885 Furness Railway Steamer 'Gondola' on Lake Coniston. ■
1885 North Staffs Railway up Manchester Express near Stoke. ■
1890 West Lancs Railway Train, 'Blackburn' on way to Southport. ■
1895 East & West Junction Railway Train at Stratford on Avon. ■
1895 Wirral Railway Train on the way to Birkenhead. ■
1900 L&Y Railway Liverpool Express at Walkden Troughs. ■
1905 Leek & Manifold Valley Railway Train at Wettonmill. ■
1905 MR Manchester Express with Loco 1000, near Millers Dale. ■
1910 Coniston Steam Motor Train, Furness Railway. ■
1910 LNWR Bus in Watford High Street. ■
1915 Electric Tram on the Burton and Ashby Light Railways. ■
1915 North Staffordshire Railway Train entering Stone Junction. ■
1920 Furness Railway Train entering Ulverston Station. ■
     Complete Set (24)

LMR Railway Architecture series
Size: A   Issued: 1952
Claude Buckle
Conway Tubular Bridge, North Wales. ▲
Curzon Street Goods Depot, Birmingham. ▲
Ditton Viaduct, Lancashire. ▲
The Entrance to Euston Station, London.
Leeds City Station Concourse. ▲
Nash Mills Bridge, Hertfordshire. ▲
South Portals of Primrose Hill Tunnels, London. ▲
St Pancras Station, London. ▲
Kenneth Steel
Britannia Tubular Bridge, North Wales. ▲
Citadel Station, Carlisle.
Monsal Dale Viaduct, Derbyshire.
Red Hill Tunnels, Trent.
Ribblehead Viaduct, Yorkshire.
Runcorn Bridge.
The School of Transport, Derby. ▲
Wolverton Viaduct. ▲
     Complete Set (16)

LMR series (A)
Size: A   Issued: 1950
Montague B Black
Abergele, Denbighshire.
Blaneau Festiniog, Merionethshire.
Deganwy, Caernarvonshire.
Rhosneigr, Anglesey.
Claude Buckle
Bedford.
Lichfield, Staffordshire.
Newby Bridge, Lancashire.

St Asaph, Flintshire.
Jack Merriott
Berkhamsted, Hertfordshire.
Cromford, Derbyshire.
Edale, Derbyshire.
Fenny Compton, Warwickshire.
Ellis Silas
Appleby, Westmorland.
Harpenden, Hertfordshire.
Nevin, Caernarvonshire.
Rolleston-on-Dove, Staffordshire.
     Complete Set (16).

LMR series (B)
Size: A   Issued: Approx 1952
David Cobb
Arnside, Westmorland.
Beaumaris, Anglesey.
Lake Windermere, Lake District. ▲
Ravenglass, Cumberland.
Charles Knight
Brackley, Northamptonshire.
Crafnant Valley, Caernarvonshire.
Eccleston Ferry, Cheshire. ■
Knutsford, Cheshire.
Llanwrst, Denbighshire.
Ormskirk, Lancashire.
Frank Sherwin
Ashbourne, Derbyshire.
Coniston Water. Lake District.
Ingleton Village, Yorkshire.
Market Harborough, Leicestershire.
     Complete Set (14)

LMR series (C)
Size: A   Issued: 1957
Ronald Lampitt
Bramall Hall near Bramhall, Cheshire.
Bredon Village, Worcestershire.
Little Moreton Hall, near Congleton, Cheshire.
Speke Hall near Liverpool. ▲
R Lander
The Lledr Valley, near Betws-Y-Coed, North Wales ▲
Penrhyn Castle, near Bangor, North Wales ▲
Ronald A Maddox
Old Bridge House, Ambleside, Westmorland.
Sizergh Castle, near Kendal, Westmorland.
Townend, near Ambleside, Westmorland.
Wordsworth's House, Cockermouth, Cumberland.
     Complete Set (10)

LMR series (D)
Sizes: A and B   Issued: 1957
Claude Buckle
MV Cambria, B.R. Holyhead-Dun Laoghaire service.
MV Swan, B.R. Lake Windermere service.
TSS Duke of Lancaster, BR Heysham-Belfast service.
Greene
The Langdale Valley near Ambleside, Lake District. ▲
The Lune Valley near Tebay, Westmorland. ▲
R Lander
The Conway River and Conway Castle, North Wales.
The Groves and River Dee at Chester.
     Complete Set (7)

LMR History series
Size: B   Issued: 1955
Edward Mortelmans
Capture of Henry VI, 1460 at Northampton by Duke of York. ▲
Edgar, King of the English on the Dee at Chester, AD 973. ▲
Elizabeth Fry at Newgate Prison, London in 1813. ▲
Famous Samuel Johnson was born in Lichfield in 1709. ▲
In 1715 Jacobite army marched; defeated at Preston. ▲
In 1854 Florence Nightingale, at Lea Hurst, Derbyshire. ▲
In 1875 P.M. Disraeli, London bought shares in Suez Canal. ▲
King Henry VIII annuls marriage at Dunstable Abbey in 1533. ▲
Peasants revolt in 1381 against poll tax at Smithfield, London. ▲
Scene in Temple Gardens, London, – led to Wars of the Roses. ▲
Sir Walter Scott, married in Carlisle Cathedral, 1797. ▲
Sir Richard Arkwright b.1732, Cotton Machine, Nottingham. ▲
Sawyer
Edward I holding Parliament at Ashridge, near Berkhamsted, 1291. ▲
Lady Jane Grey, at Bradgate House, Leicester in early 1550's. ▲
St Comgall settled in Bangor Co. Down, Ireland in AD 555. ▲
Samuel Pepys, diarist watching the great fire of London, 1666. ▲
Charles I setting up his standard at Nottingham Castle, 1642. ▲
John Bunyan (1628-88) spent many years in Bedford Prison. ▲
Last battle on English soil was fought at Clifton, Westmorland, 1745. ▲
Wigan was Charles I's H.Q. for the North West in Civil War, 1651. ▲
John Peel, the man whose fame as a fox hunter in Lake District. ▲
Poet William Wordsworth (1770-1850) was born in Lakeland. ▲
Robert the Bruce, storming Castle Rushen, Isle of Man, 1313. ▲
Cromwell, Lord Protector, dissolving parliament, 1653 (London). ▲
A R Whitear
Conspirators in Gunpowder Plot 1605 at Ashby St Ledgers. ▲
Edward V, the boy King arrested at Stony Stratford in 1483. ▲
Albanus, a Roman officer – our first martyr at St Albans, AD 303. ▲
Francis Bacon, philosopher and essayist lived at St Albans. ▲
Romans 20th Legion based on Deva (Chester) 2000 years ago. ▲
Richard the III at Leicester, before being slain at Bosworth, 1485. ▲
Edward I and his Queen, Eleanor of Castile at Conway Castle. ▲
A jousting tournament at the Castle of Ashby De La Zouch. ▲
Edward I hawking at Rhuddlan Castle, built in 11th century. ▲
Mary Queen of Scots in 1570 at Chatsworth Place (Derbys). ▲
Tynwald Hill in the Isle of Man, derives its name from. . . . ▲
In 1788, William Wilberforce the British reformer . . . (London). ▲
Winslade
Thomas Wolsey, Cardinal & Statesman, Leicester Abbey, 1530. ▲
Robin Hood, legendary outlaw of Sherwood Forest, Notts. ▲
Heroic defence, 1645 of Lathom House, Ormskirk, by Charlotte. ▲
Robert Dudley, Earl of Leicester at Kenilworth Castle, 1562. ▲
William Caxton with his printing press at Westminster, 1476. ▲
At St Albans in 1455 was the first battle of the Wars of the Roses. ▲
Charles I at the top of the Phoenix Tower in city walls of Chester. ▲
William the Conqueror, offered crown of England at Berkhamsted. ▲
Henry Tudor proclaimed Henry VII, Battle of Bosworth, 1485. ▲
First Prince of Wales, presented at Caernarvon Castle, 1301. ▲
According to Legend, Lady Godiva rode naked through Coventry. ▲
Crown jewels were stolen by Colonel Blood, 1671 (London). ▲
    Complete Set (48)

LNER series
Size: B   Issued: (see individual prints)

Acanthus

Blakeney, Norfolk.	1948-55
Overy Staithe, Norfolk.	1948-55

John E Aitken RSW.

Dirleton Village, East Lothian, Scotland.	1948-55
East Linton, East Lothian, Scotland.	1948-55

S R Badmin RWS

Alnmouth, Northumberland.	1945-7
Berwick-on-Tweed, Northumberland.	1945-7
Croxdale Viaduct, near Durham.	1945-7
Kelso, Roxburghshire.	1945-7
Welwyn Viaduct, Hertfordshire.	1945-7
Yarm, Yorkshire.	1945-7

John L Baker

London, Horse Guards, Whitehall.	1948-55
London, Tower Bridge.	1948-55

F W Baldwin

Aldeburgh, Suffolk.	1948-55
Beccles, Suffolk.	1948-55
Bury St Edmunds, Suffolk.	1948-55
Cavendish, Suffolk.	1948-55
Cromer, Norfolk.	1948-55
Debenham, Suffolk.	1948-55
Felixstowe, Suffolk.	1948-55
Great Yarmouth, Norfolk. ▲	1948-55
Halesworth, Suffolk.	1948-55
Laxfield, near Halesworth, Suffolk.	1948-55
Leiston Abbey, Suffolk.	1948-55
Lowestoft, Suffolk. ▲	1948-55
Saffron Walden, Essex. ▲	1948-55
Southwold, Suffolk. ▲	1948-55
St Osyth Priory near Clacton-on-Sea, Essex.	1948-55
Thaxted, near Elsenham, Essex.	1948-55

John Bee

Sulgrave Manor near Helmdon, Northants.	1945-7
Town Bridge, Stamford, Lincs.	1945-7

F Donald Blake

Braintree, Essex.	1945-55
Bridlington, Yorkshire. ▲	1948-55
Bury St Edmunds, Suffolk.	1945-55
Finchingfield, Essex.	1945-55
Gorleston-on-Sea, Norfolk.	1948-55
Great Easton, Dunmow, Essex.	1945-55
The Roosevelt Memorial, London.	1945-55

Edwin Byatt RI

Constable Country (Flatford Bridge and Cottage)	1937-9
Durham Cathedral.	1937-9
Edinburgh.	1937-9
Rievaulx Abbey.	1937-9

Sidney Causer RI

Beverley Minster, Yorkshire.	1945-7
Durham.	1945-7
Edinburgh.	1945-7
Wakefield Chantry, Yorkshire.	1945-7

R T Cowern RWS

St Johns College from Trinity Bridge, Cambridge.	1948-55
Trinity Great Court, Cambridge.	1948-55

Henry J Denham SMA/SGA

Blythburgh, near Halesworth, Suffolk. ▲	1948-55
Maldon, Essex.	1948-55

W Fairclough

High Wycombe, Buckinghamshire.	1945-7
Welbeck Abbey, Nottinghamshire. ▲	1945-7

Francis R Flint ROI/SMA

St Ives, Huntingdonshire.	1948-55
Tilbury Hailing Station, Essex. ▲	1948-55

E W Haslehust RI

Braemar Castle, Aberdeenshire. ▲	1937-9
Byland Abbey, Yorkshire. ▲	1937-9
High Force, Teesdale. ▲	1937-9
Loch Shiel, Inverness-shire.	1937-9

Rowland Hilder RI

Ben Nevis, Inverness-shire.	1937-9
Brightlingsea, Essex.	1937-9
Ely Cathedral.	1937-9
Lavenham, Suffolk.	1937-9
Loch Lomond.	1937-9
Robin Hood's Bay, Yorkshire.	1937-9
Whitby, Yorkshire.	1937-9
Yorkshire Dales.	1937-9

E T Holding RWS

Great Yarmouth, Norfolk. ▲	1945-7
Grimsby, Lincolnshire. ▲	1945-7
Hull, Entrance to Victoria Dock. ▲	1945-7
Lowestoft, Suffolk. ▲	1945-7
Sunderland, Co Durham.	1945-7

R E Jordan

Cley, near Holt, Norfolk. ▲	1948-55
Ely, Cambridgeshire.	1948-55

Charles King

Harwich, Essex. ▲	1953
Leigh-on-Sea, Essex.	1953
Pinmill, near Ipswich, Suffolk.	1953
Westcliff-on-Sea, Essex.	1953

Alexander Macpherson RSW

Loch Long, Dunbartonshire.	1945-7

Freda Marston ROI

Boston, Lincolnshire.	1945-7
Coxwold, Yorkshire.	1945-7
Deeping St James, Lincolnshire.	1945-7
Duncombe Park, Yorkshire.	1945-7
Lastingham, Yorkshire.	1945-7
Lincolnshire Wolds, near Horncastle.	1945-7
Rievaulx Abbey, Yorkshire.	1945-7
Tattershall, Lincolnshire.	1945-7

Frank H Mason RI

Firth of Clyde.	1945-7
Firth of Clyde. (different image)	1947-54
Immingham Docks, Lincolnshire. ▲	1947
Loch Lomond.	1945-7
London, River Thames (Kings Reach).	1945-7
Norfolk Broads.	1945-7

S Agnew Mercer FRSA

Archbishops Palace, Bishopsthorpe, York.	1954
The River Ouse, Naburn, York. ▲	1954

Jack Merriott RI

Aberfeldy, Perthshire.	1945-7
Bamburgh, Northumberland.	1945-55
Dunfermline Abbey, Fifeshire. ■	1945-7
Dunkeld, Perthshire.	1945-7
Harrogate, Yorkshire.	1948-55
Killiecrankie, Perthshire.	1945-7
Lincoln.	1948-55
London, Cleopatras Needle and Embankment. ■	1945-55
Pickering, Yorkshire.	1948-55

Richmond, Yorkshire.	1948-55
The River Nidd, Knaresborough, Yorkshire.	1945-55
Roman Camp, Corstopitam, Northumberland.	1945-55
Sandsend, nr Whitby, Yorkshire.	1948-55
Seahouses, Northumberland,	1945-55
Stirling Bridge, Stirlingshire.	1945-7
Twizel Bridge, Northumberland.	1945-55
Wivenhoe, Essex.	1948-55
Woodbridge, Suffolk.	1948-55

John C Moody RE/RI

Barnard Castle, Co. Durham. ▲	1937-9
Berwick-on-Tweed, Northumberland.	1937-9
Durham.	1937-9
Hitchin, Hertfordshire.	1937-9

Claud Muncaster RWS

Temple Bar, Cheshunt, Hertfordshire.	1945-7
Ware, Hertfordshire.	1945-7
West Mill, Hertfordshire.	1945-7

J Mcintosh Patrick

Dunnottar Castle, Kincardineshire.	1945-7
St Monance, Fifeshire.	1945-7

Henry Rushbury RA

Castle Acre Priory, Norfolk.	1937-9
Felixstowe.	1937-9
Fort Augustus, Inverness-shire.	1945-7
Palace of Holyroodhouse, Edinburgh.	1945-7
Rievaulx Abbey, Yorkshire.	1937-9
Royal Baths, Harrogate.	1937-9
Scarborough, Yorkshire.	1945-7
Stirling Castle, Stirlingshire.	1945-7

Gyrth Russell RI/SMA

Anstey, Hertfordshire.	1948-55
Kings Lynn, Norfolk. ▲	1948-55
The River Ouse, York.	1948-55
River Wharfe, near Ilkley, Yorkshire.	1948-55
Staithes, Yorkshire.	1948-55
Theddlethorpe, Lincolnshire. ▲	1948-55
Wisbech, Cambridgeshire.	1948-55

Eric Scott

Blythburgh, near Halesworth, Suffolk.	1945-55
The River Blyth at Southwold nr Halesworth, Suffk.	1945-55

Frank Sherwin RI

Bolton Abbey, Wharfedale, Yorkshire.	1948-55
The River Wharfe, Ilkley, Yorkshire. ▲	1948-55
Robin Hoods Bay, Yorkshire. ■	1948-55

Leonard Squirrell RWS/RE

Bamburgh Castle, Northumberland.	1945-55
Bishops Stortford, Hertfordshire. ▲	1948-55
Brightlingsea, Essex.	1948-55
Colne Valley Viaduct, Chappel, Essex.	1945-55
Felixstowe Ferry, Suffolk.	1948-55
Hemingford Grey, Huntingdonshire.	1945-55
Inverlochy Castle, Inverness-shire.	1945-7
Melrose Abbey, Roxburghshire.	1945-7
Richmond, Yorkshire. ■	1948-55
River Allen, near Bardon Mill, County Durham.	1948-55
The River Orwell at Ipswich, Suffolk.	1948-55
Saturday Market Place, Kings Lynn, Norfolk.	1945-55
Sible Hedingham, Essex.	1945-55
Stowmarket Station, Suffolk. ▲	1945-55
Ufford, near Melton, Suffolk.	1945-55
Wymondham, Norfolk.	1945-55

Kenneth Steel RBA/SGA

Abbotsford, Roxburghshire.	1948-55
Bramham Cross, Yorkshire.	1948-55
Crowland, Lincolnshire.	1948-55
Dryburgh Abbey, Berwickshire.	1945-7
Fen Drayton, Cambridgeshire.	1945-7
Flatford Mill (near Manningtree), Suffolk.	1948-55
Forth Bridge, Scotland.	1948-55
Hemingford Abbots, Huntingdonshire.	1948-55
King Edward Bridge, Newcastle-upon-Tyne.	1948-54
Lavenham, Suffolk. ■	1948-55
Linlithgow Palace, Linlithgowshire.	1945-7
London, Kensington Palace.	1945-7
London, Lambeth Bridge.	1948-55
London, Waterloo Bridge.	1948-55
Newark Castle, Nottinghamshire.	1945-55
Norton (near Billingham) Co. Durham. ▲	1948-55
Norwich, Pulls Ferry.	1948-55
Peterborough Cathedral, Northamptonshire.	1948-55
Priory Gatehouse, Worksop, Nottinghamshire.	1945-55
Rufford Abbey, Nottinghamshire.	1945-55
Selby, Yorkshire. ▲	1945-55

Henry Stringer

Welwyn Garden City, Hertfordshire.	1948-55

Fred Taylor RI

Alnwick Castle, Northumberland. ▲	1937-9
Fountains Abbey, Yorkshire. ▲	1937-9
John Knox's House, Edinburgh.	1937-9
Lincoln.	1937-9
Peterborough Cathedral. ▲	1937-9
St Johns College, Cambridge.	1937-9
Stonegate, York.	1937-9

H Tittensor RI

Norwich.	1937-9
Old Abbey Gate, Bury St Edmunds.	1937-9
Petergate, York.	1937-9
Richmond, Yorkshire.	1937-9
St Ives, Huntingdonshire.	1937-9
Thetford, Norfolk.	1937-9

Edward Walker ARCA(Lond)

Buckden Palace, Huntingdonshire.	1945-7
Hinchingbrooke, Huntingdonshire.	1945-7

J Fletcher Watson

Dereham, Norfolk.	1945-7
Horstead Mill, Coltishall, Norfolk.	1945-7
Norwich, Tombland Alley. ▲	1945-7
Wells-next-the-Sea, Norfolk.	1945-7

A J Wilson

London, Marble Arch.	1954
London, The River Thames at Putney.	1954

L J Wood FRIBA

Hutton Le Hole, near Pickering, Yorkshire.	1954
Lastingham, near Pickering, Yorkshire.	1954

Horace Wright

Amersham, Buckinghamshire.	1945-7
Bildeston, Suffolk.	1945-7
Hatfield, Hertfordshire.	1945-7
Kersey, Suffolk.	1945-7
Much Hadham, Hertfordshire.	1945-7
West Wycombe, Buckinghamshire.	1945-7

Possibly Complete List (207)

Originally issued in Intermediate Series

Scottish Region series

Size: A and B   Issued: 1956-7

F Donald Blake RI

Ben Nevis from Corpach, Western Highlands.
The Castle, Inverness.

Lance Cattermole ROI

Glen Tanner, near Aboyne, Aberdeenshire.
River Dee at Cambus O'May, Aberdeenshire.

Edward Lawson

Braemar Castle, Aberdeenshire.
Bridge of Balgie, Glen Lyon, Perthshire.
Brig O'Balgownie, near Aberdeen.
Castle of Broughty, Broughty Ferry, Angus.
Crathie Church, near Balmoral Castle, Aberdeenshire.
Glamis Castle, Angus.
Loch Garry, Dalnaspidal, Perthshire.
River Spey near Craigellachie, Banffshire.

Alasdair Macfarlane

Ettrick Bay, Island of Bute.
Kyles of Bute, Firth of Clyde.
Gourock and Dunoon Car Ferry, Firth of Clyde.
Wemyss Bay and Rothesay Car Ferry, Firth of Clyde.

W Douglas Macleod

Ben Loyal, Sutherland.
Ben Slioch & Loch Maree, Wester Ross.
Loch Morar, Inverness-shire.
Loch Shiel, Western Highlands.
Schiehallion near Kinloch Rannoch, Perthshire.
Torridon Hills, Wester Ross.

Jack Merriott RI SMA

Inveraray Castle, Loch Fyne, Argyll.
Loch Etive, Argyll.
Loch Katrine and Ben Venue, Perthshire.
Loch Leven, near North Ballachulish, Western Highlands.
Loch Linnhe and Morven Hills, Western Highlands. ■
The River Tweed and Neidpath Castle, Peebles-shire.
Wallace Monument, near Stirling.
Western Highlands near Morar.

J Mcintosh Patrick ARSA ROI

Loch Awe, Argyll.
The Lomond Hills from Tarvit, near Cupar, Fife.
Strathmore from the Sidlaws Hills, Perthshire.
The Tay Bridge, Scotland.

Frank Sherwin RI

Loch Eck, Argyll.
The Three Sisters, Pass of Glencoe, Argyll.

Kenneth Steel RBA SGA

Balmoral Castle, Aberdeenshire.
Culzean Castle, near Maybole, Ayrshire.
Eilean Donan Castle, Loch Duich, Western Highlands.
The Falls, Invermoriston, Inverness-shire.
Kyle of Lochalsh-Kyleakin Ferry, Western Highlands. ■
Old Bridge of Dee, near Braemar, Aberdeenshire.
Complete Set (42)

Southern Region series (A)
Size: A and D   Issued: 1952
Claude Buckle
Canterbury Cathedral, Kent. ▲
Exeter Cathedral, Devonshire.▲
Salisbury Cathedral, Wiltshire.▲
Winchester Cathedral, Hampshire.
Jack Merriott RI
The Cinque Port of Dover, Kent. ■
The Cinque Port of Hastings, Sussex.
The Cinque Port of Hythe, Kent.
The Cinque Port of New Romney, Kent.
The Cinque Port of Sandwich, Kent. ■
   Complete Set (9)

Southern Region series (B)
Size: B   Issued: 1956
Claude Buckle
St Helier, Jersey. ▲
St Peter Port, Guernsey. ▲
Alan Gray
Arundel, Sussex. ▲
Eynsford, Kent. ▲
Frank Sherwin RI
Bournemouth, Hampshire.
Brighton, Sussex.
Gorey Harbour, Jersey.
Hastings, Sussex.
Richard Ward
Atlantic Coast Express, London and the West Country.
Direct Electric Services, London-Brighton. ▲
Golden Arrow, Continental Express. ▲
Ocean Liner Express, Southampton Docks-London. ▲
   Complete Set (12)

Western Region series
Size: B   Issued: 1954
Claude Buckle
Bourton-on-the-Water, Gloucestershire. ■
Marlborough, Wiltshire.
Marlow, Buckinghamshire.
Tewkesbury, Gloucestershire.
R Lander
Cockington, near Torquay, Devon.
Dunster, Somerset.
Selworthy, near Minehead, Somerset.
Frank H Mason RI
Brixham, Devon.
Dartmouth, Devon.
Pendennis Castle, Falmouth, Cornwall.
Jack Merriott RI
Cadgwith, via Helston, Cornwall.
Mousehole, near Penzance, Cornwall.
Widecombe-in-the-Moor, near Ashburton, Devon.
Arthur G Mills
Camp Coach Holidays. (advert)
Holiday Runabout Ticket. (advert)
Gyrth Russell RI
St Mawes, near Falmouth, Cornwall.
Frank Sherwin RI
The Booth Hall, Evesham, Worcestershire.
Broadway, Worcestershire.
Stokesay Castle, near Ludlow, Shropshire.
Worcester Cathedral. ■
   Complete Set (20)

Non–standard print series

LNER Original etchings series (mounted)
Size: B   Issued: 1936
Cyril H Barraud
Cambridge.
Edinburgh.
Felixstowe.
Holland, via Harwich.
Knaresborough, near Harrogate.
Lincoln.
Royal Deeside.
York.
Frank H Mason
Bruges.
Durham.
Fountains Abbey, Yorkshire.
Lowestoft.
The Night Parade, Harwich.
The Rhine.
Scarborough.
The West Highlands.
   Complete Set (16)

LNER Intermediate series (mounted)
Size: B   Issued: Approx 1937
Cyril H Barraud
Boston?
Ely.
Kings Lynn.
Peterborough Cathedral.
W Lee-Hankey
Holy Loch from Dunoon.
Norwich.
Whitby.
Wroxham, Norfolk.
Henry Rushbury
Peterborough.
Rievaulx Abbey, Yorkshire.@
Lincoln.
   Probably incomplete List.
@ Also issued as standard-format print

LMS Liverpool-Manchester Railway series
Size: F   Issued: ?
I Shaw
Travelling on the Liv-Man Rly Plate I & II
Travelling on the Liv-Man Rly Plate III & IV
  Complete Set (2)

Southern Railway original series (mounted)
Size: C   Issued: 1936
Donald Maxwell
Maidstone, Kent – Ancient.
Maidstone, Kent – Modern.
HMS Victory, Portsmouth.
Rochester, Kent.
Aldington, Kent?
Kipling Country, Pooks Hill.
South Downs, Sussex.
Ba . . . .Abbey.
Exeter Cathedral.
Freshwater Bay, Isle of Wight.
Carisbrooke Castle, Isle of Wight.
Winchester Cathedral.
North Downs, Surrey.
Tintagel, North Cornwall.
Hardy Country, Stinsford.
Boscastle, North Cornwall.
HMS Hood, Portsmouth.
Southampton Bargate.
Bucklers Hard, Beaulieu.
Canterbury Cathedral.
Incomplete List?

Southern Railway post–war series
Size: D   Issued: 1945-8
Adrian Allinson
Cornish Vale.
East Devon.
North Cornwall.
Red Devon.
Hesketh Hubbard
Alfriston.
Bideford.
Corfe Castle.
Exmoor.
Guernsey.
Hockworthy Bridge, Dartmoor.
New Forest.
Padstow.
Porchester Castle.
St Catherine's Lighthouse, IOW.
St Cross, Winchester.
Thomas Hardy's Birthplace, Dorchester.
   Possibly Incomplete List.

Southern Region series (C)
Size: E   Issued: 1965
A Brenet
Dorset Coast, Go by train.
Langhammer
Atlantic Coast, Go by train.
Hampshire Coast, Go by train.
   Complete Set (3)

The author would be pleased to know of any additions or amendments to the following lists and will be glad to enter into correspondence. Please write or send an e-mail to the author c/o the publisher (details on page 4) or visit website www.carriageprints.com

Appendix C
Listing of Western Region's intended carriage prints

This original listing of print subjects for the WR Series was produced by Paddington H.Q. and should be self–explanatory. K.W.C.Grand was the WR General Manager at the time.
The print sizes are: A = 17'' x 11¼'', B = 17'' x 8¾'', C = 20'' x 10'', X = Not Known. (Sizes A & B were non-standard and were therefore not suitable for use in WR coaches).

Title	Commissioned/ Received	Outcome	Size
John Bee			
Bickleigh Bridge, near Tiverton, Devon		Not shown to Mr Grand in 1954	B
Dartmoor, Devon	11/5/49	Not shown to Mr Grand in 1954	B
Exe Estuary, Devon	11/5/49	Not shown to Mr Grand in 1954	B
Exeter Cathedral, Devon	11/5/49	Fate?	A
Higher Ashton, Teign Valley, Devon		Not shown to Mr Grand in 1954	X
Lustleigh, Devon	11/5/49	Fate?	A
Starcross, Devon		Not shown to Mr Grand in 1954	B
Claude Buckle			
Marlow, Buckinghamshire		Published	C
Bourton-on-the-Water, Gloucestershire		Published	C
Tewkesbury, Gloucestershire		Published	C
Oxford, Oxfordshire		Not shown to Mr Grand in 1954	X
Lacock, Wiltshire		Not shown to Mr Grand in 1954	X
Marlborough, Wiltshire		Published	C
Francis Russell Flint			
Haverfordwest, Pembrokeshire		In course of preparation list	X
Manorbier, Pembrokeshire		In course of preparation list	X
Pembroke, Pembrokeshire		In course of preparation list	X
Penally, Pembrokeshire		In course of preparation list	X
St Davids, Pembrokeshire		In course of preparation list	X
Tenby, Pembrokeshire		In course of preparation list	X
Reginald M Lander			
Cockington, near Torquay, Devon		Published	C
Totnes, Devon		Not shown to Mr Grand in 1954	X
Monnow Bridge, Monmouth, Mon.		Rejected by Mr Grand in 1954	X
Dunster, Somerset		Published	C
Selworthy, near Minehead, Somerset		Published	C
Stratford upon Avon, Warwickshire		Not shown to Mr Grand in 1954	X
Frank H Mason			
Newlyn, Cornwall	21/6/49	Not shown to Mr Grand in 1954	X
Pendennis Castle, Falmouth, Cornwall	21/6/49	Published	C
Penzance, Cornwall	21/6/49	Not shown to Mr Grand in 1954	A
St Ives, Cornwall		Rejected by Mr Grand in 1954	C
Brixham, Devon	21/6/49	Published	C
Dartmouth, Devon	21/6/49	Published	C
Exmoor, Somerset	14/6/49	Not shown to Mr Grand in 1954	C
Porlock Weir, Somerset	14/6/49	Rejected by Mr Grand in 1954	A

Title	Commissioned/ Received	Outcome	Size
Jack Merriott			
Cadgwith, via Helston, Cornwall	14/6/49	Published	C
Mousehole, near Penzance, Cornwall	14/6/49	Published	C
Salcombe, Devon	14/6/49	Not shown to Mr Grand in 1954	A
Widecombe-in-the-Moor, Devon	14/6/49	Published	C
Hereford, Herefordshire		In course of preparation list	X
Kerne Bridge, Herefordshire		In course of preparation list	X
Ross-on-Wye, Herefordshire		In course of preparation list	X
Symonds Yat, Herefordshire		In course of preparation list	X
Chepstow, Monmouthshire		In course of preparation list	X
Tintern, Monmouthshire		In course of preparation list	X
Arthur G Mills			
Camp Coach Holidays [advert]		Published	C
Holiday Runabout Ticket [advert]		Published	C
Gyrth Russell			
Fowey, Cornwall	31/5/49	Rejected by Mr Grand in 1954	C
Gorran Haven, Cornwall	31/5/49	Fate?	A
Looe, Cornwall	31/5/49	Rejected by Mr Grand in 1954	C
Mevagissey, Cornwall	31/5/49	Rejected by Mr Grand in 1954	C
Polperro, Cornwall	31/5/49	Not shown to Mr Grand in 1954	A
St Mawes, near Falmouth, Cornwall	31/5/49	Published	C
Frank Sherwin			
Broad Street, Ludlow, Shropshire	1/7/49	Not shown to Mr Grand in 1954	X
Stokesay Castle, near Ludlow, Shropshire	1/7/49 19/7/49	Published	C
Booth Hall, Evesham, Worcestershire	1/7/49 19/7/49	Published	C
Broadway, Worcestershire	1/7/49	Published	C
Malvern, Worcestershire	1/7/49 19/7/49	Not shown to Mr Grand in 1954	A
Worcester Cathedral, Worcestershire	1/7/49 19/7/49	Published	C
Frank Wootton			
Dawlish, Devon		In course of preparation list	X
Kingswear, Devon		In course of preparation list	X
Paignton, Devon		Not shown to Mr Grand in 1954	X
Teignmouth, Devon		In course of preparation list	X
Torquay, Devon		In course of preparation list	X
Total: 63			

Appendix D
Bibliography

As mentioned previously, very little has been written on the subject of carriage panels. There are only two books which include short accounts of the subject and one of them is a purely fictional one by John Brooks, entitled *Railway Ghosts* – not exactly the most helpful reference on the subject! However, the following publications have proved useful:

Railway Relics & Regalia, General Editor P. B. Whitehouse, Country Life Publications 1975. ISBN 0600375722 – this book includes a chapter on carriage panels by George Dow. (p. 122–125).

Rarity & Price Guide to Railway Carriage Prints by Greg Norden (issued regularly - details from the author - address on page 4). A detailed guide for all prints.

Collecting Railwayana by John Mander (Moorland Publishing, 1988. ISBN 0861903129) – a general book on railway relics but includes a brief mention on the subject (p. 78–80).

Steam Railway Magazine, September 1990, (EMAP Publications), featured a condensed, but very useful, history of carriage panels in an article entitled 'Through the Looking Glass' by Allan Middleton.

The World of Trains Magazine, part 67, 1993 (Eaglemoss Publications Ltd) include a very small article on the subject in their 'Railway Relics' feature.

Many of the carriage panel artists also produced posters for the railways. Readers may find the following poster books of interest:

The Golden Age of the Railway Poster by J. T. Shackleton (New English Library, 1976. ISBN 0450010090).

Happy as a Sand Boy by Beverley Cole & Richard Durak (London HMSO, 1990. ISBN 0112904882).

Railway Posters 1923–47 by Beverley Cole & Richard Durak (Lawrence King, 1992. ISBN 1856690148).

Happy Holidays (The Golden Age of Railway Posters) by Michael Palin (Pavilion Books, 1987. ISBN 1851451307).

The following reference works have been invaluable in helping to compile the Index of Carriage Panel Artists in Appendix A:

Who's Who in Art, The Art Trade Press, various dates from 1927.

Dictionary of British Artists Working 1900–1950, Grant M Waters (Eastbourne Fine Art, 1975. ISBN 0902010069).

Dictionary of British Artists 1800–1940 (Antique Collectors Club. ISBN 0902028367).

British Landscape Painters by Charles Hemming (Gollancz 1989. ISBN 0575039574). This is useful for those interested in the history of this distinctive British art form and its relationship with the land's changing fortunes.

Index

QUOTES FROM REVIEWS ON
LANDSCAPES UNDER THE LUGGAGE RACK...

"The next best thing to a journey in the carriages themselves!" *Railway Magazine*

"A delightfully nostalgic book... it should enthral almost anyone with an eye for a gift that is rather different and rather special" *Scotsman*

"This delightful and beautifully produced book is a poignant memoir of the steam age" *Heritage Today (English Heritage) Magazine*

"One of the great railway books of all time... it is unquestionably the most attractive book produced so far on any aspect of railwayana" *Railway Collectors Journal*

"An ideal Christmas gift... his book is one of the best of its kind I have ever seen" *Runcorn Weekly News*

"Numerous superb colour illustrations" *The Scots Magazine*

"Thorough and painstaking research, not only into the life and work of the artists but also into the scenes they depicted, is evident in this beautifully produced book" Roly Smith - *Countryman Magazine*

"A superb compilation" *Lincolnshire Life Magazine*

"A Who's who of prominent watercolour artists for the period" *Antiques Bulletin Magazine*

"Undoubtedly the definitive work on the subject" *Steam World Magazine*

"Well-captioned pictures are complemented by a very readable and often humorous text" *Rail News*

"Represents extraordinary good value for money" *Great Eastern News*

"Every now and again, the publishing world is blessed by the arrival of a book providing a refreshing change - this is such a publication and will delight all." *Nick Pigott - Railway Magazine*

"A sumptuous full-colour volume" *Cathy Brown - East Anglian Daily Times*

"The book provides useful information on the artists and prints" *The Artist Magazine*

"Beautiful pictures... thoroughly researched" *Hertfordshire Countryside Magazine*

"A delightful book... highly recommended" *Friends of the National Railway Museum*

"There can be no finer present... a treasured book that will remind you of a lost Britain" *Best of British Magazine*